DISCARDED

NATIONAL GALLERY OF ART
U.S.A.

A PAGEANT OF PAINTING

FROM THE NATIONAL GALLERY OF ART

A PAGEANT OF PAINTING

FROM THE

NATIONAL GALLERY OF ART

Edited by HUNTINGTON CAIRNS

and JOHN WALKER

VOLUME I

THE MACMILLAN COMPANY : NEW YORK

NATIONAL GALLERY OF ART

WASHINGTON, D.C.

155740

QQ
759
D58
v. 1

Copyright ©, 1966, by Publications Fund, National Gallery of Art

FIRST PRINTING

The Macmillan Company, New York
Collier-Macmillan Limited, London
Collier-Macmillan Canada, Ltd., Toronto, Ontario

Library of Congress catalog card number: 66–11576

PRINTED IN THE UNITED STATES OF AMERICA

ENGRAVED BY THE BECK ENGRAVING COMPANY, INC.
PRINTED BY PUBLISHERS PRINTING–ADMIRAL PRESS

ACKNOWLEDGMENTS

The editors wish to thank members of the staff of the National Gallery of Art who aided in the preparation of this volume.

The following institutions have been of assistance in making source material available: Brooklyn Museum, Brooklyn, N.Y.; Bryn Mawr College Library, Bryn Mawr, Pa.; Catholic University Library, Washington, D.C.; Detroit Public Library, Detroit, Mich.; Dumbarton Oaks Library, Washington, D.C.; Enoch Pratt Free Library, Baltimore, Md.; Folger Shakespeare Library, Washington, D.C.; Freer Gallery of Art, Washington, D.C.; Georgetown University Library, Washington, D.C.; Girard College Library, Philadelphia, Pa.; Grosvenor Library, Buffalo, N.Y.; Harvard University Library, Cambridge, Mass.; Library of Congress, Washington, D.C.; Mount Holyoke University Library, South Hadley, Mass.; National Collection of Fine Arts, Washington, D.C.; New York Historical Society, New York City; New York Public Library, New York City; New York University Library, New York City; Ohio State University Library, Columbus, Ohio; Peabody Institute Library, Baltimore, Md.; Philadelphia Museum of Art, Philadelphia, Pa.; Phillips Collection, Washington, D.C.; Princeton University Library, Princeton, N.J.; Public Library of the District of Columbia, Washington, D.C.; University of Illinois Library, Urbana, Ill.; Walters Art Galleries, Baltimore, Md.; Yale University Library, New Haven, Conn.

For permission to reproduce copyrighted material in this work acknowledgment is made to the following publishers and others: from *Mont Saint Michel and Chartres,* by Henry Adams, copyright 1904, by permission of Houghton Mifflin Company; from *The Life of Reason,* by George Santayana, copyright 1905, by permission of Charles Scribner's Sons; from *The Golden Legend* of Jacobus de Voragine, copyright 1941, by permission of Longmans, Green and Co.; from *Giovanni di Paolo,* by John Pope-Hennessy, by permission of Chatto and Windus, London; from *The Italian Painters of the Renaissance,* by Bernard Berenson, 1930, by permission of the Clarendon Press, Oxford; from *Collected Poems 1909–1935,* by T. S. Eliot, copyright 1936, by permission of Harcourt, Brace & World, Inc., and Faber and Faber, Ltd.; from *Alesso Baldovinetti,* by Ruth Wedgwood Kennedy, copyright 1938, by permission of Yale University Press; from *The Testament of Beauty,* by Robert Bridges, by permission of the Clarendon Press, Oxford; from *Along the Road,* by Aldous Huxley, copyright 1925, by permission of Harper & Brothers; from *The Notebooks of Leonardo da Vinci,* 1939, by permission of Reynal and Hitchcock; from *Vision and Design,* by Roger Fry, 1920, by courtesy of Coward McCann, Inc.; from *Stephen Hero,* by James Joyce, copyright 1955, by permission of New Directions, Publishers; from *The Oxford Dictionary of Nursery Rhymes,* by Iona and Peter Opie, copyright 1952, by permission of the Clarendon Press; from *Sandro Botticelli,* by Yukio Yashiro, by permission of The Medici Society Ltd., London; from *Italian Backgrounds,* by Edith Wharton, copyright 1905, 1933 by Frederic R. King, by permission of A. Watkins, Inc.; from *Religious Art from the Twelfth to the Eighteenth Century,* by Émile Mâle, by permission of Pantheon Books, Inc., New York, and Routledge and Kegan Paul Ltd., London; from *The Poems of John Donne,* by permission of the Clarendon Press, Oxford; reprinted by permission of Dodd, Mead & Company, New York, and Faber and Faber Ltd., London, from *The Anatomy of Art,* by Herbert Read; from *Mysticism and Logic,* by Bertrand Russell, by permission of W. W. Norton & Company, Inc., New York, and George Allen & Unwin Ltd., London; from *The Divine Names and Mystical Theology,* by Dionysius the Areopagite, translated by C. E. Rolt, copyright 1920, by permission of The Society for Promoting Christian Knowledge; from *A History of Spanish Painting,* by Chandler Rathfon Post, copyright 1933, by permission of Harvard University Press; from *Collected Poems of W. B. Yeats,* copyright 1933, by The Macmillan Company and used with their permission and by Macmillan and Co., Ltd. and Mrs. W. B. Yeats; from *The Collected Poems of Edith Sitwell,* copyright 1949, 1954, by Edith Sitwell, by permission of The Vanguard Press; from *The Sense of Form in Art,* by Heinrich Wölfflin, copyright 1958, by permission of Chelsea Publishing Co.; from *Hans Holbein the Younger,* by Ford Madox Ford, by permission of E. P. Dutton & Co., Inc., New York, and Gerald Duckworth & Co. Ltd., London; from *Four Quartets,* by T. S. Eliot, copyright 1943, by permission of Harcourt, Brace & Co.; from *History of Italian Literature,* by Francesco De Sanctis, copyright 1931, by permission of Harcourt, Brace & Co.; from *A Portrait of the Artist as a Young Man,* by James Joyce, by permission of The Viking Press, Inc., New York, and Jonathan Cape Limited, London; from *The Civilization of the Renaissance in Italy,* by Jacob Burckhardt, by permission of George Allen & Unwin Ltd., London; from *Biographia Literaria,* by S. T. Coleridge, by permission of the Clarendon Press, Oxford; from *The Note-Books of Samuel Butler,* by permission of E. P. Dutton & Co., Inc., New York, and Jonathan Cape Limited, London, and the executors of Samuel Butler; from *The Leadership of Giorgione,* by Duncan Phillips, by permission of the author; from *History of Art,* by Élie Faure, by permission of Harper & Brothers, New York; from *Landscape into Art,* by Kenneth Clark, by permission of Charles Scribner's Sons, New York, and John Murray (Publishers) Ltd., London; reprinted from *Poems: 1922–1947,* by Allen Tate, copyright 1932, 1937, 1948 by Charles Scribner's Sons, New York, used by permission of the publishers, and by permission of Eyre & Spottiswoode (Publishers), Limited, London; from *Laws,* by Plato, by permission of Harvard University Press; from *Titian,* by Charles Ricketts, copyright 1910, by permission of Methuen & Co., Ltd.; from *The Paintings of George Bellows*, by George Bellows, by permission of Alfred A. Knopf, Inc., New York; from *The Introduction to Hegel's Philosophy*, by G. W. F. Hegel, copyright 1905, by permission of Routledge & Kegan Paul, Ltd.; from *The Analects of Confucius*, by permission of George Allen & Unwin Ltd., London; from *Italian Hours*, by Henry James, copyright 1909, by permission of Houghton Mifflin Company; from *The Spanish Journey*, by Julius Meier-Graefe, copyright 1927, by permission of Harcourt, Brace & World, Inc.; from *Don Fernando*, by W. Somerset Maugham, copyright 1935, reprinted by permission of Doubleday, Doran & Co., Inc.; from *A Call to Order*, by Jean Cocteau, translated by Rollo H. Myers, by permission of Jean Cocteau, and Faber and Faber Ltd., London; from *The Gentle Art of Making Enemies*, by James A. McNeill Whistler, by permission of G. P. Putnam's Sons, New York, and William Heinemann, Ltd., London; from *The Soul of Spain*, by Havelock Ellis, copyright 1908, by permission of Houghton Mifflin Company; from *The Essays of Montaigne*, by permission of Oxford University Press, London; from *Promenades of an Impressionist*, by James Huneker, copyright 1910, by permission of Charles Scribner's Sons; from *The Art Spirit*, by Robert Henri, copyright 1923, by permission of J. B. Lippincott Co.; from *Rembrandt*, by Jakob Rosenberg, copyright 1948, by permission of Harvard University Press; from *Academies of Art, Past and Present*, by Nikolaus Pevsner, copyright 1940, by permission of Cambridge University Press; from *Longinus on the Sublime*, by permission of the Clarendon Press, Oxford; from *The Masters of Past Time*, by Eugène Fromentin, copyright 1913, by permission of J. M. Dent & Sons, Ltd., and E. P. Dutton & Co., Inc.; from *Bird-Watching and Bird Behaviour*, by Julian Huxley, by permission of Chatto and Windus, London; from *Vermeer of Delft*, by E. V. Lucas, by permission of Methuen & Co., Ltd., London; from *Galateo*, by Giovanni della Casa, copyright 1958, by permission of Penguin Books, Inc.; from *The Life of Forms in Art*, by Henri Focillon, copyright 1934, by permission of Yale University Press; from *The Enchantress*, by HelenW. Henderson, copyright 1928, by permission of Methuen & Co., Ltd.; from *The Georgics of Virgil*, translated by C. Day Lewis, by permission of A. D. Peters Ltd., London, and Jonathan Cape Limited, London; from *Artists on Art*, compiled and edited by Robert Goldwater and Marco Treves, by permission of Pantheon Books, Inc., New York, and Routledge & Kegan Paul Ltd.; from *Chardin*, by Herbert E. A. Furst, copyright 1911, by permission of Methuen & Co., Ltd.; from *Art and Science*, by Adrian Stokes, by permission of Faber and Faber, Ltd., London; from *Collected Poems*, by Thomas Hardy, copyright 1925, The Macmillan Company and used with their permission, and Macmillan and Co., Ltd.; from *Fragonard*, by James Laver (The Faber Gallery), by permission of Faber and Faber, Ltd.; from *Canaletto and His Contemporaries*, by Decio Gioseffi, copyright 1960 by Instituto Italiano d'Arti Grafiche, by permission of Crown Publishers, Inc.; from *A History of Italian Painting* and *Western European Painting of the Renaissance*, by Frank Jewett Mather, Jr., by permission of Henry Holt and Company, Inc., New York; from *Metamorphoses*, by Ovid, copyright 1955, by permission of Indiana University Press; from *Goya*, by William Rothenstein, by permission of The Unicorn Press Ltd., London; from *Francisco de Goya*, by August L. Mayer, copyright 1924, by permission of J. M. Dent & Sons, Ltd.; from *An Essay on Landscape Painting*, by Kuo Hsi, The Wisdom of the East Series, by permission of John Murray (Publishers) Ltd., London; from *Heartbreak House*, by George Bernard Shaw, copyright 1919, by permission of The Public Trustee and the Society of Authors; from *"Taste"* by Osbert Sitwell and Margaret Barton (*Johnson's England*, edited by A. S. Turberville, the Clarendon Press, Oxford, 1933); from *Speculations*, by T. E. Hulme, by permission of Routledge and Kegan Paul Ltd., London; from *Gilbert Stuart*, by William T. Whitley, 1932, reprinted by permission of Harvard University Press, Cambridge, Mass.; from *The Aristocratic Journey; Being the Letters of Mrs. Basil Hall*, edited by Una Pope-Hennessy, copyright 1931, by courtesy of G. P. Putnam's Sons; from *Alexander Hamilton*, by Frederick Scott Oliver, copyright 1906, by permission of Constable and Co., Ltd.; from *John Singleton Copley*, by James Thomas Flexner, copyright 1948, by permission of Houghton Mifflin Co.; from *Ingres*, by Walter Pach, copyright 1939, by permission of Harper & Brothers; from *The Journal of Eugène Delacroix*, translated by Walter Pach, copyright 1948, Crown Publishers, by permission of Crown Publishers, Inc., New York; from *Sixteen to Sixty*, by Louisine W. Havemeyer, copyright 1961, by permission of The Metropolitan Museum of Art; from *Degas, Manet, Morisot*, by Paul Valéry, copyright 1960, by permission of Bollingen Foundation; from *"Time, Distance, and Form in Proust,"* by José Ortega y Gasset, copyright 1959, by permission of *The Hudson Review*, Vol. XI, No. 4, Winter 1958–59; from *The Journals of André Gide*, translated by Justin O'Brien, by permission of Alfred A. Knopf, Inc., New York; from *Renoir, An Intimate Record*, by Ambroise Vollard, copyright 1925, by permission of Alfred A. Knopf; from *The Life and Art of Renoir*, by William Gaunt, copyright 1952, by permission of Phaidon Press, Ltd.; from *Pots and Pans*, by Arthur Edwin Bye, copyright 1921, by permission of Princeton University Press; from *Art and Reality*, by Joyce Cary, copyright 1958, by permission of Harper & Brothers and Cambridge University Press; from *The History of Impressionism*, by John Rewald, by permission of The Museum of Modern Art, New York; from *The Autobiography of William Carlos Williams*, copyright 1951, by William Carlos Williams, reprinted by courtesy of Random House, Inc., New York; from *Letters of Rainer Maria Rilke*, 1892–1910, Vol. I, copyright 1945, by permission of W. W. Norton & Co., Inc.; from *The Paintings of D. H. Lawrence*, 1929, by permission of Mrs. Frieda Lawrence; from *An Essay on Man*, by Ernst Cassirer, copyright 1944, by permission of Yale University Press; quoted from *The Unquiet Grave*, by permission of the author, Cyril Connolly, and the publishers, Harper & Brothers, New York, and Hamish Hamilton Ltd., London; from "*Art and Ideas*" in *Essays*, by William Butler Yeats, copyright 1924, by The Macmillan Company, New York, and used with their permission, and by permission of Mrs. W. B. Yeats; from *Gauguin the Rebel*, by Cyril Connolly, copyright November 14, 1954, by permission of *The Sunday Times;* from *Toulouse-Lautrec to Rodin,* by Arthur Symons, copyright 1929, by permission of the Bodley Head Ltd.; from *Life, Art, and Letters of George Inness,* by George Inness, Jr., by permission of Appleton-Century-Crofts, Inc., New York; from *The Shape of Content,* by Ben Shahn, copyright 1957, by permission of Harvard University Press; from *Painting and Reality,* by Étienne Gilson, copyright 1957, by permission of Bollingen Foundation; from *Adventures in the Arts,* by Marsden Hartley, copyright by Boni & Liveright, Inc., 1921 and 1949, published by Liveright Publishing Corporation, New York; from *"Remington and Winslow Homer,"* by John Wheelwright, *Hound & Horn,* 1933, by permission of Lincoln Kirstein; from *Winslow Homer,* by Lloyd Goodrich, copyright 1944, by The Macmillan Company, New York, and used with their permission; from *The Life and Works of Winslow Homer,* by William Howe Downes, by permission of Houghton Mifflin Company, Boston; from *Studies in Seven Arts,* by Arthur Symons, copyright 1906, by permission of E. P. Dutton & Co.; from *Landmarks in Nineteenth-Century Painting,* by Clive Bell, by permission of Harcourt, Brace and Company, Inc., New York, and Chatto and Windus, London; from *Modigliani,* by Jean Cocteau, © 1951, Fernand Hazan, Editeur, Paris; from *Neroccio de' Landi,* by Gertrude Coor, copyright 1961, by permission of Princeton University Press; from *The Poetry of Father Tabb,* edited by Francis E. Litz, copyright 1928, by permission of Dodd, Mead & Co.; from *Baudelaire,* by Jean-Paul Sartre, translated by Martin Turnell, copyright 1950 by New Directions, reprinted by permission of New Directions and Hamish Hamilton Ltd.; from *The Poems of John Milton,* edited by Helen Darbishire, copyright 1961, by permission of the Clarendon Press, Oxford; from *The Bible Designed To Be Read As Living Literature,* edited by Ernest Sutherland Bates, copyright 1936, by permission of Simon and Schuster, Inc. and Heinemann Publishers Ltd.; from *Galateo,* by Giovanni della Casa, translated by R. S. Pine-Coffin, copyright 1958, by permission of Penguin Books Ltd.; from *Plato: Selected Passages,* edited by Sir R. W. Livingston, copyright 1960, by permission of the Clarendon Press, Oxford; from *Lemprière's Classical Dictionary,* by Dr. J. Lemprière (revised by F. A. Wright), copyright 1949, by permission of E. P. Dutton & Co. and Routledge & Kegan Paul Ltd.; from *The Diary of John Evelyn,* Vol. II, edited by E. S. de Beer, copyright 1955, by permission of the Clarendon Press, Oxford; from *The Jade Mountain,* translated by Witter Bynner from the texts of Kiang Kang-Hu, copyright 1929, by permission of Alfred A. Knopf, Inc.; from *Nicholas Poussin,* by Anthony Blunt, The A. W. Mellon Lectures in the Fine Arts (1958), Bollingen Series XXXV/7, by permission of the Bollingen Foundation; from *French Painting,* by Basil Taylor, copyright 1951, by permission of Thames and Hudson Ltd., London; from *The Enlightenment* 1687–1776 (Vol. II of *A History of Modern Culture*), by Preserved Smith, copyright 1934 by Holt, Rinehart and Winston, Inc. (copyright renewed in the name of Priscilla Robertson), by permission also of Routledge & Kegan Paul Ltd.; from *Vigée-Lebrun,* by W. H. Helm, copyright 1915, by Hutchinson & Company Ltd. (the records of this volume were destroyed in World War II; present owner of copyright unknown); from *Jerusalem Delivered,* by Torquato Tasso, translated by Edward Fairfax, copyright 1962, reprinted by permission of Centaur Press Ltd.; from *The Annals* of Tacitus, Books I–VI, translated by George Gilbert Ramsay, copyright 1909, by permission of John Murray Ltd.; from *Amid These Storms,* by Winston S. Churchill, copyright 1932, by permission of Charles Scribner's Sons, *Thoughts and Adventures,* copyright 1932, by permission of Odhams Books Ltd., proprietors of the copyright; from "Winthrop Chandler: An Eighteenth-Century Artisan Painter", *Magazine of Art,* November 1947, Vol. 40, reprinted by permission of The American Federation of Arts; from *Prejudices: Fourth Series,* by H. L. Mencken, copyright 1924, by permission of Alfred A. Knopf, Inc.; from *The Characteristics of French Art,* by Roger Fry, copyright 1932, by permission of Chatto and Windus Ltd.; from *The Guermantes Way* (Vol. II of *Remembrance of Things Past*), by Marcel Proust, translated by C. K. Scott Moncrieff, copyright 1925 and renewed 1952 by Random House, Inc., reprinted by permission of Random House, Inc., and Chatto and Windus Ltd.; from *From Renoir to Picasso,* by Michel Georges-Michel, copyright 1954 by F. Brouty, F. Fayard et Cie, by permission of the publisher, Houghton Mifflin Company; from *Cities of Italy,* by Arthur Symons, copyright 1907, by permission of E. P. Dutton & Company; from *Vuillard, His Life and Work,* by Claude Roger-Marx, translated by Edmund B. d'Auvergne, Paul Elek Publishers Ltd., London, 1946, copyright 1946 by Arts et Metiers Graphiques, Paris, reproduced by permission of Elek Books Ltd., London; from *Life with Picasso,* by Françoise Gilot and Carlton Lake, copyright © 1964, McGraw-Hill, Inc., used by permission of McGraw-Hill Book Company and Thomas Nelson & Sons Ltd.; from *Matisse: His Art and His Public,* by Alfred H. Barr, Jr., copyright 1951 by The Museum of Modern Art, New York, and reprinted with its permission, "Notes d'un peintre" was originally published in *La Grande Revue,* Paris, December 25, 1908 (the first complete English translation by Margaret Scolari Barr was published in *Henri-Matisse,* The Museum of Modern Art, 1931, and then again in *Matisse: His Art and His Public*); from *Duino Elegies,* by Rainer Maria Rilke, translated by J. B. Leishman and Stephen Spender, copyright 1939, by permission of W. W. Norton & Co., Inc., and The Hogarth Press Ltd.; from *The Cubist Painters,* by Guillaume Apollinaire, translated by Lionel Abel, copyright 1949, by permission of George Wittenborn Inc., New York; from *Chapman's Homer,* Vol. II, edited by Allardyce Nicoll, copyright 1956, by permission of The Bollingen Foundation and Routledge & Kegan Paul Ltd.

For some selections the editors have made use of translations already available, as follows: Boccaccio, *The Decameron,* translated by W. K. Kelly; Dante, *The Divine Comedy* (*Paradiso*), translated by Philip Henry Wicksteed; Jacobus de Voragine, *The Golden Legend,* translated and adapted by Granger Ryan and Helmut Ripperger; Alberti, *The Painting of Leon Battista Alberti,* translated by Giacomo Leoni; Leonardo da Vinci, *Notebooks,* arranged and translated by Edward MacCurdy; Faure, *History of Art,* translated by Walter Pach; Lessing, *Laokoon,* anonymous revision of E. C.

Beasley's translation; Aristotle, *Poetics,* translated by W. Hamilton Fyfe; Vasari, *Lives,* translated by Gaston du C. de Vere; Mâle, *Religious Art from the Twelfth to the Eighteenth Century,* anonymous translation; Castiglione, *The Courtier,* translated by A. P. Castiglione; Kristeller, *Andrea Mantegna,* translated by S. Arthur Strong; Huizinga, *The Waning of the Middle Ages,* translated by F. Hopman; *The Aeneid of Virgil,* translated by John Dryden; *The Ante-Nicene Fathers,* Vol. 8, translated by Alexander Walker; Dürer, in *The Life of Albrecht Dürer,* translated by Mary M. Heaton; Wölfflin, *The Sense of Form in Art,* translated by Alice Muehsam and Norma Shatan; Sartre, *Baudelaire,* translated by Martin Turnell; De Sanctis, *History of Italian Literature,* translated by Joan Redfern; Balzac, *The Unknown Masterpiece,* translated by Ellen Marriage; Burckhardt, *The Civilization of the Renaissance in Italy,* translated by S. G. C. Middlemore; Machiavelli, *The Art of War,* anonymous translation; Ovid, *Fasti,* translated by Henry T. Riley; Plato, *Symposium,* translated by Sir R. W. Livingstone; Francisco de Hollanda, *Four Dialogues on Painting,* translated by Aubrey F. G. Bell; Anonymous, *Pervigilium Veneris,* translated by Allen Tate (*Poems: 1922–1947*); Plato, *Laws,* translated by R. G. Bury; Schopenhauer, *The World as Will and Idea,* translated by R. B. Haldane and J. Kemp, with revisions by the editors; Hegel, *The Introduction to Hegel's Philosophy,* translated by Bernard Bosanquet; *The Analects of Confucius,* translated by Arthur Waley; Meier-Graefe, *The Spanish Journey,* translated by J. Holroyd-Reece; Cocteau, *A Call to Order,* translated by Rollo H. Myers; Cascales y Muñoz, *Francisco de Zurbarán,* translated by Nellie Sulye Evans; *The Essays of Montaigne,* translated by E. J. Trechmann; *Longinus on the Sublime,* translated by A. O. Prickard; Fromentin, *The Masters of Past Time,* anonymous translation; *Conversations of Goethe with Eckermann,* translated by John Oxenford; Liu Chang-ch'ing, in *The Jade Mountain,* translated by Witter Bynner; Virgil, *Georgics,* translated by John Dryden; Hourticq, *Rubens,* translated by Frederic Street; de Piles, *The Principles of Painting,* anonymous translation; della Casa, *Galateo,* translated by R. S. Pine-Coffin; Focillon, *The Life of Forms in Art,* translated by C. Beecher Hogan and George Kubler; Clouet, in *The Enchantress,* translated by Helen W. Henderson; *The Georgics of Virgil,* translated by C. Day Lewis; Homeric Hymn, *Chapman's Homer,* translated by George Chapman; Grimm, *Correspondence,* anonymous translation; Sainte-Beuve, *Causeries du lundi,* translated by E. J. Trechmann; Aeschylus, *Agamemnon,* translated by Edith Hamilton; Tasso, *Gerusalemme Liberata,* translated by Edward Fairfax; Tacitus, *Annals,* translated by George Gilbert Ramsay; Ovid, *Metamorphoses,* translated by Rolfe Humphries; Mayer, *Francisco de Goya,* translated by Robert West; Kuo Hsi, *An Essay on Landscape Painting,* translated by Shio Sakanishi; Aristotle, *Rhetoric,* translated by W. Rhys Roberts; Tocqueville, *Democracy in America,* translated by Henry Reeve; Ingres, in *Ingres,* translated by Walter Pach; *The Journal of Eugène Delacroix,* translated by Walter Pach; Goethe, *Conversations of Goethe with Eckermann and Soret,* translated by John Oxenford; Poussin, Boudin, and Courbet, in *Artists on Art,* translated by Robert Goldwater and Marco Treves; Valéry, *Degas, Manet, Morisot,* translated by David Paul; Ortega y Gasset, *"Time, Distance, and Form in Proust,"* translated by Irving Singer; *The Journals of André Gide,* translated by Justin O'Brien; Vollard, *Renoir, An Intimate Record,* translated by Harold L. Van Doren and Randolph T. Weaver; Proust, *Le Coté de Guermantes,* translated by C. K. Scott Moncrieff; Rilke, *Letters of Rainer Maria Rilke,* translated by Jane Bannard Greene and M. D. Herter Norton; van Gogh, *Further Letters of Vincent van Gogh,* anonymous translation; Roger-Marx, *Vuillard, His Life and Work,* translated by Edmund B. d'Auvergne; Cocteau, *Modigliani,* translated by F. A. McFarland; Rilke, *Duino Elegies,* translated by J. B. Leishman and Stephen Spender; Apollinaire, *Un Fantôme de nuées,* translated by Lionel Abel; Matisse, "Notes d'un peintre", translated by Margaret Scolari Barr.

INTRODUCTION

Unless some fundamental change in the world takes place it seems probable that the National Gallery of Art will remain the last great national collection of its kind ever to be formed. We say this because the masterpieces of the past are now largely locked into existing museums. Not only has the export of national treasures become immensely difficult, but great private collections of old masterpieces no longer exist. Assuming that all the paintings and sculpture remaining in private hands in any single country on either side of the Atlantic were to be shown together, the result would not, as far as one can judge, equal the collection in the National Gallery of Art.

It is true that there are important Spanish paintings privately owned in Spain, French paintings in France, German paintings in Germany, and Impressionist and Post-Impressionist paintings in the United States. Specialized collections of this kind containing superb masterpieces still exist. Certain public museums in Europe, in Italy, Belgium, and Holland are outstanding for a particular aspect or period of painting. But what is remarkable about the National Gallery is the scope of its collection: the balanced representation of the achievements of the various schools of European and American painting and sculpture between the thirteenth century, the date of the earliest painting in the Gallery, and the beginning of the twentieth century, the date of the most recent in the permanent collection.

So rapidly have private treasures in our day become public property that in 1937 when Andrew Mellon established, endowed, and gave his collection to the National Gallery it was almost too late. The time for great acquisitions had nearly run out. A few years' delay and his vision of a new museum exhibiting as it now does more than a thousand paintings and over a hundred pieces of sculpture, all extraordinarily high in quality, would have been impossible to realize. The collectors who, along with Andrew Mellon, were to become the principal benefactors of the Gallery, Samuel Kress, Joseph Widener, Chester Dale, and Lessing Rosenwald, were about to commit their collections elsewhere. In erecting one of the most beautiful museum buildings in the world, Mr. Mellon felt confident its magnetic power would draw such uncommitted collections to Washington. The National Gallery of Art has been open for exactly twenty-five years, and Mr. Mellon's intuition has proved correct. Not only have these immense gifts been made, but more than a hundred other collectors have joined their donations to those of the major benefactors.

Andrew Mellon, Secretary of the Treasury under three administrations, and Ambassador to the Court of St. James, was one of America's most notable industrialists. As an experienced man of affairs intent upon the creation of a great institution that would endure for generations he attached few conditions to his offer of gift, none of them burdensome. He stipulated that the Gallery should not bear his name. He wished the new building identified as a gallery of art of the National Government to which the public should forever have access. Although he was a modest man this condition was not based on modesty. He saw that the attachment of his name to the institution would contradict the very idea of a National Gallery, and would act as a deterrent to future gifts from other donors. He named John Russell Pope of New York as the architect. He chose the site of the building as the one most readily accessible to the public. There was also sufficient surrounding property, under control of public authorities, to protect the building from undesirable encroachments. He stipulated that the upkeep of the Gallery building and certain other administrative expenses be borne by the United States, and he proposed that the Gallery be administered by a board to be composed of the Chief Justice of the United States, the Secretary of State, the Secretary of the Treasury, the Secretary of the Smithsonian Institution, all *ex officio,* and five general trustees who would choose their successors by majority vote. To maintain quality in the works of art to be exhibited he stipulated that no painting or sculpture should be included in the permanent collection unless it were of a standard of excellence equal to those in his own collection.

It was a statesmanlike proposal the soundness of which bore immediate fruits. President Franklin D. Roosevelt at once approved the offer and commended the matter of enabling legislation to Congress for its consideration. The bill passed with little delay, although efforts were made to change certain of its provisions. The most important was that the nature of the Board of Trustees be modified, but Mr. Mellon was unyielding. He wished the private trustees to be self-perpetuating. After much debate in the Senate it was concluded that the Board, being composed of responsible men, would undoubtedly act as a unit, as in fact it has without exception.

Andrew Mellon, who died before the Gallery opened, had secured for the trustees a workable charter. It was their business to develop the rules which would allow the Gallery to become all that he had hoped. As he saw it, a national gallery should collect and exhibit masterpieces of painting and sculpture, and its purpose should be that of "encouraging and developing a study of the fine arts." No suggestions were offered and no conditions were imposed on the methods to be used for the accomplishment of that end. The matter was completely the responsibility of the trustees. Before the Gallery opened they had determined the broad policies which have governed it for a quarter of a century.

They decided that it should be primarily a gallery of European and American painting and sculpture. Washington and the nation already possessed in the Freer Gallery of Art one of the world's great museums of oriental art, and it would serve no useful purpose for the National Gallery to attempt to duplicate the Freer's resources. The trustees determined that the works of art should be arranged chronologically by schools. This would permit a visitor on entering the Gallery to see in Gallery One the oldest painting in the collection, executed during the thirteenth century, and reproduced here on page three. He could then proceed through the galleries seriatim until he reached the chronological end of the collection typified by the paintings which conclude this volume. The alternative was to exhibit the various individual collections as units without reference to chronology. It was felt this would be confusing to visitors. However, it was agreed that when a donor's collection contained sufficient paintings of a particular school to fill a single gallery they could be shown as a unit in their proper chronological place. Thus the Gallery has the Mellon and Widener Rembrandt rooms, the Kress Venetian gallery, and the Dale Nineteenth-Century rooms. Throughout its history the trustees have maintained this policy firmly although it has meant declining two important gifts which carried the condition that they be shown as units outside their chronological sequence. The trustees also decided that no work of art should be admitted to the permanent collection until the artist had been deceased for twenty years. This rule is an adaptation of the one that prevails in the National Gallery in London and in the Louvre. In the world of painting and sculpture, quality is not always immediately determinable even by the most accomplished connoisseurs, but a testing period of twenty years can usually be counted upon to winnow the good from the bad. "People tell me this is the art of my period," said Ingres, "but suppose my period is bad?" This rule produces comment in the press from time to time, but it has been misunderstood. It does not mean that the National Gallery does not exhibit the works of contemporary artists. It has done so and will continue to do so. It does not mean that the works of contemporary artists may not be acquired. Several of the paintings reproduced in this volume are contemporary. It means only that the works of artists still alive or deceased for less than twenty years do not pass into the permanent collection, which entails the final seal of approval of the trustees, and also involves more restrictive lending conditions, until there is reasonable certainty that the painting or sculpture has achieved the level of quality contemplated by the charter. Contemporary art is kept separate from the work of the established masters. In London, paintings and sculpture are tested in the Tate Gallery before they move to the National Gallery. In Paris they are tested in the Musée d'Art Moderne. Until Washington possesses a gallery equivalent to the Tate or the Musée d'Art Moderne the present rule appears a workable solution of the problem.

To house the collections, the trustees had been presented with one of the largest marble buildings in the world. The task of the staff was to exhibit the collections, in an old phrase, in a place of rest and refreshment for the public. The work of art is not an end in itself. It must be shown in a manner that will permit the establishment of a relationship between it and the spectator. An art museum, to reverse Santayana's dictum, should be a place where the Muses intend to dwell. A closed gallery of the type of the Wallace Collection in London, is pervaded with a sense of intimacy which the great State museums can hardly hope to achieve. As a step in this direction different backgrounds in the National Gallery of Art were chosen for the different schools of painting. The early Italian, Flemish, and German are hung on plastered walls. Damask is used for the later Italian canvases. The Rubens, van Dyck, Rembrandt, and other Dutch pictures are shown against oak paneling, while the French, English, and American paintings are in rooms with painted paneling. The wainscoting, moldings, and lintels suggest the dominant architectural styles of the periods to which the paintings belong. The pictures are hung twice as far apart as they are usually shown in other galleries, and not above each other. Since many of the paintings are on paneled walls, which in effect provide a second framing, the visitor is thus afforded an undisturbed view of each work of art. In the garden courts at each end of the Gallery's main axis there are fountains and changing exhibitions of flowers, thus relating art to nature and providing places of rest and refreshment.

This volume is a pictorial accounting of the Gallery's collection of painting as it stands at the end of the first twenty-five years of its life. It was preceded by three volumes similar in format, the first published in 1944, the second in 1952, and the third in 1962. All three volumes are now out-of-print. The present book contains a selection of two hundred and fifty-five four-color reproductions of the principal paintings in the Gallery's collections. It is also a pictorial history of Western painting in its important aspects from the thirteenth century to Picasso. A comment is printed opposite each reproduction. It may deal directly with the painting, the artist, his philosophy, his period, or the subject. It may show what a great writer has done in verse or prose with the same material. In all cases the comments have been chosen from the point of view of intrinsic interest and a bearing, direct or indirect, upon the painting. A catalogue note giving the date, dimensions, provenance, and other information about the painting is also provided for each reproduction.

H. C.
J. W.

CONTENTS

CONTENTS — Volume II

A PAGEANT OF PAINTING

FROM THE NATIONAL GALLERY OF ART

BYZANTINE SCHOOL · XIII Century

Enthroned Madonna and Child

You can start at Byzantium with the Empress Helena in 326, or with the Council of Ephesus in 431. You will find the Virgin acting as the patron saint of Constantinople and of the imperial residence, under as many names as Artemis or Aphrodite had borne. As God-mother (θεομητηρ), Deipara (θεοτοκος), Path-finder (Ὁδηγητρια), she was the chief favorite of the eastern empire, and her picture was carried at the head of every procession and hung on the wall of every hut and hovel, as it is still wherever the Greek Church goes. In the year 610, when Heraclius sailed from Carthage to dethrone Phocas at Constantinople, his ships carried the image of the Virgin at their mast-heads. In 1143, just before the *flèche* on the Chartres *clocher* was begun, the Basileus John Comnenus died, and so devoted was he to the Virgin that, on a triumphal entry into Constantinople, he put the image of the Mother of God in his chariot, while he himself walked. In the western Church the Virgin had always been highly honored, but it was not until the crusades that she began to overshadow the Trinity itself. Then her miracles became more frequent and her shrines more frequented, so that Chartres, soon after 1100, was rich enough to build its western Portal with Byzantine splendor. . . .

The Church had crowned and enthroned her almost from the beginning, and could not have dethroned her if it would. In all Christian art,—sculpture or mosaic, painting or poetry,—the Virgin's rank was expressly asserted. Saint Bernard like John Comnenus, and probably at the same time (1120-1140) chanted hymns to the Virgin as Queen:

O salutaris Virgo Stella Maris
Generans prolem, Aequitatis solem,
Lucis auctorem, Retinens pudorem,
Suscipe laudem!

Coeli Regina Per quam medicina
Datur aegrotis, Gratia devotis,
Gaudium moestis, Mundo lux cœlestis,
Spesque salutis;

Aula regalis, Virgo specialis,
Posce medelam Nobis et tutelam,
Suscipe vota, Precibusque cuncta
Pelle molesta!

O savior Virgin, Star of Sea,
Who bore for child the Sun of Justice,
The source of Light, Virgin always
Hear our praise!

Queen of Heaven who have given
Medicine to the sick, Grace to the devout,
Joy to the sad, heaven's light to the world
And hope of salvation;

Court royal, Virgin typical,
Grant us cure and guard,
Accept our vows, and by prayers
Drive all griefs away!

Henry Adams
Mont Saint Michel and Chartres (1904)

This painting was discovered about 1920 in a Spanish convent, which possessed a similar Madonna also now in the National Gallery of Art. Both Madonnas may have been brought to Spain by some crusading knight or ecclesiastic returned from a pilgrimage to the East. Collections: A convent in Calahorra, Aragon, Spain. *Andrew Mellon Collection,* 1937. Wood. Height 32⅛ in.; width 19⅜ in. (0.815 x 0.49).

DUCCIO DI BUONINSEGNA · Sienese Active 1278-1318/19

Nativity with the Prophets Isaiah and Ezekiel

This is the Month, and this the happy morn
Wherin the Son of Heav'ns eternal King,
Of wedded Maid, and Virgin Mother born,
Our great redemption from above did bring;
For so the holy sages once did sing,
    That he our deadly forfeit should release,
And with his Father work us a perpetual peace.

John Milton
On the Morning of Christs Nativity (1629)

O my deir hert, young Jesus sweit,
Prepare thy creddil in my spreit,
And I sall rock thee in my hert
And never mair from thee depart.

But I sall praise thee evermoir
With sangis sweit unto thy gloir;
The knees of my hert sall I bow,
And sing that richt *Balulalow!*

James, John, and Robert Wedderburn (c. 1567)

These three panels were originally part of the predella from the front of Duccio's Maestà, commissioned by Giacomo Mariscotti for the Duomo of Siena. When this great altarpiece was completed a contemporary chronicler described the celebration in its honor as follows: "On the day that it was carried to the Duomo the shops were shut; and the Bishop bade that a goodly and devout company of priests and friars should go in solemn procession, accompanied by the *Signori Nove* and all the officers of the Commune and all the people; all the most worthy followed close upon the picture, according to their degree, with lights burning in their hands; and then behind them came the women and children, with great devotion. And they accompanied the said picture as far as the Duomo, making procession round the Campo as is the use, all the bells sounding joyously for the devotion of so noble a picture as is this. And all that day they offered up prayers, with great alms to the poor, praying God and His Mother who is our advocate, that He may defend us in His infinite mercy from all adversity and all evil, and that He may keep us from the hands of traitors and enemies of Siena." Another panel from the Maestà, the Calling of the Apostles Peter and Andrew, is also in the National Gallery of Art, Samuel H. Kress Collection (see page 7). Collections: Cathedral, Siena; Kaiser Friedrich Museum, Berlin. *Andrew Mellon Collection,* 1937. Wood. Center panel, height 17¼ in.; width 17½ in. (0.438 x 0.444). Each side panel, height 17¼ in.; width 6½ in. (0.438 x 0.165). Dated by documents between 1308 and 1311.

DUCCIO DI BUONINSEGNA · Sienese Active 1278-1318/19

The Calling of the Apostles Peter and Andrew

The whole history of painting may be strung on this single thread—the effort to reconstitute impressions, first the dramatic impression and then the sensuous. A summary and symbolic representation of things is all that at first is demanded; the point is to describe something pictorially and recall people's names and actions. It is characteristic of archaic painting to be quite discursive and symbolic; each figure is treated separately and stuck side by side with the others upon a golden ground. The painter is here smothered in the recorder, in the annalist; only those perceptions are allowed to stand which have individual names or chronicle facts mentioned in the story. But vision is really more sensuous and rich than report, if art is only able to hold vision in suspense and make it explicit. When painting is still at this stage, and is employed on hieroglyphics, it may reach the maximum of decorative splendour. Whatever sensuous glow finer representations may later acquire will be not sensuous merely, but poetical.

· · · ·

Illustration has nevertheless an intellectual function by which it diverges altogether from decoration and even, in the narrowest sense of the word, from art: for the essence of illustration lies neither in use nor in beauty. The illustrator's impulse is to reproduce and describe given objects. He wishes in the first place to force observers—overlooking all logical scruples—to call his work by the name of its subject matter; and then he wishes to inform them further, through his representation, and to teach them to apprehend the real object as, in its natural existence, it might never have been apprehended. His first task is to translate the object faithfully into his special medium; his second task, somewhat more ambitious, is so to penetrate into the object during that process of translation that this translation may become at the same time analytic and imaginative, in that it signalises the object's structure and emphasises its ideal suggestions. In such reproduction both hand and mind are called upon to construct and build up a new apparition; but here construction has ceased to be chiefly decorative or absolute in order to become representative. The æsthetic element in art has begun to recede before the intellectual; and sensuous effects, while of course retained and still studied, seem to be impressed into the service of ideas.

George Santayana
The Life of Reason (1905)

The Byzantine tradition of painting culminated in the Maestà, or Virgin in Majesty, executed by Duccio for the Cathedral of Siena between 1308 and 1311. This great double altarpiece was later removed from the cathedral, dismembered, and placed in the Opera del Duomo, where most of it may be seen today. Ten sections of the predella are now in England and the United States. The present picture formed part of the predella which faced the east end of the church. Another panel from the Maestà, the Nativity with the Prophets Isaiah and Ezekiel, is also in the National Gallery of Art (see page 5). Collections: Cathedral, Siena; Charles Fairfax Murray, London; Robert H. and Evelyn Benson, London; Clarence H. Mackay, Roslyn, New York. *Samuel H. Kress Collection,* 1939. Wood. Height 17⅛ in.; width 18⅛ in. (0.435 x 0.46).

GIOTTO · Florentine c. 1266(?)-1337

Madonna and Child

As it often happens that fortune hides, under the meanest trades in life, the greatest virtues, which has been proved by Pampinea, so are the greatest geniuses found frequently lodged by nature in the most deformed and misshapen bodies. This truth was verified in two of our own citizens, as I am now going to relate. For the one, who was called Forese da Rabatta, being a little deformed mortal, with a flat Dutch face, worse than any of the family of the Baronci, was yet esteemed by most men a repository of the civil law. And the other, whose name was Giotto, had such a prodigious fancy, that there was nothing in Nature, the parent of all things, but he could imitate it with his pencil so well, and draw it so like, as to deceive our very senses, making them imagine that to be the very thing itself which was only his painting; therefore, having brought that art again to light, which had lain buried for many ages, under the errors of such as aimed more to captivate the eyes of the ignorant, than to please the understandings of those who were really judges, he may deservedly be called one of the lights and glories of our city, and the rather as being master of his art, notwithstanding his modesty would never suffer himself to be so esteemed.... But though his excellence in his profession was so wonderful, yet as to his person and aspect he had no way the advantage of Signor Forese....

These two worthies had each his country seat at Mugello, and Forese being gone thither in the vacation time, and riding upon an unsightly steed, chanced to meet there with Giotto, who was no better equipped than himself, and they returned together to Florence. Travelling slowly along, as they were able to go no faster, they were overtaken by a great shower of rain, and forced to take shelter in a poor man's house, who was well known to them both; and as there was no appearance of the weather's clearing up, and each was desirous of getting home that night, they borrowed two old russet cloaks, and two rusty hats, and proceeded on their journey. After they had got a good part of their way, thoroughly wet, and covered with dirt and mire, which their two shuffling steeds had thrown upon them, and which by no means improved their looks, it began to clear up at last, and they, who had hitherto said but little to each other, now turned to discourse together. Forese, as he jogged on, listening to Giotto, who was excellent at telling a story, began at last to view him attentively from head to foot, and seeing him in that wretched dirty pickle, without ever thinking of his own plight, he fell a laughing, and said, "Do you suppose, Giotto, if a stranger were to meet with you now, who had never seen you before, that he would imagine you to be the best painter in the world, as you really are?" Giotto readily replied, "Yes, sir, I believe he might think so, if looking at you at the same time, he could ever conclude that you had learned your A, B, C." At this Forese was sensible of his mistake, finding himself well paid in his own coin.

Giovanni Boccaccio
Il Decamerone (1353)

It is believed that this painting was once the central panel of an altarpiece to which the Saint Stephen of the Horne Foundation, Florence, originally belonged. Longhi has also suggested (*Dedalo,* 1930) that the two panels in the Musée André, Châalis, representing Saint John the Evangelist and Saint Lawrence, were formerly part of the same polyptych, and he believes that this was the altarpiece mentioned by Ghiberti and Vasari as having been painted by Giotto for the Badia, Florence. Collections: Édouard-Alexandre Max, Paris; Henry Goldman, New York. *Samuel H. Kress Collection,* 1939. Wood. Height 33⅝ in.; width 24⅜ in. (0.855 x 0.62). Painted probably between 1320 and 1330.

GENTILE DA FABRIANO · UMBRIAN c. 1360/70-1427

Madonna and Child

Vergine madre, figlia del tuo figlio,
umile ed alta più che creatura,
termine fisso d' eterno consiglio,

tu se' colei, che l' umana natura
nobilitasti sì che il suo Fattore
non disdegnò di farsi sua fattura.

Nel ventre tuo si raccese l' amore,
per lo cui caldo nell' eterna pace
così è germinato questo fiore.

Qui sei a noi meridiana face
di caritate, e giuso, intra i mortali,
sei di speranza fontana vivace.

Donna, sei tanto grande e tanto vali,
che qual vuol grazia ed a te non ricorre,
sua disianza vuol volar senz' ali.

La tua benignità non pur soccorre
a chi domanda, ma molte fiate
liberamente al domandar precorre.

In te misericordia, in te pietate,
in te magnificenza, in te s' aduna
quantunque in creatura è di bontate.

Or questi, che dall' infima lacuna
dell' universo infin qui ha vedute
le vite spiritali ad una ad una,

supplica a te, per grazia, di virtute
tanto che possa con gli occhi levarsi
più alto verso l' ultima salute;

ed io, che mai per mio veder non arsi
più ch' io fo per lo suo, tutti i miei preghi
ti porgo, e prego che non sieno scarsi,

perchè tu ogni nube gli disleghi
di sua mortalità coi preghi tuoi,
sì che il sommo piacer gli si dispieghi.

Ancor ti prego, Regina che puoi
ciò che tu vuoli, che conservi sani,
dopo tanto veder, gli affetti suoi.

Vinca tua guardia i movimenti umani;
vedi Beatrice con quanti beati
per li miei preghi ti chiudon le mani.

Virgin mother, daughter of thy son, lowly
and uplifted more than any creature,
fixed goal of the eternal counsel,

thou art she who didst human nature so
ennoble that its own Maker scorned
not to become its making.

In thy womb was lit again the love under
whose warmth in the eternal peace
this flower hath thus unfolded.

Here art thou unto us the meridian
torch of love, and there below with
mortals art a living spring of hope.

Lady, thou art so great and hast such worth,
that if there be who would have grace yet
betaketh not himself to thee, his longing
seeketh to fly without wings.

Thy kindliness not only succoureth whoso
requesteth, but doth oftentimes freely
forerun request.

In thee is tenderness, in thee is pity, in
thee munificence, in thee united whatever
in created being is of excellence.

Now he who from the deepest pool of the universe even to here hath seen the spirit-
lives, one by one,

imploreth thee, of grace, for so much
power as to be able to uplift his eyes
more high towards final bliss;

and I, who never burned for my own vision
more than I do for his, proffer thee all
my prayers, and pray they be not scant,

that thou do scatter for him every cloud of
his mortality with prayers of thine, so
that the joy supreme may be unfolded to him.

And further do I pray thee, Queen who canst do
all that thou wilt, that thou keep sound
for him, after so great a vision, his affections.

Let thy protection vanquish human ferments;
see Beatrice, with how many Saints, for
my prayers folding hands.

DANTE ALIGHIERI
La Divina Commedia (c. 1305-c. 1320)

This panel is thought to have been painted just before Gentile's Adoration of the Magi, dated 1423 and now in the Uffizi, Florence. It is generally recognized as the most important example of his transitional style. Collections: Alexander Barker, London; Madame E. J. Sartoris, Paris; Henry Goldman, New York. *Samuel H. Kress Collection,* 1939. Wood. Height 37¾ in.; width 22¼ in. (0.96 x 0.57). Painted c. 1422.

SASSETTA AND ASSISTANT · Sienese Active 1423-1450

The Meeting of Saint Anthony and Saint Paul

Saint Paul fled into the desert. And when Saint Anthony in his turn repaired to the wilderness, thinking that he was the first hermit, he learned in a dream that another anchorite, better than himself, had a claim to his homage. Therefore Saint Anthony bent every effort to discover the whereabouts of this other hermit. And searching through the forests, he came first upon a hippocentaurus (centaur), half man and half horse, who told him to go to the right. Next he met an animal who was carrying some dates; the upper part of his body was that of a man, but he had the belly and the feet of a goat. Anthony asked him what he was; and he answered that he was a satyr, that is, one of those creatures which the pagans mistook for wood-gods. Finally Saint Anthony came face to face with a wolf, who led him to the cell where Saint Paul dwelt. But he, being aware of the approach of a man, had closed his door. Anthony besought him to open to him, declaring that he would die on the spot rather than go away. And Paul, yielding to his prayers, opened the door, and at once the two hermits embraced each other with great affection.

When the noon-hour drew near, a crow flew down, bearing a loaf formed of two halves. Anthony wondered at this, but Paul told him that God provided him daily with food in this manner: this day the quantity was doubled, on account of Anthony's visit. Thereupon they disputed piously over which of them was more worthy to divide the loaf. Paul wished that Anthony should do it, since he was the guest. Anthony insisted that it be Paul, who was the older. In the end both took hold of the loaf, and broke it in two.

As Anthony was on his way back to his cell, he saw two angels passing overhead, bearing the soul of Saint Paul. He hastened to retrace his steps, and found Paul's body kneeling in the attitude of prayer, so that Anthony thought he was still alive. But the saint was dead. And Anthony cried out: 'O blessed spirit, even in death thou showest still that which thou didst throughout thy life!' And while he was pondering over means of giving burial to Paul, thither came two lions, who dug a grave, helped to lay the body therein, and then returned to their forest. And Anthony took Paul's mantle, which was fashioned of palm-leaves; and thereafter he wore it on high feast days.

Jacobus de Voragine
Legenda aurea (c. 1255-66)

This panel formed part of a large altarpiece representing Saint Anthony Abbot and scenes from his life. In the upper right hand corner of the panel reproduced, Saint Anthony sets out on his journey. On his way he meets a centaur, a symbol of the gods of paganism. The centaur, holding a palm branch, beats on his breast as a sign of penitence and receives a blessing—an indication of the conversion to Christianity of the ancient divinities of the woods. At the bottom of the picture the two old men at last find each other. Their deep emotion is beautifully suggested by their tender embrace. Seven other scenes have been identified as belonging to the same polyptych: Saint Anthony at Mass, in the Berlin Museum; Saint Anthony Distributing His Money to the Poor, and Saint Anthony Leaving His Monastery, both in the Samuel H. Kress Collection, National Gallery of Art; the Temptation of Saint Anthony, and Saint Anthony Beaten by Devils, both in the Jarves Collection, Yale University; Saint Anthony and the Porringer, in the Lehman Collection, New York; and finally, the Death of Saint Anthony, in the Samuel H. Kress Collection, National Gallery of Art. Collections: Viscount Allendale, London. *Samuel H. Kress Collection,* 1939. Wood. Height 18¾ in.; width 13⅝ in. (0.475 x 0.345). Painted c. 1440.

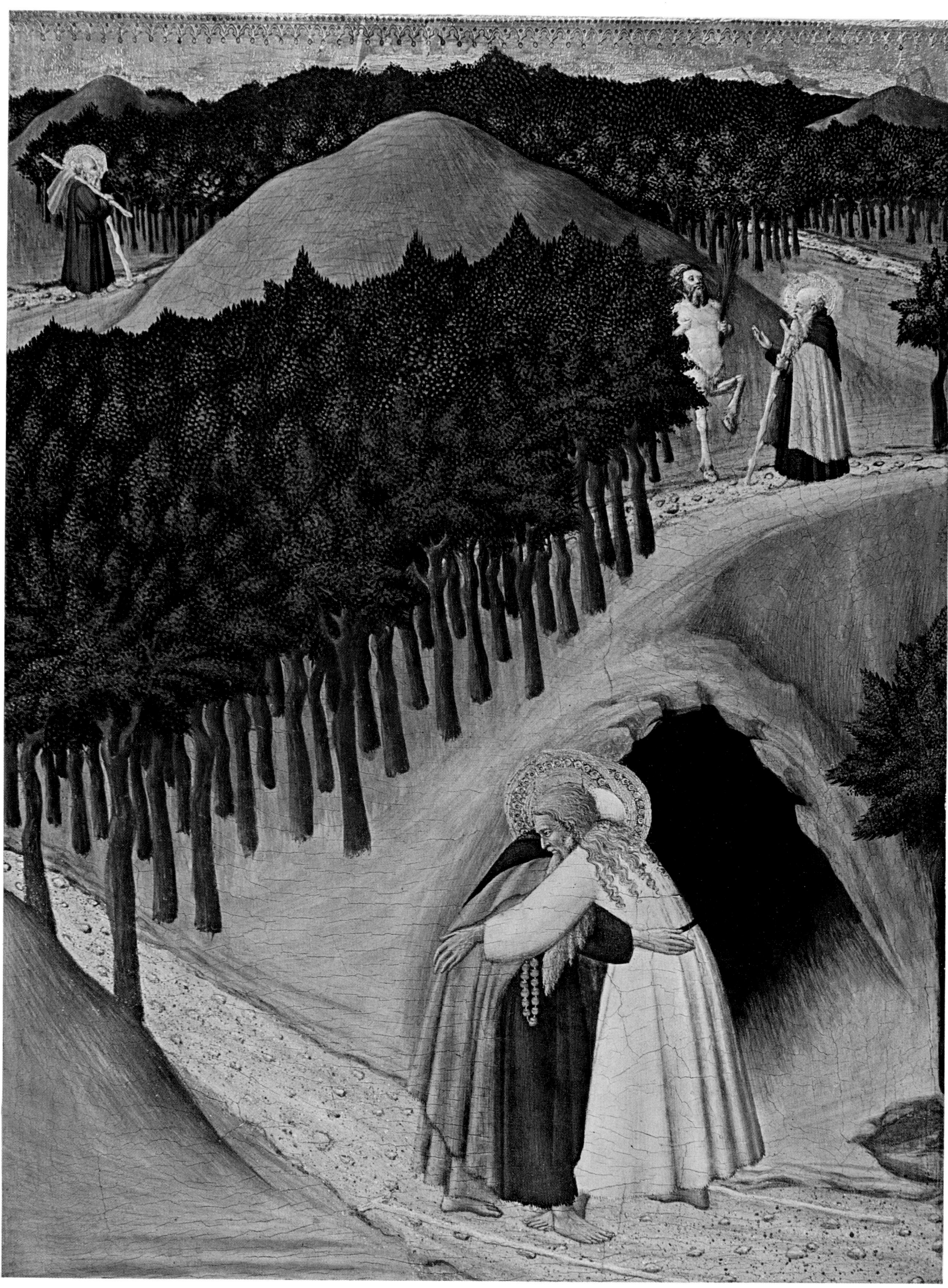

GIOVANNI DI PAOLO · Sienese Active 1420-1482

The Annunciation

The germ of Giovanni di Paolo's stylistic growth was a vivid imagination inflamed by a deeply religious temperament. Emotional stress was not uncommon at the time. The revivalism of S. Bernardino was achieved by simple descriptive methods. A comparable directness gives Giovanni di Paolo's pictures their peculiar mystical intensity. The religious mystic is a person who, gifted with a literal faith in events or dogmas too far outside the range of the experience of the ordinary individual to be generally credible in a literal sense, goes on to endow with a symbolist significance concepts he had at first accepted as simple facts. Giovanni di Paolo's realism and super-realism seem to argue an emotional conviction of this literal, yet transcendental nature.

That literary painting has its peculiar validity we cannot doubt. The twin elements of form and narrative in the finite work of art are susceptible of individual extension to an infinite degree. We can conceive of some paintings whose form is so subtilised that the spectator is unconscious of emotional deficiencies, and of others so direct and so passionate that he ignores their fundamental formal incoherence. Giovanni di Paolo is one of the few Italian painters to have created a convincing and original imaginative world. As he emerged from the predominantly æsthetic orbit of Sassetta, the force of his own disposition slowly compelled him to transcribe his imaginative impressions with decreasing reference to æsthetic dictates. When we remember that at the end of his life he was working in competition with Matteo di Giovanni, Benvenuto di Giovanni and Neroccio dei Landi, painters whose object for the most part was a merely æsthetic appeal, the nonconformist character of his style appears most striking. Giovanni di Paolo was a Gerard Hopkins in a world of Swinburnes. He is often grotesque and sometimes rude. But his faults are the expression of an inner strain few other painters felt, and his pictures at their best provide us with a unique example of style heated to receive the impress of a vital and candescent personality.

John Pope-Hennessy
Giovanni di Paolo (1938)

The theme of the painting is the Fall and Redemption of Man, with Joseph and Mary shown as the counterparts of Adam and Eve. Saint Joseph is an unusual figure in scenes of the Annunciation (see Shapiro, *Art Bulletin,* 1945). His appearance here may perhaps be explained by the sudden growth of his cult during the first half of the fifteenth century. It is significant that he warms his hands before a golden fire. "Since fire is the most noble element, its virtue is wonderfully diffused," wrote Berchorius a century before this picture was painted. "For fire lurks secretly in all things, as is evident when two solid bodies are struck together, for then the fire breaks out, though it was not at all believed to be hidden there. Thus God is truly in all things, though invisible. . . . Indeed, we may well speak of the fire of charity, or the fire of the Holy Spirit, and especially of the fire of divine love, which is in many people who are not believed to possess it" (see Miess, *Art Bulletin,* 1945). The panel belonged to a predella, other parts of which are: the Nativity, in the Vatican Gallery; the Crucifixion, in the Berlin Museum; the Presentation in the Temple, in the Metropolitan Museum, New York; and the Adoration of the Magi, in the Cleveland Museum. Collections: Sir William J. Farrer, London; Sir J. Charles Robinson, London; Charles Fairfax Murray, London; Robert H. and Evelyn Benson, London. *Samuel H. Kress Collection,* 1939. Wood. Height 15¾ in.; width 18¼ in. (0.40 x 0.46). Painted c. 1445.

NEROCCIO DE' LANDI · SIENESE 1447-1500

Portrait of a Lady

In the general composition, the Widener portrait is related to Leonardo's portrait of *Ginevra de' Benci* of ca. 1474, which, however, perhaps included the sitter's hands. Leonardo's portrait is psychologically much more penetrating and is much more individualized than Neroccio's, and the mood is very different. In the Florentine representation the sitter and landscape have a melancholy, brooding aspect, whereas in the Sienese they are wistful and dreamy. They too are contemplative, but they lack the mysterious, introvert quality of Leonardo's representation. Both young women fascinate, but in different ways: the rather severe-looking Florentine maiden puzzles—the gentle-faced Sienese enchants; the pale, brown-haired girl makes us ponder—the fair one, dream. In Leonardo's portrait one senses tensions among body, mind, and soul—in Neroccio's all three are in harmony. The simply attired Ginevra has a masculine quality—the expensively (but unostentatiously) dressed, Sienese lady is completely feminine.

Leonardo's *Ginevra de' Benci* and Neroccio's unknown *Lady* belong to the earliest Italian portraits in which the landscape reflects the sitter's psychological temper and thus forms an integral part of the painting. Characteristically, Leonardo filled almost the entire background with a dense mass of foliage and depicted the body of water as isolated and reflecting. Also characteristically, Neroccio placed the sitter's head against a serene summer sky and conceived the body of water in the background as a broad river bordered by towns.

The idealized loveliness of Neroccio's young sitter brings to mind Francesco Laurana's contemporary marble busts of *Beatrix of Aragon* in the Louvre and the Museo Nazionale in Palermo. It brings to mind furthermore Petrarch's emotional description of Simone Martini's portrait of the poet's beloved, Laura:

Ma certo il mio Simon fu in paradiso,
    onde questa gentil donna si parte;
    ivi la vide, e la ritrasse in carte,
    per far fede qua giù del suo bel viso.
L'opra fu ben di quelle che nel cielo
    si ponno imaginar, non qui tra noi,
    ove le membra fanno a l'alma velo.

GERTRUDE COOR
Neroccio de' Landi (1961)

In the fifteenth century portraiture flourished in almost every Italian city, attracting artists as great as Leonardo da Vinci, but in Siena portraits were of such rarity that the picture reproduced is virtually unique. The inscription at the bottom of the picture may be translated: "Although by wondrous dexterity I may reach the summit of human achievement, yet am I doomed to failure. A mortal, I am pitting my art against that of the gods." Mrs. Coor translates Petrarch's lines as follows: But surely my Simone was in Paradise, from where this gentle lady comes; there he saw her and drew her on paper to give testimony below of her beautiful face. The work was indeed one of those which we can imagine to have been made in heaven, not here among us where the flesh veils the spirit. *Widener Collection,* 1942. Wood. Height 18⅜ in.; width 12 in. (0.465 x 0.305). Painted c. 1490.

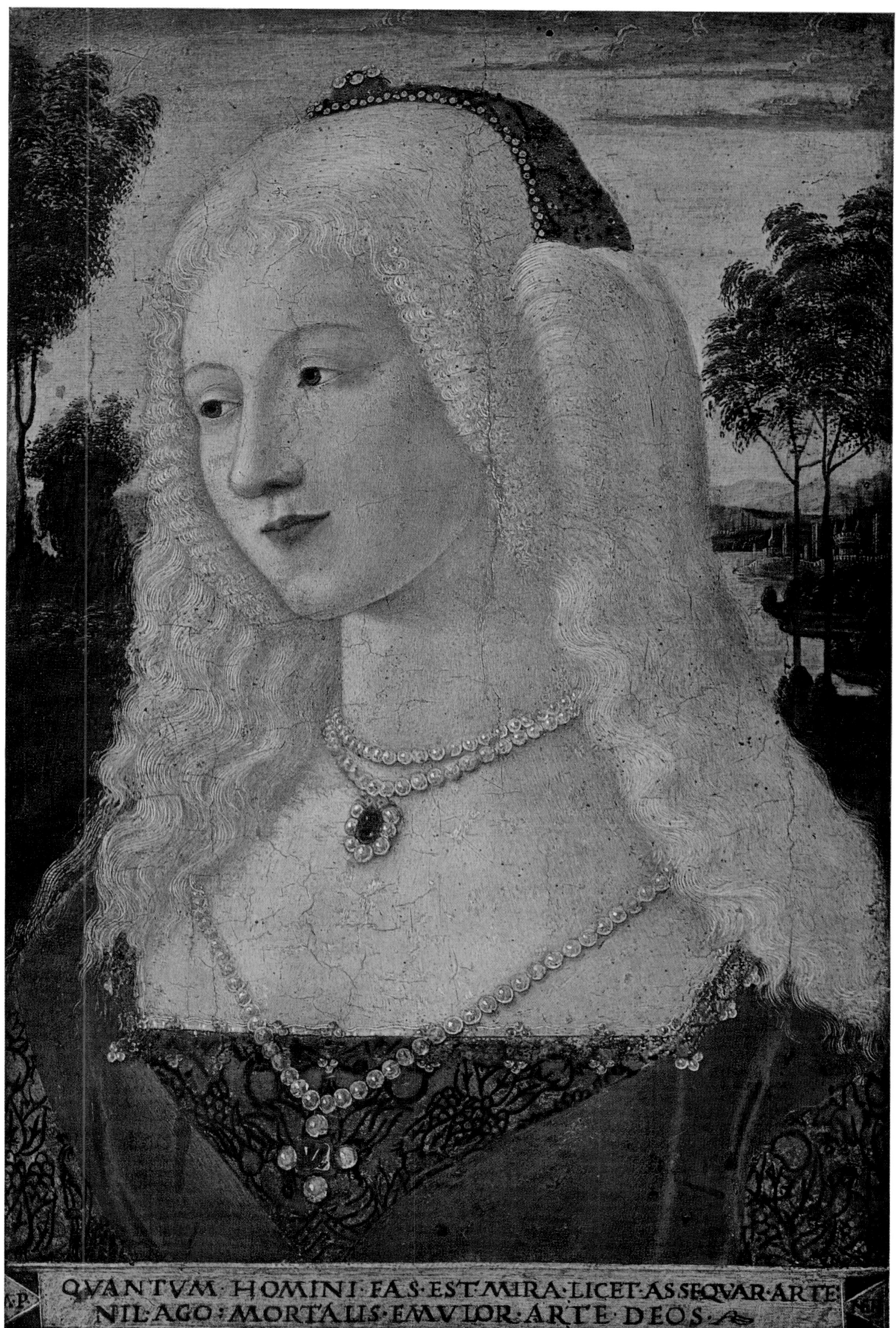
QVANTVM·HOMINI·FAS·EST·MIRA·LICET·ASSEQVAR·ARTE
NIL·AGO: MORTALIS·EMVLOR·ARTE·DEOS·

MASOLINO · Florentine 1383/84-Active to 1432

The Annunciation

As I lay up on a night
My thought was on a berd so bright
That men clepen Marye full of might,
    Redemptoris mater.

To here cam Gabriel with light,
And seid 'Heil be thou, blissful wight,
To ben clepėd now art thou dight
    Redemptoris mater.'

At that wurd that lady bright
Anon conseived God full of might.
Than men wist weel that sche hight
    Redemptoris mater.

Whan Jhesu on the rode was pight,
Mary was doolful of that sight,
Til sche sey him rise up right,
    Redemptoris mater.

Jhesu, thou sittest in hevenė light,
Graunt us to comen beforn thy sight,
With that berd that is so bright,
    Redemptoris mater.

Anonymous (15th Century)

Poetry and picture are arts of a like nature, and both are busy about imitation. It was excellently said of Plutarch, poetry was a speaking picture, and picture a mute poesy. For they both invent, feign, and devise many things, and accommodate all they invent to the use and service of Nature. Yet of the two the pen is more noble than the pencil; for that can speak to the understanding, the other but to the sense. They both behold pleasure and profit as their common object; but should abstain from all base pleasures, lest they should err from their end, and, while they seek to better men's minds, destroy their manners. They both are born artificers, not made. Nature is more powerful in them than study.

Ben Jonson
Timber: or, Discoveries (1640)

Glossary: *berd,* maiden; *pight,* fastened.

The elaborate architecture and the rich patterns and sinuous folds of drapery in this panel are characteristic of a way of painting found throughout Europe toward the end of the fourteenth and the beginning of the fifteenth century. But Masolino, though himself conservative and familiar with this International style as practiced not only in Italy but also in Hungary where he traveled, formed a partnership with one of the greatest innovators in art, Masaccio. From this association with a young and brilliant genius, Masolino must have received certain progressive ideas, especially regarding the linear representation of perspective. Longhi (*Critica d'Arte,* 1940) has suggested that this painting was originally in the Church of San Niccolò Oltrarno, and therefore was the picture which Vasari saw in that church a hundred years later and praised for its accurate perspective rendering. Collections: The Earls of Wemyss, Gosford House, Longniddry, Scotland; Henry Goldman, New York. *Andrew Mellon Collection,* 1937. Wood. Height 58¼ in.; width 45¼ in. (1.48 x 1.15). Painted probably 1425-30.

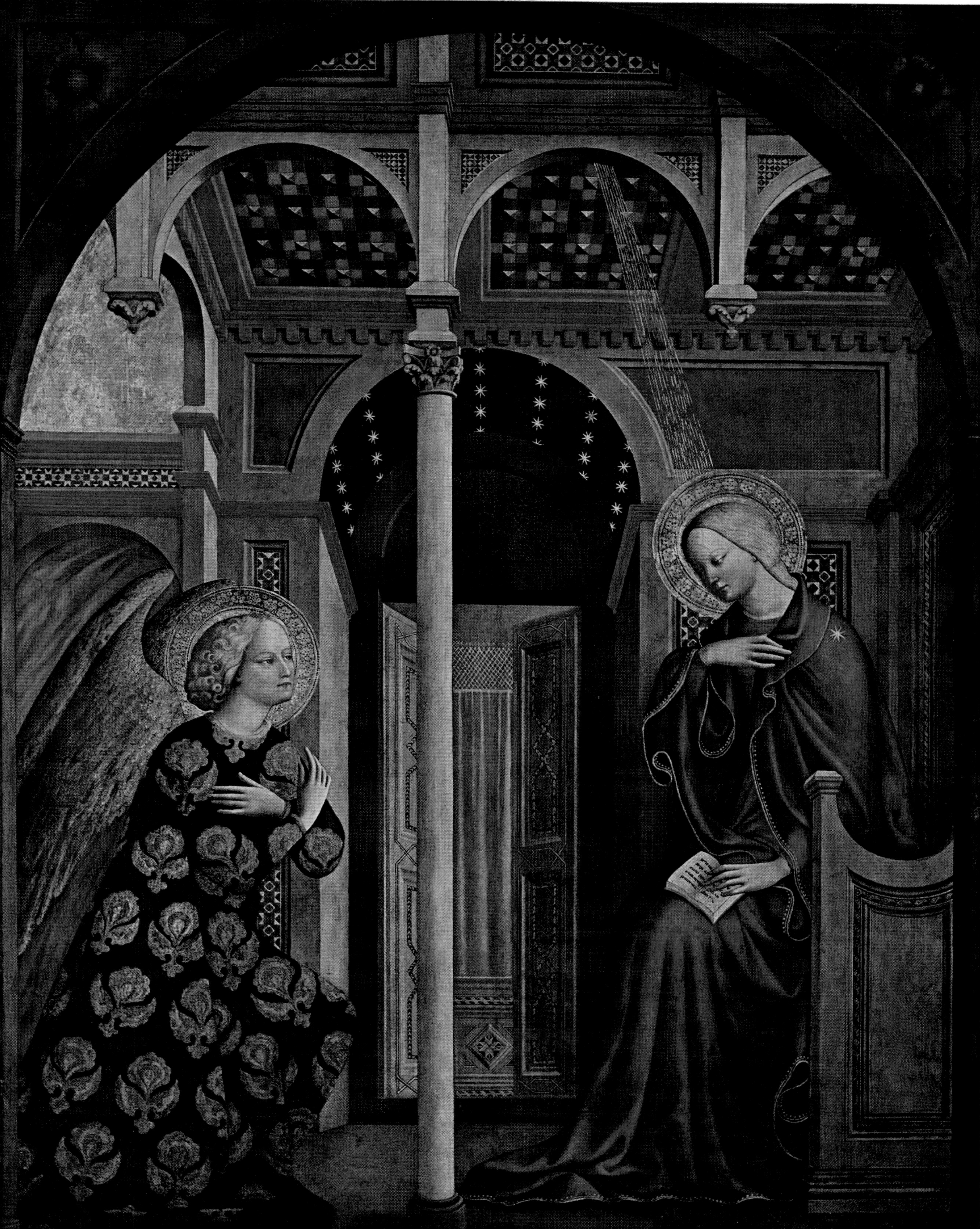

MASACCIO · Florentine 1401-1427/29

Profile Portrait of a Young Man

Giotto born again, starting where death had cut short his advance, instantly making his own all that had been gained during his absence, and profiting by the new conditions, the new demands —imagine such an avatar, and you will understand Masaccio.

Giotto we know already, but what were the new conditions, the new demands? The medieval skies had been torn asunder and a new heaven and a new earth had appeared, which the abler spirits were already inhabiting and enjoying. Here new interests and new values prevailed. The thing of sovereign price was the power to subdue and to create; of sovereign interest all that helped man to know the world he was living in and his power over it. To the artist the change offered a field of the freest activity. It is always his business to reveal to an age its ideals. But what room was there for sculpture and painting—arts whose first purpose it is to make us realize the material significance of things—in a period like the Middle Ages, when the human body was denied all intrinsic significance? In such an age the figure artist can thrive, as Giotto did, only in spite of it, and as an isolated phenomenon. In the Renaissance, on the contrary, the figure artist had a demand made on him such as had not been made since the great Greek days, to reveal to a generation believing in man's power to subdue and to possess the world, the physical types best fitted for the task. . . .

Types, in themselves of the manliest, he presents with a sense for the materially significant which makes us realize to the utmost their power and dignity; and the spiritual significance thus gained he uses to give the highest import to the event he is portraying; this import, in turn, gives a higher value to the types, and thus, whether we devote our attention to his types or to his action, Masaccio keeps us on a high plane of reality and significance. In later painting we shall easily find greater science, greater craft, and greater perfection of detail, but greater reality, greater significance, I venture to say, never. Dust-bitten and ruined though his Brancacci Chapel frescoes now are, I never see them without the strongest stimulation of my tactile consciousness. I feel that I could touch every figure, that it would yield a definite resistance to my touch, that I should have to expend thus much effort to displace it, that I could walk around it. In short, I scarcely could realize it more, and in real life I should scarcely realize it so well, the attention of each of us being too apt to concentrate itself upon some dynamic quality, before we have at all begun to realize the full material significance of the person before us. . . .

Masaccio, then, like Giotto a century earlier—himself the Giotto of an artistically more propitious world—was, as an artist, a great master of the significant, and, as a painter, endowed to the highest degree with a sense of tactile values, and with a skill in rendering them. In a career of but few years he gave to Florentine painting the direction it pursued to the end. In many ways he reminds us of the young Bellini. Who knows? Had he but lived as long, he might have laid the foundation for a painting not less delightful and far more profound than that of Venice.

Bernard Berenson
The Italian Painters of the Renaissance (1930)

The present painting has been incorrectly grouped by some critics with the Olivieri portraits, which have been ascribed to Domenico Veneziano and Paolo Uccello. The attribution to Masaccio, on the convincing evidence of style, was first published in the 1843 catalogue of the Artaud de Montor Collection, and is supported by Berenson. One other portrait on panel, Profile of a Young Man, in the Isabella Gardner Museum, Boston, has been ascribed to Masaccio's own hand. Collections: Artaud de Montor, Paris. *Andrew Mellon Collection,* 1937. Wood. Height 16⅝ in.; width 12¾ in. (0.42 x 0.32). Painted c. 1425.

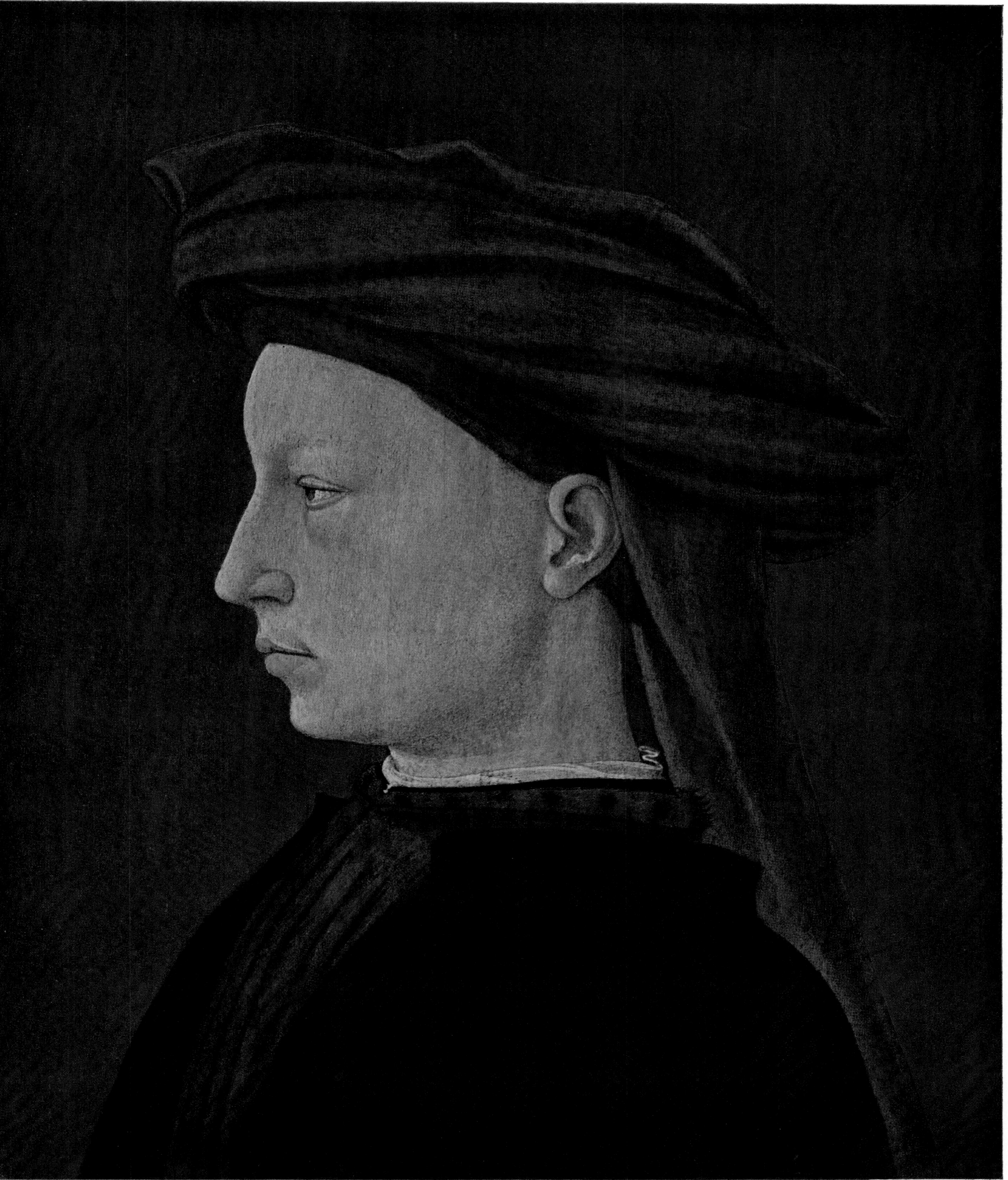

FRA ANGELICO · Florentine 1387-1455

The Healing of Palladia by Saint Cosmas and Saint Damian

This variation of colour in uneven superficies, is what confounds an unskilful Painter; but if he takes care to mark the Out-lines of his Superficie and the seat of his lights in the manner I have before taught, he will find the true colouring no such difficult matter: for first he will alter the superficies properly as far as the line of separation, either with white or black sparingly as only with gentle dew; then he will in the same manner bedew the other side of the line, if I may be allow'd the expression, then this again, and so on by turns, till the light side is brightened with a more transparent colour, and the same colour on the other side dies away like smoak into an easy shade. But you shou'd always remember that no Superficie shou'd ever be made so white, that you cannot make it still brighter: even in Painting the whitest cloaths you shou'd abstain from coming near the strongest of that colour; because the Painter has nothing but white wherewith to imitate the polish of the most shining Superficie whatsoever, as I know of none but black, with which he can represent the utmost shade and obscurity of night. For this reason when he paints a white habit, he shou'd take one of the four kinds of colours that are clear and open; and so again in painting any black habit, let him use another extreme, but not absolute black, as for instance the colour of the sea where it is very deep, which is extremely dark. In a word this composition of black and white has so much power, that when practised with art and method, it is capable of representing in painting the Superficie either of gold or of silver, and even of the clearest glass. Those Painters therefore are greatly to be condemned, who make use of white immoderately, and of black without judgment; for which reason I cou'd wish that the Painters were obliged to buy their white at a greater price than the most costly gems, and that both white and black were to be made of those Pearls which *Cleopatrea* dissolved in vinegar; that they might be more chary of it: it wou'd make their works more graceful and come nearer to truth.

Leon Battista Alberti
De Pictura (1435)

In this painting, as Alberti recommends, the whites are not pure white nor the blacks absolute black. A piece of drapery, for example, is modeled from deep shades of color in the depth of the fold to less intense and more transparent color at the top of the fold. Beginning about 1500, however, painters developed a tendency to ignore the fact that color "dies away like smoak into an easy shade" and made shadows brown or black instead of "the colour of the sea where it is very deep." This tendency finally evolved into the exaggerations which characterized fashionable painting in the last century, and which provoked Whistler's remark: "Lights have been heightened until the white of the tube alone remains—shadows have been deepened until black alone is left." Collections: Lord Northwick, Thirlestane House, near Cheltenham, Gloucestershire; Albert Keller, New York. *Samuel H. Kress Collection,* 1952. Wood. Height 14⅜ in.; width 18⅜ in. (0.365 x 0.467). Painted between 1438 and 1440 if, as most critics assume, it originally formed a part of the predella of the altarpiece which Fra Angelico painted at this time for the high altar of the church of San Marco, Florence.

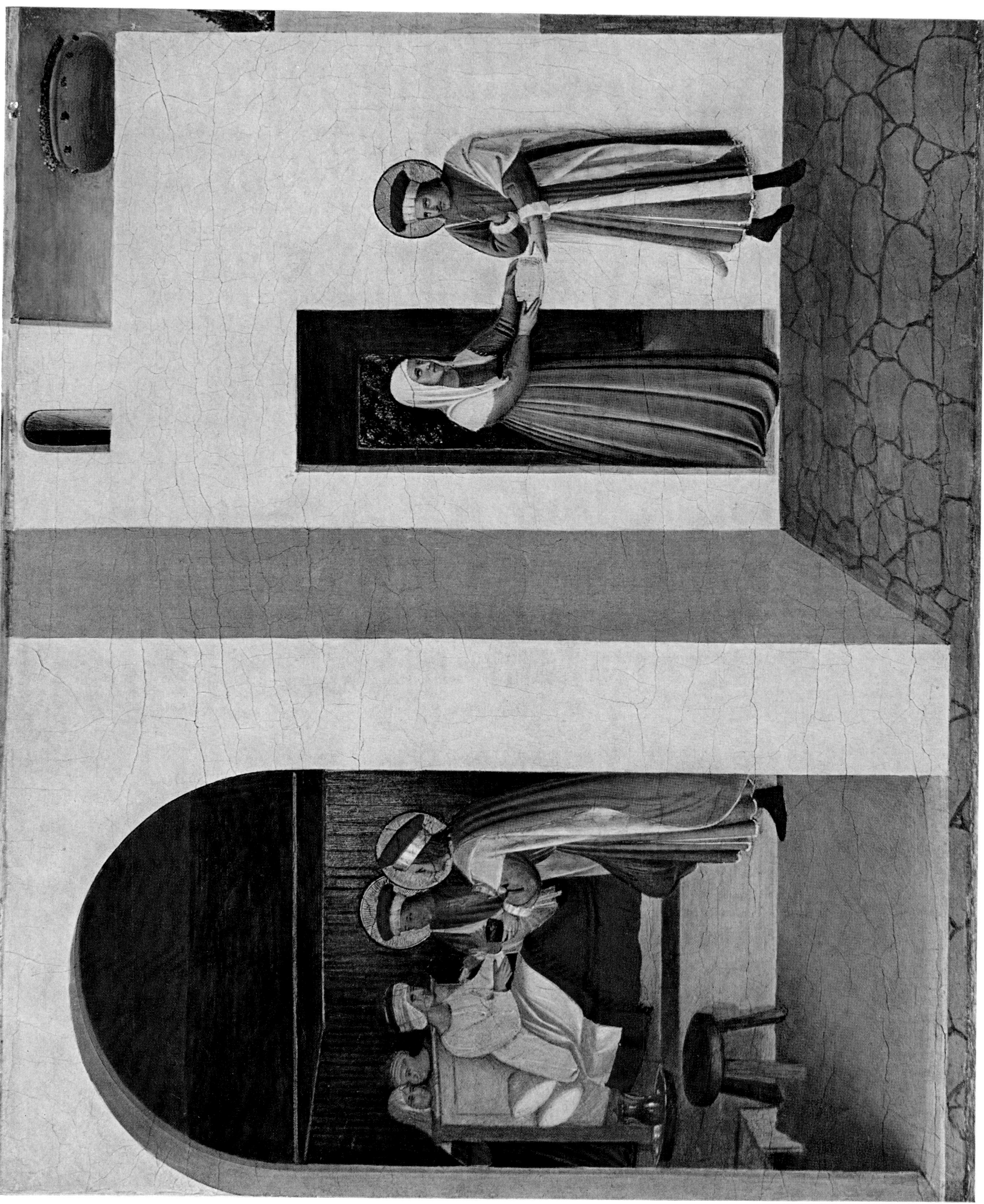

FRA ANGELICO AND FRA FILIPPO LIPPI

FLORENTINE 1387-1455 AND PROBABLY c. 1406-1469

The Adoration of the Magi

'A cold coming we had of it,
Just the worst time of the year
For a journey, and such a long journey:
The ways deep and the weather sharp,
The very dead of winter.'
And the camels galled, sore-footed, refractory,
Lying down in the melting snow.
There were times we regretted
The summer palaces on slopes, the terraces,
And the silken girls bringing sherbet.
Then the camel men cursing and grumbling
And running away, and wanting their liquor
 and women,
And the night-fires going out, and the lack
 of shelters,
And the cities hostile and the towns unfriendly
And the villages dirty and charging high
 prices:
A hard time we had of it.
At the end we preferred to travel all night,
Sleeping in snatches,
With the voices singing in our ears, saying
That this was all folly.

Then at dawn we came down to a
 temperate valley,
Wet, below the snow line, smelling of
 vegetation;
With a running stream and a water-mill
 beating the darkness,
And three trees on the low sky,
And an old white horse galloped away in the
 meadow.
Then we came to a tavern with vine-leaves
 over the lintel,
Six hands at an open door dicing for pieces of
 silver,
And feet kicking the empty wine-skins.
But there was no information, and so we
 continued
And arrived at evening, not a moment too soon
Finding the place; it was (you may say)
 satisfactory.

All this was a long time ago, I remember,
And I would do it again, but set down
This set down
This: were we led all that way for
Birth or Death? There was a Birth, certainly,
We had evidence and no doubt. I had seen
 birth and death,
But had thought they were different; this
 Birth was
Hard and bitter agony for us, like Death,
 our death.
We returned to our places, these Kingdoms,
But no longer at ease here, in the old
 dispensation,
With an alien people clutching their gods.
I should be glad of another death.

T. S. ELIOT
Journey of the Magi (1927)

This tondo ranks among the greatest Florentine paintings of the fifteenth century. It has been identified with an entry in the Medici inventory of 1492 made after the death of Lorenzo the Magnificent, which reads: "A tondo with its golden frame representing the Madonna and Our Lord and the Magi offering gifts, from the hand of Fra Giovanni (Fra Angelico) worth 100 florins"—an extraordinarily high appraisal for a painting in the fifteenth century. This was the highest price in the inventory. Some critics believe the painting to have been executed by Fra Filippo Lippi under the strong influence of Fra Angelico. Collections: Probably Guicciardini Palace, Florence; probably M. Dubois, Florence; William Coningham, London; Alexander Barker, London; Cook, Doughty House, Richmond, Surrey. *Samuel H. Kress Collection,* 1952. Wood. Diameter 54 in. (1.372). Painted probably c. 1445.

FRA FILIPPO LIPPI · Florentine Probably c. 1406-1469

Madonna and Child

And between spiritual emotion and sensuous form
the same living compact maketh our Art, wherein
material appearances engage the soul's depth;
and if in men untrain'd without habit of thought
the ear is more æsthetic than the eye is, this cometh
from thatt sense being the earlier endow'd in animals
who, tho' they be all vacant in a picture-gallery
nor see themselves in a mirror, attend to music
and yield to fascination or vague wonder thereat.
So if we, changing Plato's old difficult term,
should rename his Ideas Influences, ther is none
would miss his meaning nor, by nebulous logic,
wish to refute his doctrin that indeed ther are
eternal Essences that exist in themselves,
supreme efficient causes of the thoughts of men.

What is Beauty? saith my sufferings then.—I answer
the lover and poet in my loose alexandrines:
Beauty is the highest of all these occult influences,
the quality of appearances that thru' the sense
wakeneth spiritual emotion in the mind of man:
And Art, as it createth new forms of beauty,
awakeneth new ideas that advance the spirit
in the life of Reason to the wisdom of God.
But highest Art must be rare as nativ faculty is,
and her surprise of magic winneth favor of men
more than her inspiration.

Robert Bridges
The Testament of Beauty (1929)

Fra Filippo Lippi set himself the task of finding a new "quality of appearances," which Bridges argues lies at the root of all art. Unlike most earlier painters, he selected as models the everyday people of Florence. As Berenson says (*Florentine Painters,* 1896): "His real place is with the genre painters; only his genre was of the soul, as that of others—of Benozzo Gozzoli, for example—was of the body." Thus his figures, though less idealized, are no less religious in feeling than the more formalized Madonnas and saints of Masolino and Domenico Veneziano. Collections: Solly, London; Kaiser Friedrich Museum, Berlin. *Samuel H. Kress Collection,* 1939. Wood. Height 31⅜ in.; width 20⅛ in. (0.80 x 0.51). Painted 1440-45.

FRA FILIPPO LIPPI · Florentine Probably c. 1406-1469

Saint Benedict Orders Saint Maurus to the Rescue of Saint Placidus

I am poor brother Lippo, by your leave!
You need not clap your torches to my face.
Zooks, what 's to blame? you think you see a monk!
What, 't is past midnight, and you go the rounds,
And here you catch me at an alley's end
Where sportive ladies leave their doors ajar? . . .
Here 's spring come, and the nights one makes up bands
To roam the town and sing out carnival,
And I've been three weeks shut within my mew,
A-painting for the great man, saints and saints
And saints again. . . .
You should not take a fellow eight years old
And make him swear to never kiss the girls. . . .
For me, I think I speak as I was taught;
I always see the garden and God there
A-making man's wife: and, my lesson learned,
The value and significance of flesh,
I can't unlearn ten minutes afterwards. . . .

Your hand, sir, and good-by: no lights, no lights!
The street 's hushed, and I know my own way back,
Don't fear me! There 's the gray beginning. Zooks!

Robert Browning
Fra Lippo Lippi (1855)

Fra Filippo's tranquil scenes from the lives of the saints, although modeled to a considerable degree on everyday people, as pointed out in the preceding note, give no indication of his turbulent private life. Browning's poem, based on Vasari, describes how Fra Filippo Lippi was shut up in a room by his great patron, Cosimo de' Medici, who wished him to complete a certain painting. Unable to endure this confinement, Fra Filippo let himself down from the window with a rope made of bed sheets, and roamed the streets of Florence seeking amusement. He is also said to have seduced a nun, who later became his wife. The present representation of the miraculous rescue of a monk who has fallen into a lake while filling his pitcher is characteristic of the narrative scenes often used to decorate the base, or predella, of an altarpiece. In this case the altar may have been the one with scenes from the lives of Saint Benedict and Saint Bernard which Vasari recorded as having been painted by Fra Filippo for the church of the Murate, Florence. Collections: Cernuschi; Édouard Aynard, Lyons. *Samuel H. Kress Collection,* 1952. Wood. Height 16⅜ in.; width 28 in. (0.416 x 0.711). Painted c. 1445.

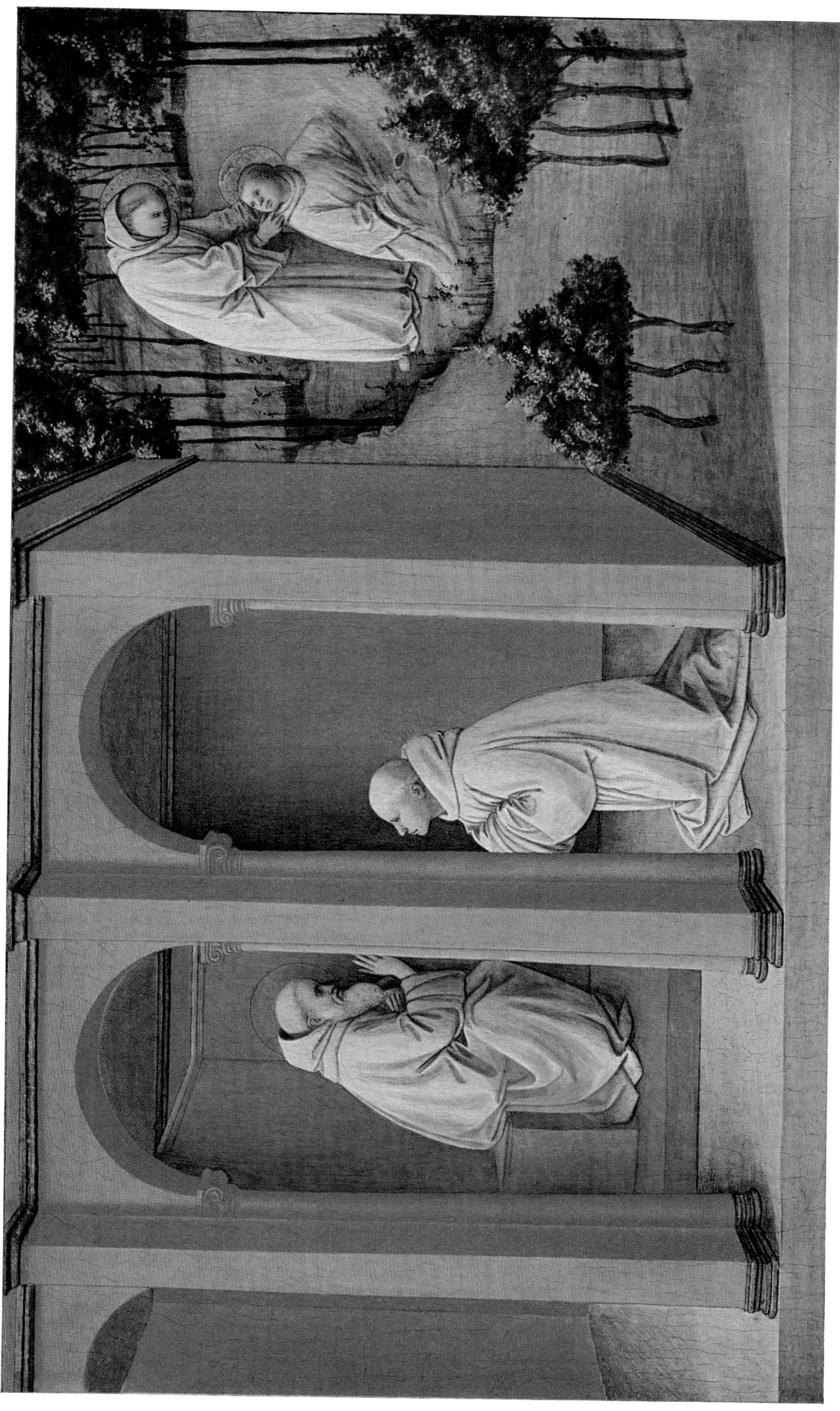

FRA FILIPPO LIPPI · Florentine Probably c. 1406-1469

The Annunciation

There was then in the Carmine a chapel that had been newly painted by Masaccio, which, being very beautiful, pleased Fra Filippo so greatly that he would haunt it every day for his recreation; and continually practising there in company with many young men, who were ever drawing in it, he surpassed the others by a great measure in dexterity and knowledge, insomuch that it was held certain that in time he would do something marvellous. Nay, not merely in his maturity, but even in his early childhood, he executed so many works worthy of praise that it was a miracle....

Having been commissioned by the Nuns of S. Margherita to paint the panel of their high-altar, he was working at this when there came before his eyes a daughter of Francesco Buti, a citizen of Florence, who was living there as a ward or as a novice. Having set eyes on Lucrezia (for this was the name of the girl), who was very beautiful and graceful, Fra Filippo contrived to persuade the nuns to allow him to make a portait of her for a figure of Our Lady in the work that he was doing for them. With this opportunity .... he stole her away from the nuns and took her off.... Whereupon the nuns were greatly disgraced by such an event, and her father, Francesco, who never smiled again, made every effort to recover her; but she, either through fear or for some other reason, refused to come back—nay, she insisted on staying with Filippo, to whom she bore a male child, who was also called Filippo, and who became, like his father, a very excellent and famous painter.

Giorgio Vasari

Le Vite de' piv eccellenti pittori, scvltori, e architettori (1568)

The most marvelous thing about him was that he so thoroughly assimilated the style of Masaccio that, after his death, people used to say in jest that the spirit of Masaccio had entered into the body of Fra Filippo.... This artist was most exceptional for his time in the accuracy of his drawing and the charm which he always strove to impart to his figures, in the beautiful expression of his heads, the variety and nobility of his drapery, and in a certain perfection and grandeur of style which is always evident, especially in the great works which he executed in fresco in the city of Prato and elsewhere, but also in his smaller pictures. These works show most remarkable judgment and that singular care which he constantly devoted to the expression, not only of actions but also of emotions. These are qualities not found in ordinary artists but only in those who have become superior to art itself through long study and wide experience in their craft.

Filippo Baldinucci

Notizie de' professori del disegno (1728)

Vasari states that Filippo Lippi painted for the Palazzo Vecchio "an Annunciation on a panel, which is over a door; and over another door in the said Palace he also painted a Saint Bernard." Albertini (*Memoriale,* 1510) says that one panel was painted for the Main Chancery and the other for the Old Chancery of the palace. It is probable that the large Annunciation reproduced, which is suitable in size and shape for an overdoor, is that mentioned by Vasari and Albertini as executed for the Palazzo Vecchio. Collections: Palazzo Vecchio, Florence (?); Achillito Chiesa, Milan; Percy S. Straus, New York. *Samuel H. Kress Collection,* 1943. Wood. Height 40½ in.; width 64 in. (1.03 x 1.63). Painted probably soon after 1440.

DOMENICO VENEZIANO · Florentine Active 1438-1461

Madonna and Child

A word as to colour. One can only give warnings against possible faults; it is clearly impossible to teach colour by words, even ever so little of it, though it can be taught in a workshop, at least partially. Well, I should say, be rather restrained than over-luxurious in colour, or you weary the eye. Do not attempt over-refinements in colour, but be frank and simple. If you look at the pieces of colouring that most delight you in ornamental work, as, e.g., a Persian carpet, or an illuminated book of the Middle Ages, and analyse its elements, you will, if you are not used to the work, be surprised at the simplicity of it, the few tints used, the modesty of the tints, and therewithal the clearness and precision of all boundary lines. In all fine flat colouring, there are regular systems of dividing colour from colour. Above all, don't attempt iridescent blendings of colour which look like decomposition. They are about as much as possible the reverse of useful.

William Morris
Address (Feb. 21, 1894)

Among Florentine artists influenced by Fra Angelico was the mysterious and rare painter Domenico Veneziano. Little is known of his life and barely a dozen of his paintings have survived. According to Vasari, Domenico was invited from Venice to Florence "on account of the new method he had acquired of painting in oil." His technique, however, now seems less unusual than his choice of color. He was fond of piquant contrasts of rose and green, of tonal dissonances new in painting. He typifies that constant search after novelty which marked Florentine art in the fifteenth century. The discoveries of his generation are also suggested by such details as the correct foreshortening of the halos and the flowers, and by the improved anatomical drawing of the Christ Child. The rose hedge in the background may be a reference to the Virgin as the mystic rose of the litany, or to her identification with the Old Testament Bride who sang in the Song of Solomon: "I am the rose of Sharon." Heavenly love is symbolized by the red roses and purity by the white. Purity is further stressed by the omission of thorns from the rose hedge, for, according to Saint Ambrose, the rose had grown in heaven without thorns and had acquired them only after the fall of man, to remind man of his sins. The Virgin is therefore sometimes described as the "rose without thorns." Collections: Edgeworth family, Edgeworthstown, Ireland. *Samuel H. Kress Collection,* 1939. Wood. Height 32½ in.; width 22¼ in. (0.83 x 0.57). Painted c. 1445.

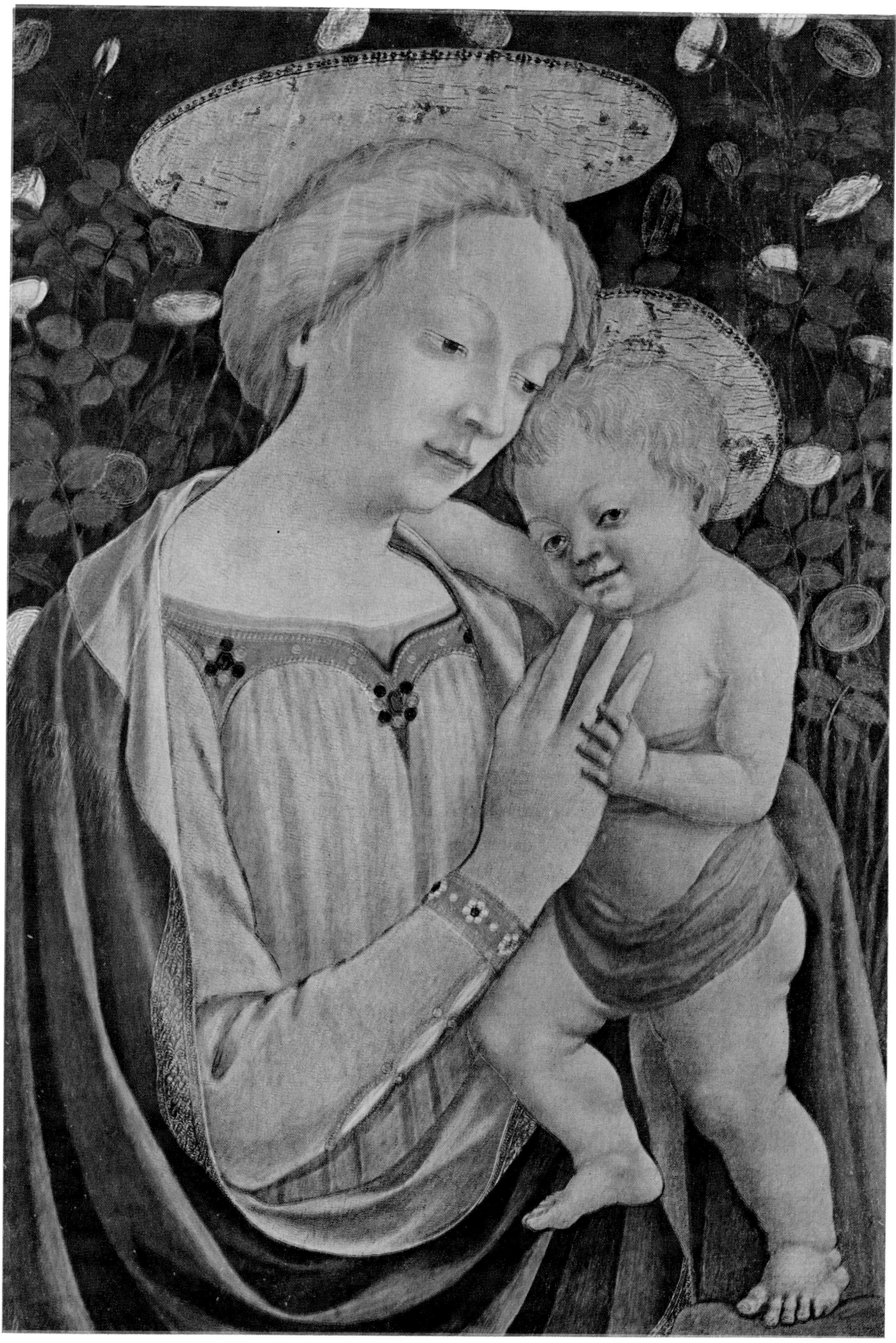

DOMENICO VENEZIANO · Florentine Active 1438-1461

Saint John in the Desert

Domenico's place in the fabric of Florentine painting is only beginning to be understood. Only in recent years has the list of his paintings lengthened from four to thirteen, and we are still in ignorance of the simplest facts about his life. But even a brief survey of his work will give us the figure of a painter whose intrinsic merit and historical significance cannot be overlooked....

Domenico was not the first Italian to look at the out-of-door world around him. Petrarch and Boccaccio had praised the spring, and gardens had become a necessary luxury to the rich *signori* to relieve the sombre austerity of their dark-eaved palaces and crenellated farms. And as the world of nature grew in importance in men's lives, it became a proper subject for painting also. Masaccio drew stark branches on bare mountain sides behind his stern followers of Christ; Masolino painted the snowy mountains he passed through between Hungary and the Lombard plain; Angelico filled his background with gentle hills and convent gardens. But Domenico, more than they, had the real landscape sense, so common north of the Alps and so often denied to Italians, and his Lago di Garda, his La Verna, and his sunny rose garden in Nazareth, have more conviction of their own intrinsic worth....

Vasari's picture of the care-free serenader, graceful and urbane, is not the man which the paintings reveal. The thousands of tiny strokes gradually working out a silken fold which in its luminosity almost foretells the brilliant cape of Velasquez's Pope, the multiplicity of planes in the face of St. John, the minute touches of a brush just wet enough so that every one suggests a leaf dazzling in the sunshine, the measured shadows from the incised cornices, all show how deeply Domenico had studied his technique, what patience and care he lavished on his work. To us, who know Fra Filippo perhaps better than his rival, Domenico's estimate of five years of constant work before the Barbadori altarpiece could be finished, seems a ridiculous exaggeration, but if we consider the methods which he used himself it seems more reasonable. The St. Lucy altarpiece might almost have taken five years! .... Even Baldovinetti, whose long line of ancestors belonged to the class which in Florence constituted its nobility in all but name, lacked that essential elegance, that refinement so aloof, so withdrawn into itself that it looks on the world through half-veiled eyes of quiet melancholy. Domenico Veneziano was an innovator but not a shattering genius. He painted little and much of that is lost. He was admired, perhaps, in his time, though never quite for what he was, and soon forgotten in the shadow of his more forceful or more prolific contemporaries.

Ruth Wedgwood Kennedy
Alesso Baldovinetti (1938)

This panel belongs to the predella of the Saint Lucy altarpiece which was originally in Santa Lucia dei Magnoli, Florence, and which is now in the Uffizi, Florence. The predella was composed of the following five paintings arranged from left to right: Saint Francis Receiving the Stigmata and the painting reproduced, both in the Samuel H. Kress Collection, National Gallery of Art; the Annunciation and the Miracle of Saint Zenobius, both in the Fitzwilliam Museum, Cambridge, England; and the Martyrdom of Saint Lucy in the Berlin Museum. In the present painting the figure of Saint John was probably inspired by some classical statue. Collections: Santa Lucia dei Magnoli, Florence; Bernard Berenson, Florence; Carl W. Hamilton, New York. *Samuel H. Kress Collection,* 1943. Wood. Height 11⅛ in.; width 12¾ in. (0.284 x 0.324). Painted c. 1445.

PIERO DELLA FRANCESCA · UMBRIAN c. 1416-1492

Saint Apollonia

A natural, spontaneous, and unpretentious grandeur—this is the leading quality of all Piero's work. He is majestic without being at all strained, theatrical or hysterical—as Handel is majestic, not as Wagner. He achieves grandeur naturally with every gesture he makes, never consciously strains after it. Like Alberti, with whose architecture, as I hope to show, his painting has certain affinities, Piero seems to have been inspired by what I may call the religion of Plutarch's *Lives*—which is not Christianity, but a worship of what is admirable in man. Even his technically religious pictures are paeans in praise of human dignity. And he is everywhere intellectual. . . .

Aesthetically, Piero's work has this resemblance to Alberti's: that it too is essentially an affair of masses. What Alberti is to Brunelleschi, Piero della Francesca is to his contemporary, Botticelli. Botticelli was fundamentally a draughtsman, a maker of supple and resilient lines, thinking in terms of arabesques inscribed on the flat. Piero, on the contrary, has a passion for solidity as such. There is something in all his works that reminds one constantly of Egyptian sculpture. Piero has that Egyptian love of the smooth rounded surface that is the external symbol and expression of a mass. The faces of his personages look as though they were carved out of some very hard rock into which it had been impossible to engrave the details of a human physiognomy—the hollows, the lines and wrinkles of real life. They are ideal, like the faces of Egyptian gods and princes, surface meeting and marrying with curved unbroken surface in an almost geometrical fashion. Look, for example, at the faces of the women in Piero's fresco at Arezzo: 'The Queen of Sheba recognizing the Holy Tree.' They are all of one peculiar cast: the foreheads are high, rounded and smooth; the necks are like cylinders of polished ivory; from the midst of the concave sockets the eyelids swell out in one uninterrupted curve into convexity; the cheeks are unbrokenly smooth and the subtle curvature of their surfaces is indicated by a very delicate chiaroscuro which suggests more powerfully the solidity and mass of the flesh than the most spectacular Caravaggioesque light and shade could do.

Piero's passion for solidity betrays itself no less strikingly in his handling of the dresses and drapery of his figures. . . . Among clothes he has a special fondness for pleated bodices and tunics. The bulge and recession of the pleated stuff fascinates him and he likes to trace the way in which the fluted folds follow the curve of the body beneath. . . .

I am attracted to his character by his intellectual power; by his capacity for unaffectedly making the grand and noble gesture; by his pride in whatever is splendid in humanity. And in the artist I find peculiarly sympathetic the lover of solidity, the painter of smooth curving surfaces, the composer who builds with masses. For myself I prefer him to Botticelli, so much so indeed, that if it were necessary to sacrifice all Botticelli's works in order to save the Resurrection, the Nativity, the Madonna della Misericordia and the Arezzo frescoes, I should unhesitatingly commit the Primavera and all the rest of them to the flames. It is unfortunate for Piero's reputation that his works should be comparatively few and in most cases rather difficult of access.

ALDOUS HUXLEY
Along the Road (1925)

This panel apparently formed part of a polyptych, other parts of which were the Saint Monica and an Augustinian monk, formerly in the Liechtenstein Gallery, and now in the Frick Collection, New York. Possibly the polyptych was painted for the high altar of Sant' Agostino at Borgo San Sepolcro. It was commissioned in 1454 and final payment made in 1469. Collections: Santa Chiara, Borgo San Sepolcro; Casa Marini-Franceschi, Borgo San Sepolcro; Philip Lehman, New York. *Samuel H. Kress Collection,* 1952. Wood. Height 15¼ in.; width 11 in. (0.39 x 0.28). Painted c. 1460.

ANDREA DEL CASTAGNO · Florentine c. 1420-1457

Portrait of a Man

If nature had only one fixed standard for the proportions of the various parts, then the faces of all men would resemble each other to such a degree that it would be impossible to distinguish one from another; but she has varied the five parts of the face in such a way that although she has made an almost universal standard as to their size, she has not observed it in the various conditions to such a degree as to prevent one from being clearly distinguished from another. . . .

A picture or any representation of figures ought to be done in such a way that those who see them may be able with ease to recognise from their attitudes what is passing through their minds. So if you have to represent a man of good repute in the act of speaking, make his gestures accord with the probity of his speech; and similarly if you have to represent a brutal man, make him with fierce movements flinging out his arms towards his hearer, and the head and chest protruding forward beyond the feet should seem to accompany the hands of the speaker.

Just so a deaf mute who sees two people talking, although being himself deprived of the power of hearing, is none the less able to divine from the movements and gestures of the speakers the subject of their discussion.

· · · ·

If you have a courtyard which, when you so please, you can cover over with a linen awning, the light will then be excellent. Or when you wish to paint a portrait, paint it in bad weather, at the fall of the evening, placing the sitter with his back to one of the walls of the courtyard. Notice in the streets at the fall of the evening when it is bad weather the faces of the men and women—what grace and softness they display! Therefore, O painter, you should have a courtyard fitted up with the walls tinted in black and with the roof projecting forward a little beyond the wall; and the width of it should be ten braccia, and the length twenty braccia, and the height ten braccia; and you should cover it over with the awning when the sun is on it, or else you should make your portrait at the hour of the fall of the evening when it is cloudy or misty, for the light then is perfect.

Leonardo da Vinci
Notebooks (c. 1483-1518)

A generation separates this painting from the date of Leonardo's *Notebooks*. Though Leonardo's remarks summarize the general principles of Renaissance portraiture, there is one important difference in style between the methods he advocates and those followed by Castagno and earlier artists. Leonardo recommends "grace" and "softness," an illumination "cloudy" and "misty," the type of lighting which encourages the indistinct, almost imperceptible gradations of modeling we find in the Mona Lisa. Castagno instead paints by a hard, clear light, models the separate planes of the figure with the sharp clarity of a relief in bronze. The difference between the sculptural approach of the Early Renaissance, as we find it in Castagno, and the pictorial methods of the High Renaissance, as described by Leonardo, is one of the most significant stylistic changes in the history of painting. Collections: Barone Cerbone del Nero, Florence; Marchese Torrigiani, Florence; Rodolphe Kann, Paris; J. Pierpont Morgan, New York. *Andrew Mellon Collection,* 1937. Wood. Height 21¼ in.; width 15⅞ in. (0.540 x 0.405). Painted c. 1455.

ANDREA DEL CASTAGNO · Florentine c. 1420-1457

The Youthful David

Curiosity about natural forms in all their variety and complexity—*naturalism* in the modern sense—first manifested itself in European art in Flanders, France, and North Italy about the second decade of the fifteenth century. It appears that Italy actually led the way in this movement, and that Lombardy was the point of origin. . . .

In Florence, too, this impulse was undoubtedly felt, but it is the great distinction of the Florentine artists that, however much their curiosity about particular forms may have been excited, their high intellectual passion for abstract ideas impelled them more to the study of some general principles underlying all appearance. They refused to admit the given facts of nature except in so far as they could become amenable to the generalising power of their art. Facts had to be digested into form before they were allowed into the system.

We can get an idea of what Florence of the fifteenth century meant for the subsequent tradition of European art if we consider that if it had not been for Florence the art of Italy might have been not altogether unlike the art of Flanders and the Rhine—a little more rhythmical, a little more gracious, perhaps, but fundamentally hardly more significant. . . .

Masaccio . . . . was helped perhaps by the fact that the new naturalism was as yet only a general perception of new aspects of natural form. It was left for his younger contemporaries to map out the new country methodically—to the group of adventurous spirits—Brunelleschi, Donatello, Castagno, and Uccello—who founded modern science, and gave to the understanding of classic art a methodical basis. It is in this group that the fierce intellectual passion of the Florentine genius manifests itself most clearly. Perspective and anatomy were the two studies which promised to reveal to them the secrets of natural form. The study of anatomy exemplifies mainly the aspect of curiosity, though even in this the desire to find the underlying principles of appearance is evident—on the other hand perspective, to its first discoverers, appeared to promise far more than an aid to verisimilitude, it may have seemed a visual revelation of the structure of space and through that a key to the construction of pictorial space. . . .

Neither perspective nor anatomy has any very immediate bearing upon art—both of them are means of ascertaining facts, and the question of art begins where the question of fact ends. But artists have always had to excite themselves with some kind of subsidiary intoxicant, and perspective and anatomy, while they were still in their infancy, acted admirably as stimulants. That they have by now become, for most artists, the dreariest of sedatives may make it difficult to conceive this. But at all events in that first generation they excited their devotees to an ardent search for abstract unity of design.

Roger Fry
Vision and Design (1920)

This is a painting on a leather shield, and was intended to be carried in parades, at jousts or tournaments. It is the only example of its kind painted by a great master which has come down to us. Not only is it unique but also Castagno's paintings are extremely rare. Apart from his frescoes in Florence and Venice, only four or five paintings by him have survived. Collections: Drury-Lowe, Locko Park, near Derby, England. *Widener Collection,* 1942. Leather. Height 45½ in.; width 30¼ in. above, 16⅛ in. below (1.156 x 0.769 above, 0.410 below). Painted c. 1450.

BENOZZO GOZZOLI · Florentine 1420-1497

The Dance of Salome

Herod—Salomé, Salomé, dance for me. I pray thee dance for me. I am sad to-night. Yes; I am passing sad to-night. When I came hither I slipped in blood, which is an evil omen; also I heard in the air a beating of wings, a beating of giant wings. I cannot tell what they mean. . . . I am sad to-night. Therefore dance for me. Dance for me, Salomé, I beseech thee. If thou dancest for me thou mayest ask of me what thou wilt, and I will give it thee, even unto the half of my kingdom.

Salomé [*Rising*]—Will you indeed give me whatsoever I shall ask of thee, Tetrarch?

Herodias—Do not dance, my daughter.

Herod—Whatsoever thou shalt ask of me, even unto the half of my kingdom. . . .

Herodias—I will not have her dance while you look at her in this fashion. In a word, I will not have her dance.

Herod—Do not rise, my wife, my queen, it will avail thee nothing. I will not go within till she hath danced. Dance, Salomé, dance for me.

Herodias—Do not dance, my daughter.

Salomé—I am ready, Tetrarch.

[Salomé *dances the dance of the seven veils.*]

Herod—Ah! wonderful! wonderful! You see that she has danced for me, your daughter. Come near, Salomé, come near, that I may give thee thy fee. Ah! I pay a royal price to those who dance for my pleasure. I will pay thee royally. I will give thee whatsoever thy soul desireth. What wouldst thou have? Speak.

Salomé [*Kneeling*]—I would that they presently bring me in a silver charger . . .

Herod [*Laughing*]—In a silver charger? Surely yes, in a silver charger. She is charming, is she not? What is it thou wouldst have in a silver charger, O sweet and fair Salomé, thou that art fairer than all the daughters of Judæa? What wouldst thou have them bring thee in a silver charger? Tell me. Whatsoever it may be, thou shalt receive it. My treasures belong to thee. What is it that thou wouldst have, Salomé?

Salomé [*Rising*]—The head of Jokanaan.

Oscar Wilde
Salomé (1893)

How self-conscious is Oscar Wilde's prose compared to the simplicity of Benozzo Gozzoli's painting! The contrast is a measure of the change that has come about in art and literature between the Renaissance and modern times. Gozzoli conveys the drama of the scene almost naïvely. The king clutches a knife and touches his heart while one courtier pleads and the others look on, fascinated but coldly indifferent. This panel is part of the predella for the altarpiece of the Virgin and Child Enthroned among Angels and Saints in the National Gallery, London. Other panels once forming the predella are a Miracle of Saint Zenobius in Berlin, the Purification of the Virgin in the Johnson Collection, Philadelphia, the Death of Simon Magus in Buckingham Palace, London, and a Miracle of Saint Dominic in the Brera, Milan. Collection: *Samuel H. Kress Collection,* 1952. Wood. Height 9⅜ in.; width 13½ in. (0.238 x 0.343). Commissioned in 1461 by the Confraternity of the Purification of the Virgin for their meeting place above the Church of San Marco, Florence.

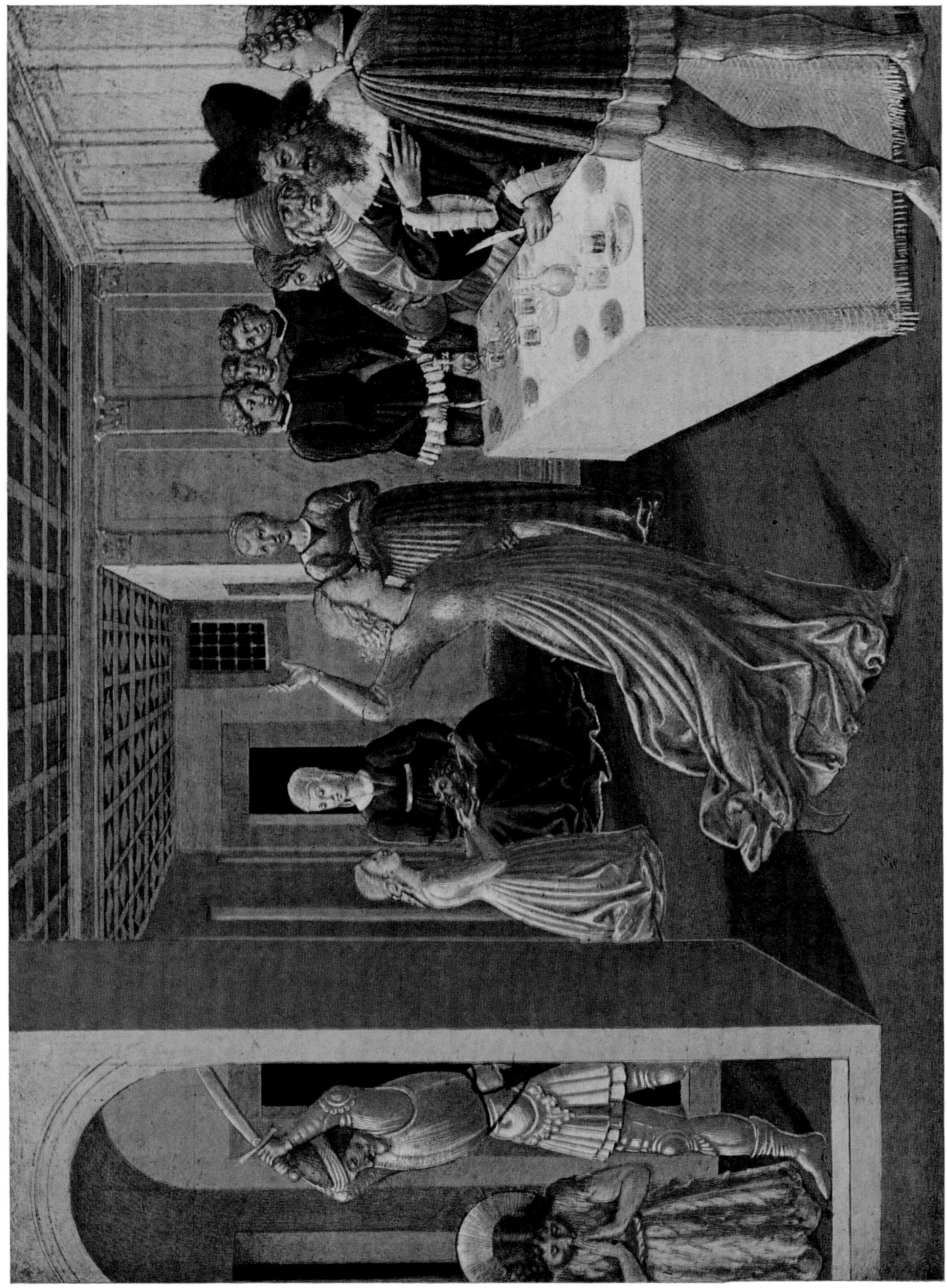

DOMENICO GHIRLANDAIO · Florentine 1449-1494

Madonna and Child

—You know what Aquinas says: The three things requisite for beauty are, integrity, a wholeness, symmetry and radiance. Some day I will expand that sentence into a treatise. Consider the performance of your own mind when confronted with any object, hypothetically beautiful. Your mind to apprehend that object divides the entire universe into two parts, the object, and the void which is not the object. To apprehend it you must lift it away from everything else: and then you perceive that it is one integral thing, that is *a* thing. You recognise its integrity. Isn't that so?

—And then?

—That is the first quality of beauty: it is declared in a simple sudden synthesis of the faculty which apprehends. What then? Analysis then. The mind considers the object in whole and in part, in relation to itself and to other objects, examines the balance of its parts, contemplates the form of the object, traverses every cranny of the structure. So the mind receives the impression of the symmetry of the object. The mind recognises that the object is in the strict sense of the word, a *thing,* a definitely constituted entity. You see?

—Let us turn back, said Cranly. They had reached the corner of Grafton St and as the footpath was overcrowded they turned back northwards. Cranly had an inclination to watch the antics of a drunkard who had been ejected from a bar in Suffolk St but Stephen took his arm summarily and led him away.

—Now for the third quality. For a long time I couldn't make out what Aquinas meant. He uses a figurative word (a very unusual thing for him) but I have solved it. *Claritas* is *quidditas.* After the analysis which discovers the second quality the mind makes the only logically possible synthesis and discovers the third quality. This is the moment which I call epiphany. First we recognise that the object is *one* integral thing, then we recognise that it is an organised composite structure, a *thing* in fact: finally, when the relation of the parts is exquisite, when the parts are adjusted to the special point, we recognise that it is *that* thing which it is. Its soul, its whatness, leaps to us from the vestment of its appearance. The soul of the commonest object, the structure of which is so adjusted, seems to us radiant. The object achieves its epiphany....

Cranly's thin lips parted for speech:—I wonder, he said ...

—What?

Cranly continued to stare towards the mouth of the Liffey like a man in a trance.... "I wonder did that bloody boat, the *Sea-Queen* ever start?"

James Joyce
Stephen Hero (1944)

This great achievement of the Florentine school of the 1470's exemplifies what Joyce means by "integrity, a wholeness, symmetry and radiance." But who painted it? Berenson and Zeri ascribe it to young Ghirlandaio. Other critics have thought it by Verrocchio. In any event it was certainly painted by an artist who formed part of that remarkable center of pictorial style, Verrocchio's studio, where so many geniuses were apprenticed, among them Leonardo da Vinci. Collections: Mrs. E. L. Scott, London. *Samuel H. Kress Collection,* 1961. Wood transferred to masonite. Height 28⅞ in.; width 20 in. (0.734 x 0.508). Painted c. 1470.

BOTTICELLI · Florentine 1444/45-1510

Giuliano de' Medici

There was a man of double deed
Sowed his garden full of seed.
When the seed began to grow,
'Twas like a garden full of snow;
When the snow began to melt,
'Twas like a ship without a belt;
When the ship began to sail,
'Twas like a bird without a tail;
When the bird began to fly,
'Twas like an eagle in the sky;
When the sky began to roar,
'Twas like a lion at the door;
When the door began to crack,
'Twas like a stick across my back;
When my back began to smart,
'Twas like a penknife in my heart;
When my heart began to bleed,
'Twas death and death and death indeed.

Anonymous
The Oxford Dictionary of Nursery Rhymes (1951)

Giuliano de' Medici
Paolo Giovio, *Elogia* (1575)

Lorenzo de' Medici's "double deeds" were numerous, but it was Giuliano, his younger and gentler brother, who suffered for them. On the 26th of April, 1478, conspirators led by members of the Pazzi family fell on the two Medici brothers while they were at Mass in the Cathedral of Florence. Lorenzo escaped but Giuliano was stabbed to the heart. The turtledove perched on a dead branch is very likely a reference to mourning; but we do not know whether it refers to the mourning of Giuliano at the death of his beloved Simonetta Vespucci, who died suddenly in 1476, or to the mourning of the Medici family and friends at the death of Giuliano himself. Collection: *Samuel H. Kress Collection,* 1952. Wood. Height 29¾ in.; width 20⅝ in. (0.756 x 0.526). Painted c. 1478.

BOTTICELLI · Florentine 1444/45-1510

The Adoration of the Magi

Botticelli lived in a generation of naturalists, and he might have been a mere naturalist among them. There are traces enough in his work of that alert sense of outward things, which, in the pictures of that period, fills the lawns with delicate living creatures, and the hillsides with pools of water, and the pools of water with flowering reeds. But this was not enough for him; he is a visionary painter, and in his visionariness he resembles Dante. Giotto, the tried companion of Dante, Masaccio, Ghirlandajo even, do but transcribe, with more or less refining, the outward image; they are dramatic, not visionary painters; they are almost impassive spectators of the action before them. But the genius of which Botticelli is the type usurps the data before it as the exponent of ideas, moods, visions of its own; in this interest it plays fast and loose with those data, rejecting some and isolating others, and always combining them anew. To him, as to Dante, the scene, the colour, the outward image or gesture, comes with all its incisive and importunate reality; but awakes in him, moreover, by some subtle law of his own structure, a mood which it awakes in no one else, of which it is the double or repetition, and which it clothes, that all may share it, with sensuous circumstance. . . .

He thus sets for himself the limits within which art, undisturbed by any moral ambition, does its most sincere and surest work. His interest is neither in the untempered goodness of Angelico's saints, nor the untempered evil of Orcagna's *Inferno;* but with men and women, in their mixed and uncertain condition, always attractive, clothed sometimes by passion with a character of loveliness and energy, but saddened perpetually by the shadow upon them of the great things from which they shrink. His morality is all sympathy; and it is this sympathy, conveying into his work somewhat more than is usual of the true complexion of humanity, which makes him, visionary as he is, so forcible a realist.

It is this which gives to his Madonnas their unique expression and charm. He has worked out in them a distinct and peculiar type, definite enough in his own mind, for he has painted it over and over again, sometimes one might think almost mechanically, as a pastime during that dark period when his thoughts were so heavy upon him.

Walter Pater
The Renaissance (1888)

Horne (*Sandro Botticelli*) has suggested that this picture, which he considered the latest of all the extant Adorations by Botticelli, may be identified with a painting mentioned in the *Codice Magliabechiano* as having been executed in Rome. On stylistic grounds it is accepted by most critics as of Botticelli's Roman period, 1481-1482. Collections: Purchased in Rome by the engraver, Peralli, it was acquired in 1808 for the Hermitage Gallery, Leningrad, by Czar Alexander I. *Andrew Mellon Collection,* 1937. Wood. Height 27⅝ in.; width 41 in. (0.702 x 1.042).

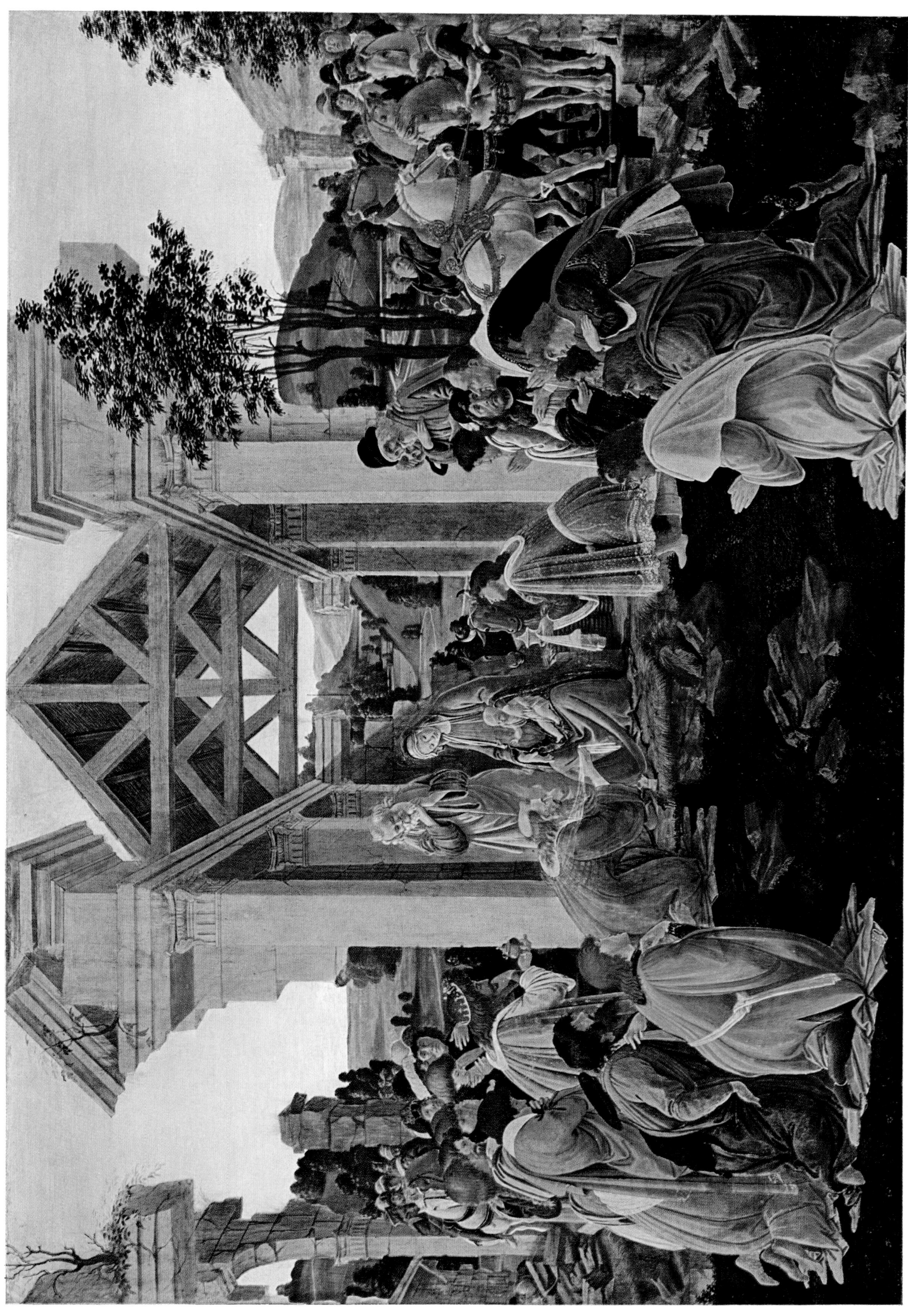

BOTTICELLI · Florentine 1444/45-1510

Portrait of a Youth

In Buddhism and other Oriental religions, all of which have strong tendencies to mysticism, hands play a large part in solemnities. The whole system of the mudras, or position of hands, in Buddhism is as complex as mysterious, which with its infinite combinations, positions of hands, their turnings, knittings of fingers and so on, serves to indicate innumerable gods and goddesses who are nothing less than the personification of different moods of the human mind. . . . All this probably came from India, where the cult of the hand and foot seems to have been always cherished. There are innumerable representations of hands, both beautiful and ugly, always very symbolic, in Indian Art and its derivatives in the Art of all Eastern lands. . . . Maple-leaves are called in Japan 'human hands,' because of their similarity in form, but I would say more, that those young pale leaves, extending in late spring, expanding visibly after sun and rain, are like the dancing hands of children. If young buds are signs of the mystery of expanding life, young hands are as well. . . .

If we trace the evolution of Botticelli's art, taking into consideration this inner development, it would appear to be of this nature: at first he was too exclusively occupied with the outward aspect of the hand and its technical difficulties; then his spiritual sense awoke; but being strictly dependent upon the still tenacious realism, its expression was at first what I called the 'characteristic,' the expression of the soul or its intentions immediately behind the exterior. And then, as his art approached more and more to its absolute domain, his outward form being gradually released from the grip of realism, the expression was also released from the immediate illustration of the character of the actual person represented, and became freer, finally arriving at symbolism, just as the outward form became a linear design. If in the outward form Botticelli's great merit lay in the linear, so in spiritual expression it must lie in the corresponding one, the symbolic. . . .

Thus, psychologically, Botticelli's hand developed. At the end of this study, let us admire the finest hand ever painted by him, in which, I may say, all the qualities I have mentioned were perfectly combined. I mean the hand of the [Portrait of a Youth]. It is the hand of an Adonis, where the soft feminine charm is mingled with a man's strength, though still young. It is a perfect hand. Except in a few of El Greco's masterpieces, you cannot see such a hand, a mere hand, with a whole mystery behind it.

Yukio Yashiro
Sandro Botticelli (1925)

Whether paintings like the one reproduced can be considered portraits at all is doubtful. They present, rather, ideal types of adolescent beauty. Yashiro points out that in looking at portraits by Botticelli: "Your interest in the persons represented is very slight. . . . Rather you are immersed in a vague ideal atmosphere, which floats above the individualistic world." Collections: Louis, Comte de Pourtalès-Gorgier, Paris; Baron Arthur de Schickler, Martinvast, France; Comtesse Hubert de Pourtalès; Clarence H. Mackay, Roslyn, New York. *Andrew Mellon Collection,* 1937. Wood. Height 16¼ in.; width 12½ in. (0.412 x 0.318). Painted c. 1483-84.

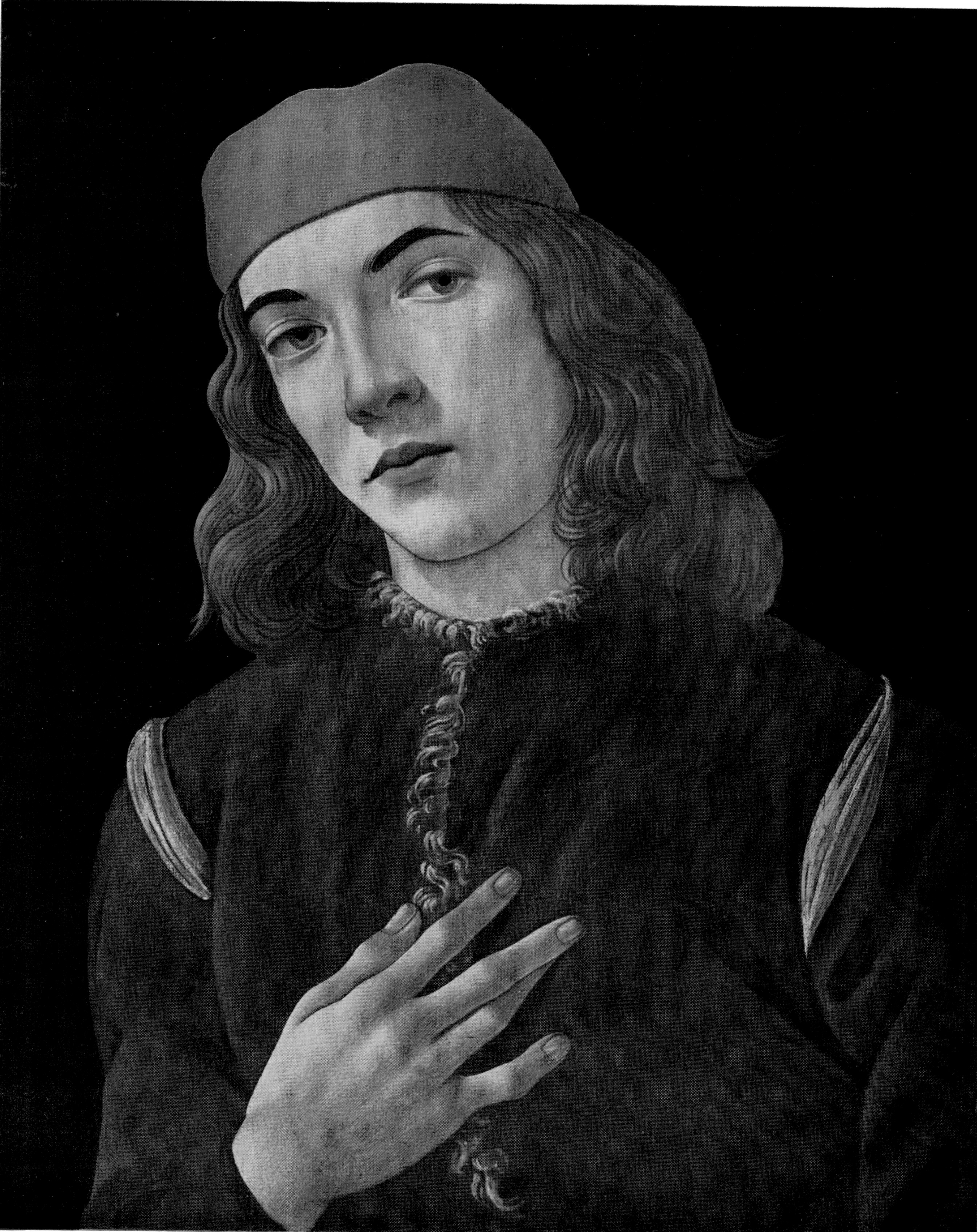

FILIPPINO LIPPI · Florentine Probably 1457-1504

Tobias and the Angel

In fact, the poet who treats a well-known story or a well-known character, has already made considerable progress towards his object. He can afford to pass over a hundred cold details, which would otherwise be indispensable to the understanding of his whole; and the more quickly his audience comprehends this, the sooner their interest will be awakened. This advantage the painter also enjoys, when his subject is not new to us, and we recognize, at the first glance, the intention and meaning of his whole composition; at once not only see that his characters are speaking, but hear what they are saying. The most important effect depends on the first glance.

Gotthold Ephraim Lessing
Laokoon (1766)

Painting is the noblest of the arts. In it are summed up all the sensations. In its presence each person can, as his imagination wishes, create his special story. With a single glance of the eye his soul can be invaded by the most profound recollections. It requires no effort of memory; everything is summarized in an instant.—Painting is the perfect art that encompasses and completes all the others.

Like music, it acts on the soul through the intermediary of tones, its harmonious colors corresponding to the harmonies of sounds; but in painting a unity is obtained that is not possible in music, where the chords follow one another and the judgment experiences an incessant fatigue if it would unite the end and the beginning. In short, the ear is an inferior sense to the eye. The hearing can grasp but a single sound at a time, while the sight takes in everything, simplifying in accordance with its wishes.

Like literature, the art of painting is able to state what it intends, with this advantage, that the *reader* knows immediately the prelude, development and outcome. Literature and music demand an effort of memory in order to appreciate the whole. . . . You can dream freely when you listen to music as well as when you look at a painting; but in reading a book you are a slave to the ideas of the author. The writer is obliged to address himself to the intelligence before he can move the heart, and God knows that a reasoned sensation is not very strong.

The sight alone produces an instantaneous impulse.

Paul Gauguin
Notes synthétiques de Paul Gauguin (1910)

The story of Tobias and the Angel was one of the most familiar themes of Renaissance painting. It was undoubtedly popular with parents of absent sons, emphasizing as it did both filial piety and divine protection. Tobias, according to the Book of Tobit, was guided by the Archangel Raphael to the banks of the river Tigris where a great fish which leaped out of the water furnished, along with other miraculous aid, the cure for the blindness of Tobias' father. In Filippino Lippi's panel not only are the central facts of the story told, but the mood of sheltering divinity is conveyed, thus achieving the wholeness of which Gauguin speaks. Collections: Robert H. and Evelyn Benson, London. *Samuel H. Kress Collection,* 1939. Wood. Height 12⅞ in.; width 9¼ in. (0.325 x 0.235). Painted c. 1480.

FILIPPINO LIPPI · Florentine Probably 1457-1504

Portrait of a Youth

The plot then is the first principle and as it were the soul of tragedy: character comes second. It is much the same also in painting; if a man smeared a canvas with the loveliest colours at random, it would not give as much pleasure as an outline in black and white. . . .

Moreover, in everything that is beautiful, whether it be a living creature or any organism composed of parts, these parts must not only be orderly arranged but must also have a certain magnitude of their own; for beauty consists in magnitude and ordered arrangement. From which it follows that neither would a very small creature be beautiful—for our view of it is almost instantaneous and therefore confused—nor a very large one, since being unable to view it all at once, we lose the effect of a single whole; for instance, suppose a creature a thousand miles long. As then creatures and other organic structures must have a certain magnitude and yet be easily taken in by the eye, so too with plots. . . .

Poetry tends to give general truths while history gives particular facts. . . .

We must copy the good portrait-painters who, while rendering the distinctive form and making a likeness, yet paint people better than they are. It is the same with the poet. . . .

Obviously the art which makes its appeal to everybody is eminently vulgar.

Aristotle
Poetics (4th Century B.C.)

In sensitive expression of the beauty of adolescence, Renaissance Florence is the closest rival of classical Greece. Filippino Lippi has attained this expression through the happy balance between imitation and idealization recommended by Aristotle for portraiture, a balance between achieving a likeness and painting "people better than they are." A number of Florentine portraits similar to the one reproduced have been preserved, and it is often difficult to attribute them with certainty. The present picture has been ascribed to Botticelli, but in view of its similarity to the portraits of the young men in the Brancacci chapel known to have been painted by Filippino Lippi, its attribution to him seems more likely. Collections: Liechtenstein Gallery, Vienna; Frank D. Stout, Chicago. *Andrew Mellon Collection,* 1937. Wood. Height 20 in.; width 13⅞ in. (0.51 x 0.355). Painted c. 1485.

CIRCLE OF VERROCCHIO (POSSIBLY LEONARDO)

FLORENTINE c. 1475

Madonna and Child with a Pomegranate

In the Italian devotional pictures of the early Renaissance there are usually two quite unrelated parts: the foreground and the background.

The foreground is conventional. Its personages—saints, angels and Holy Family—are the direct descendants of a long line of similar figures. Every detail of dress and attitude has been settled beforehand by laws which the artist accepts as passively as the fact that his models have two eyes apiece, and noses in the middle of their faces. Though now and then some daring painter introduces a happy modification, such as the little violin-playing angels on the steps of the Virgin's throne, in the pictures of the Venetian school, such changes are too rare and unimportant to affect the general truth of the statement. It is only in the background that the artist finds himself free to express his personality. Here he depicts not what some one else has long since designed for him, in another land and under different conceptions of life and faith, but what he actually sees about him, in the Lombard plains, in the delicately-modelled Tuscan hill-country, or in the fantastic serrated landscape of the Friulian Alps. One must look past and beyond the central figures, in their typical attitudes and symbolical dress, to catch a glimpse of the life amid which the painting originated. Relegated to the middle distance, and reduced to insignificant size, is the real picture, the picture which had its birth in the artist's brain and reflects his impression of the life about him. . . .

No one who has studied the backgrounds of old Italian pictures can imagine that realistic landscape-painting is a modern art. The technique of the early landscape-painters was not that of the modern interpreter of nature, but their purpose was the same; they sought to render with fidelity and precision what they saw about them. It is this directness of vision which gives to their backgrounds such vividness and charm. In these distances one may discover the actual foreground of the artist's life. Here one may learn what was veritably happening in fifteenth-century Venice, Florence and Perugia; here see what horizons the old masters looked out on, and note that the general aspect of the country is still almost as unchanged as the folds of the Umbrian mountains and the curves of the Tuscan streams.

EDITH WHARTON
Italian Backgrounds (1905)

The authorship of this painting is a mystery. It was undoubtedly executed by an artist working in the studio of Verrocchio. The scholars who have studied the problem are about evenly divided between an attribution to Lorenzo di Credi and to the youthful Leonardo da Vinci. A strong evidence for Leonardo is the background, and the background, as Mrs. Wharton points out, is where "the artist finds himself free to express his personality." The exquisite glimpse of the Arno Valley is one of the most sensitive pieces of landscape painting in the National Gallery of Art. Note the way in which the artist has introduced a favorite Christian symbol. In her left hand, the Virgin holds an open pomegranate, from which the Child has taken some seeds, holding them up for His mother to see. The meaning given by Pope Gregory the Great to this old symbol of fertility, the pomegranate, is the unity of the Church in the multiplicity of its members. Collections: John Watkins Brett, London; Charles Timbal, Paris; Gustave Dreyfus, Paris. *Samuel H. Kress Collection,* 1952. Wood. Height 6⅛ in.; width 5 in. (0.157 x 0.128). Painted c. 1475.

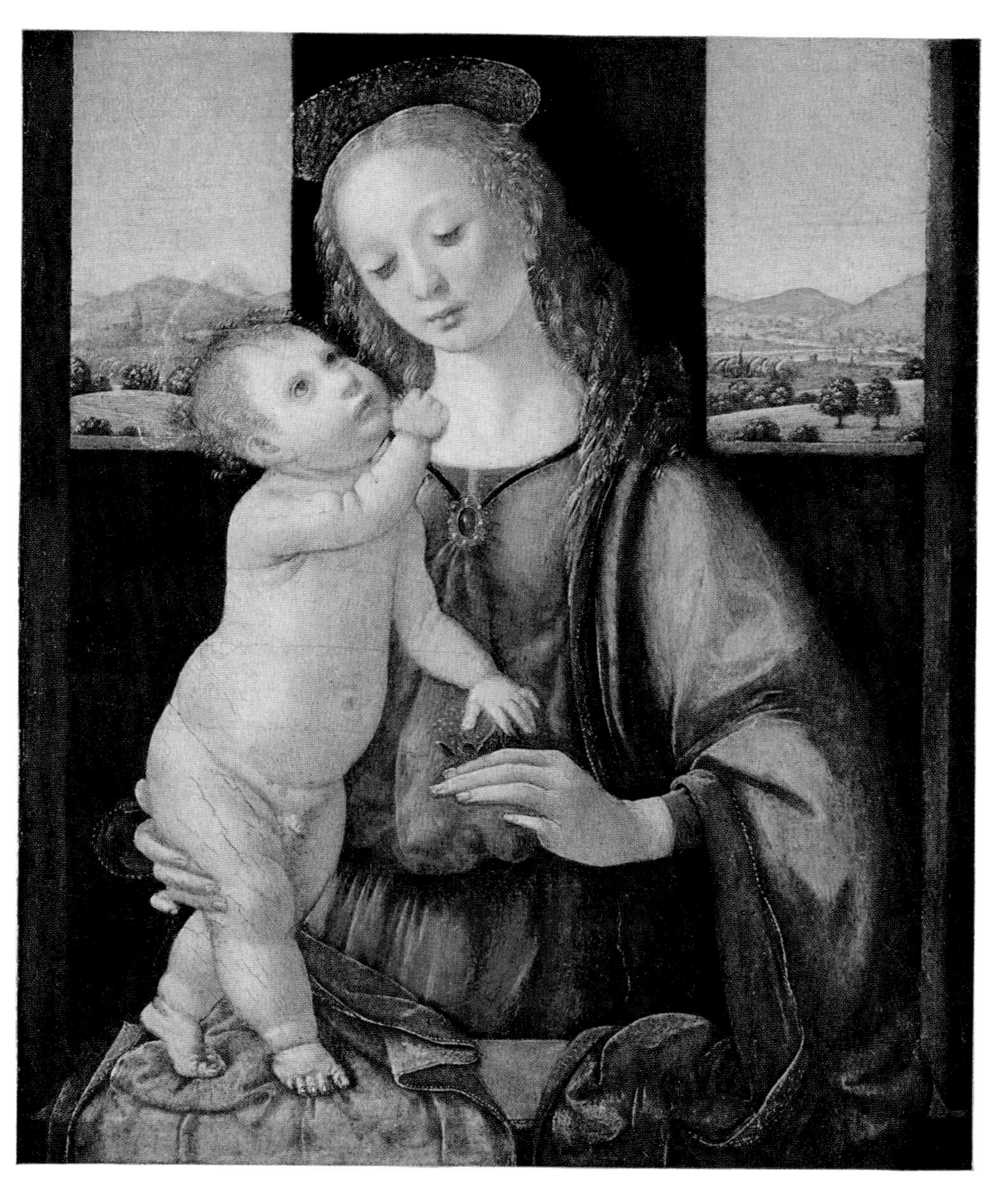

PIERO DI COSIMO · Florentine 1462-c. 1521

The Visitation with Saint Nicholas and Saint Anthony Abbot

And in truth, in all that there is to be seen by his hand, one recognizes a spirit very different and far distant from that of other painters, and a certain subtlety in the investigation of some of the deepest and most subtle secrets of Nature, without grudging time or labour, but only for his own delight and for his pleasure in the art. And it could not well be otherwise; since, having grown enamoured of her, he cared nothing for his own comfort, and reduced himself to eating nothing but boiled eggs, which, in order to save firing, he cooked when he was boiling his glue, and not six or eight at a time, but in fifties; and, keeping them in a basket, he would eat them one by one. In this life he found such peculiar pleasure that any other, in comparison with his own, seemed to him slavery. He could not bear the crying of children, the coughing of men, the sound of bells, and the chanting of friars; and when the rain was pouring in torrents from the sky, it pleased him to see it streaming straight down from the roofs and splashing on the ground. He had the greatest terror of lightning; and, when he heard very loud thunder, he wrapped himself in his mantle, and, having closed the windows and the door of the room, he crouched in a corner until the storm should pass. He was very varied and original in his discourse, and sometimes said such beautiful things, that he made his hearers burst with laughter. But when he was old, and near the age of eighty, he had become so strange and eccentric that nothing could be done with him. He would not have assistants standing round him, so that his misanthropy had robbed him of all possible aid. He was sometimes seized by a desire to work, but was not able, by reason of the palsy, and fell into such a rage that he tried to force his hands to labour; but, as he muttered to himself, the mahl-stick fell from his grasp, and even his brushes, so that it was pitiable to behold. Flies enraged him, and even shadows annoyed him.

· · · ·

In Florence, he painted many pictures for a number of citizens, which are dispersed among their various houses, and of such I have seen some that are very good; and so, also, various things for many other persons. . . . For the Chapel of Gino Capponi, in the Church of S. Spirito at Florence, he painted a panel wherein is the Visitation of Our Lady, with S. Nicholas, and a S. Anthony who is reading with a pair of spectacles on his nose, a very spirited figure. Here he counterfeited a book bound in parchment, somewhat old, which seems to be real, and also some balls that he gave to the S. Nicholas, shining and casting gleams of light and reflections from one to another; from which even by that time men could perceive the strangeness of his brain, and his constant seeking after difficulties.

Giorgio Vasari
Le Vite de' piv eccellenti pittori, scvltori, e architettori (1568)

Painted for the chapel of Gino Capponi in Santo Spirito, Florence. Vasari refers to this picture, which has been preserved exactly as he describes it. Drawings for the Visitation group and for several heads are in the Uffizi, Florence. The Biblical text on the book in the hands of Saint Nicholas is taken from the Wisdom of Solomon (i: 1-5): "Love righteousness, ye that be judges of the earth, . . . For the holy spirit of discipline will flee deceit, . . . and will not abide when unrighteousness cometh in." Collections: Chapel of Gino Capponi, Santo Spirito, Florence; Marchese Gaetano Capponi, Florence; Colonel W. Cornwallis-West, Newlands Manor, Hampshire, England. *Samuel H. Kress Collection,* 1939. Wood. Height 72½ in.; width 74¼ in. (1.84 x 1.89). Painted in the late 1480's.

COSIMO TURA · FERRARESE c. 1430-1495

Madonna and Child in a Garden

Of all holy men and women the Virgin was the most honored and the most loved. Art exalted her above all creatures, and conceived her as an eternal thought of God. . . .

Inside monastery walls the world was spiritualized by the habit of contemplation; realities trembled, dissolved, and evaporated in prayers. The perfumes which mounted from flowers were likened to virtues—modesty, charity, forgetfulness of self. Since he was always meditating on the Virgin, the monk saw her everywhere. The clear spring in the cloister was her purity. The high mountain which closed off the horizon was her grandeur. She was the springtime, coming adorned with a garland of flowers that was a garland of virtues. When the monk stepped out of the monastery all the magnificent things he saw about him were only diminished aspects of the beauty he contemplated in the Virgin. She was the field of grain nourishing within us the bread of eternity, she was the rainbow colored by a ray of God's evening, she was the star from which a drop of dew falls upon our interior aridity. . . .

Like the concept of the girl-Virgin, the grouping of the biblical emblems around Our Lady was also the slow growth of time. Long before, the liturgical writers had chosen the most beautiful biblical metaphors for the adornment of the offices of the Virgin. "Star of the sea," "closed garden," "rose without thorns"—all the lovely biblical phrases came to compose together the richest of ornaments, the most marvelous of diadems:

Botrus, uva, favus, hortus,
Thalamus, triclinium.
Arca, navis, aura, portus,
Luna, lampas, atrium.

Grape and cluster, honey, garden,
Marriage bed and banquet-room,
Ark and ship and breeze and haven,
Moon and lamp and coming home.

So reads the Missal of Evreux. All the missals convey the same mild music by whole columns of nouns: flowers, perfumes, precious metals, colors, honeycombs, all that is most delicious in nature. The most delicate poets of later times have not been more sensitive to the enchantment of words. Thus, the litanies of the Virgin, which, in their present form, did not appear until 1576, have a distant origin. These beautiful words were recited perhaps less for the sake of a specific prayer than for the solace the words alone brought to the heart.

ÉMILE MÂLE
L'Art religieux du XIIe au XVIIIe siècle (1949)

Cosimo Tura was a master of pattern, and from that point of view the present picture is pleasing when looked at in any position—right side up, sideways, or upside down. Note the repetitive rhythm in the scrolls, the floral background and the wiry lines of the Virgin's robes. Contemporary documents tell of Tura's using an aromatic moss paste for relief decorations on gilded chests. In Ferrara this technique became very popular because of the resulting fragrance. It is possible that such a paste formed the scroll reliefs in the painting reproduced. Collections: Harold I. Pratt, New York. *Samuel H. Kress Collection,* 1952. Wood. Height 20¾ in.; width 14⅝ in. (0.53 x 0.37). Painted c. 1455.

FRANCESCO DEL COSSA · Ferrarese c. 1435-c. 1477

The Crucifixion

Who can blot out the Crosse, which th'instrument
Of God, dew'd on mee in the Sacrament?
Who can deny mee power, and liberty
To stretch mine armes, and mine owne Crosse to be?
Swimme, and at every stroake, thou art thy Crosse;
The Mast and yard make one, where seas do tosse;
Looke downe, thou spiest out Crosses in small things;
Looke up, thou seest birds rais'd on crossed wings;
All the Globes frame, and spheares, is nothing else
But the Meridians crossing Parallels.
Materiall Crosses then, good physicke bee,
But yet spirituall have chiefe dignity.
These for extracted chimique medicine serve,
And cure much better, and as well preserve;
Then are you your own physicke, or need none,
When Still'd, or purg'd by tribulation.
For when that Crosse ungrudg'd, unto you stickes,
Then are you to your selfe, a Crucifixe.
As perchance, Carvers do not faces make,
But that away, which hid them there, do take;
Let Crosses, soe, take what hid Christ in thee,
And be his image, or not his, but hee.

John Donne
The Crosse (c. 1615)

The stark intensity of meaning in Donne's poem is analogous to the almost brutal severity of Cossa's picture. To both poet and painter, the image of the Cross is a brand to be burned into the soul. This small tondo, according to a reconstruction plausibly proposed by Longhi, was at the peak of a great altarpiece painted by Cossa for San Petronio, Bologna. Thus it was the climactic point the eye would reach, beyond the images and episodes of the saints which were painted on the other panels. Collections: Costabili, Ferrara; Philip Lehman, New York. *Samuel H. Kress Collection,* 1952. Wood. Diameter 25⅛ in. (0.64) Painted 1470-75.

I·N·R·I

ERCOLE ROBERTI · Ferrarese c. 1456-1496

Giovanni II Bentivoglio

I look upon the true and principal Profession of a Courtier to consist in the Skill of Arms, which I would have him exercise with much Life and Activity; and to be distinguish'd among others for his Bravery, and Courage, and Fidelity....

Let him converse with all with Chearfulness and Familiarity, and not decline such Amusements as others engage in; provided he refuse not at any time a commendable Action, and govern himself with so much Judgment, as not to be guilty of what would make him ridiculous. Let him laugh, joke, and dance, but always in such a manner as shall discover both his Wit and his Discretion, and let his Conversation and Actions be attended with a certain Grace and Dignity....

The Courtier ought to set off all his Actions, Gestures, and Habits, and every Motion with a Grace: And this you seem to apply as a Sawce for everything, without which all his other Virtues and Qualifications would be of small Account. And I am verily persuaded that every Man would soon be convinced thereof, for by Virtue of the Expression we may affirm, that whosoever hath Grace is gracious....

What therefore is the principal and most necessary Ingredient for a Courtier, in Order to his writing and speaking well, in my Opinion, is Knowledge and Understanding: For unless he comprehend the Subject well, which he proposes to treat of, he can neither speak or write to any Purpose. Then must he range it in good Method and Order, and afterward endeavour to cloath it in beautiful Expressions....

I return again to our Courtier: Whom in Letters I would have to be more than moderately instructed, especially in what they style Polite Literature, and to understand not only the Latin Tongue but the Greek, because of the Variety of Things which are written in it with great Accuracy and Beauty....

I am not satisfied with our Courtier, unless he be a Master of Musick: And beside his Understanding to play by Book, have Skill likewise in Variety of Instruments....

Our Courtier ought to have some Skill in Painting, since it is attended with such Credit and Advantage, and more valued in those Days, when Men were more eminent and remarkable for their Courage than they are at present. And though he never reap any other Profit or Pleasure from it, (besides the Help it gives him to judge of the Excellency of Statues, both Ancient and Modern, of Vessels, Buildings, Medals, Gravings, and such like,) it gives him a better Taste and Knowledge of living Beauty.

Baldassare Castiglione
Il Cortegiano (1528)

The identity of the sitter and his wife (whose portrait is on page 67) is established by their portraits included in Lorenzo Costa's altarpiece, dated 1488, in San Giacomo Maggiore, Bologna. The present panels are probably the most distinguished examples of Ferrarese portraiture. Collections: Charles Timbal, Paris; Gustave Dreyfus, Paris. *Samuel H. Kress Collection,* 1939. Wood. Height 21⅛ in.; width 15 in. (0.54 x 0.38). Painted c. 1480.

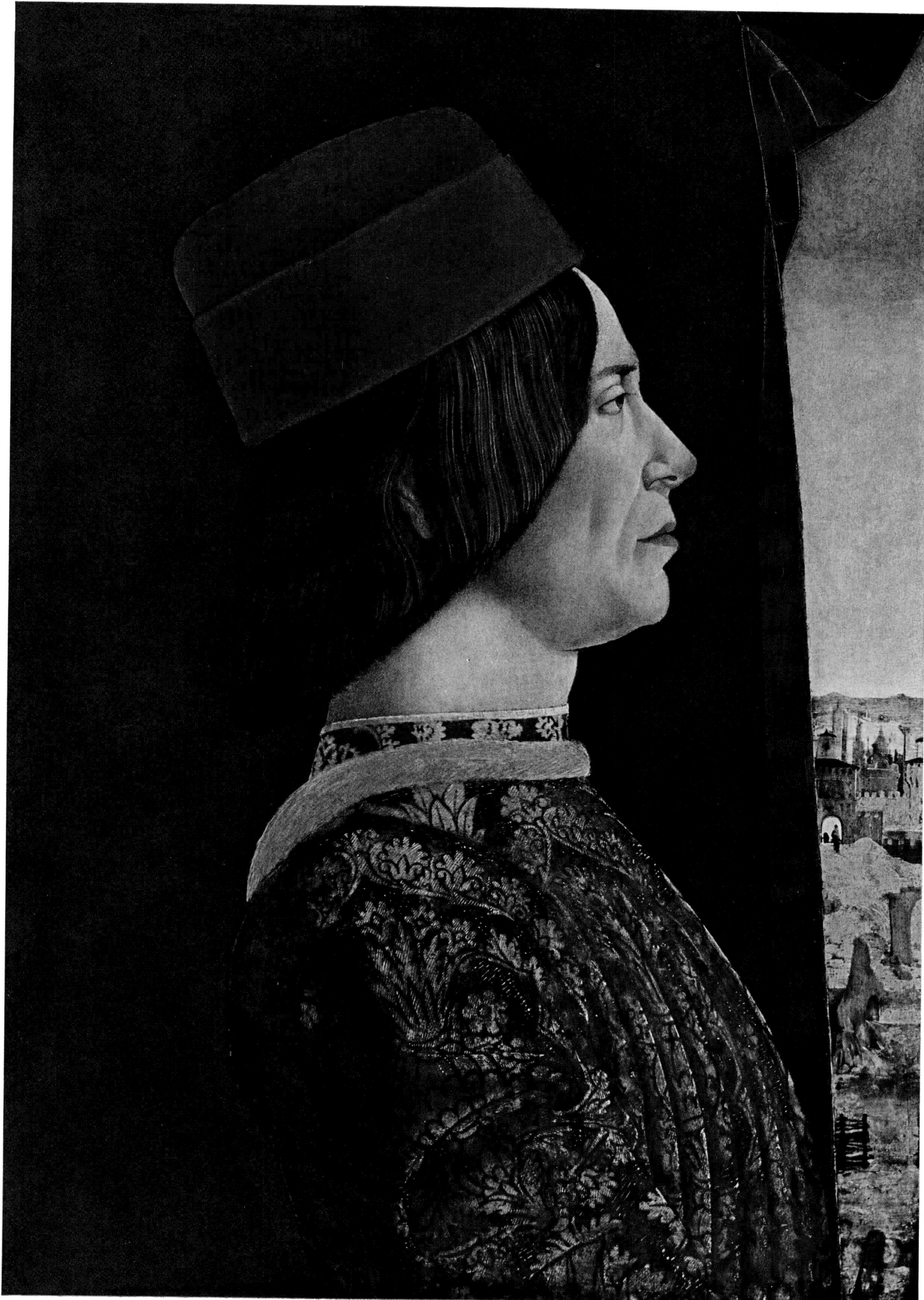

ERCOLE ROBERTI · FERRARESE c. 1456-1496

Ginevra Bentivoglio

Ginevra, distinguished wife of the famous Golden Knight, Giovanni Bentivoglio, Prince of Bologna, and daughter of Alessandro Sforza, Lord of Pesaro, shines by her many virtues and must be mentioned among the famous ladies of our time. Through the great light of the virtues which shine within her, she is an ornament to the City of Bologna, mother of students. In the first place she is famous for her very elegant appearance, gestures and carriage. She moves with a composure which is truly regal. Having lost her first husband and married again, she proved extremely fecund and has already borne sixteen handsome children, both boys and girls. She has a certain remarkable charm in her face and a certain gravity of expression equal to her charm. Her prudence and intelligence are even greater, and beauty of manners is her constant adornment. She speaks with exceeding probity and simple modesty. In all her actions, whether standing, walking, or sitting, she evinces the greatest grace and composure. She does not forget favors, is always grateful, generous and gentle in her speech. She is indeed most affable in entertaining her friends and kinsmen, and is extremely obliging and polite. In her you may see a certain domestic modesty and uncorrupted self-restraint. She loves and cultivates solitude rather than public gatherings, remaining secluded at home most of the time in the manner of pious people. There she occupies herself with religion, nor does she despise secular literature. She takes pleasure in frequently hearing about those women who have acquired fame because of their virtues. She hates and despises shameful words and ignoble talk. She worships God most devoutly, particularly in that she prefers to frequent holy places. She is most charitable towards the servants of Christ and the poor, nor is she any the less diligent in her prayers to God and frequent homage to the Saints. She most ardently listens to the word of God and holds it in her heart above all things, so that other women beholding her example are easily encouraged to imitate and to follow in her footsteps. She is moderate in eating and drinking and does not dress sumptuously. She takes delight in association with those persons who are distinguished for their modesty. In all her doings this great woman shows to a remarkable degree the qualities which all are wont to require of a ruler.... For this reason we have decided to write down this account of her outstanding virtues so that any woman desirous of moral comeliness and fame, and anxious to obtain the favor of God, may read of her virtues and may not refuse or be unwilling to imitate her example, through which life may be made more joyful and immortality assured.

JACOBUS PHILIPPUS BERGOMENSIS
De Claris Mulieribus (1497)

Ginevra Bentivoglio was the sister of the Duchess of Urbino. The Duke of Urbino had commissioned Piero della Francesca to paint the double portrait of himself and his wife, now in the Uffizi, Florence, and it seems probable that Bentivoglio, the tyrant of Bologna, impressed with the fame of the Piero della Francesca double portrait, desired that he and his consort should be similarly commemorated. *Samuel H. Kress Collection,* 1939. Wood. Height 21⅛ in.; width 15¼ in. (0.54 x 0.39). For date and provenance see note on page 64.

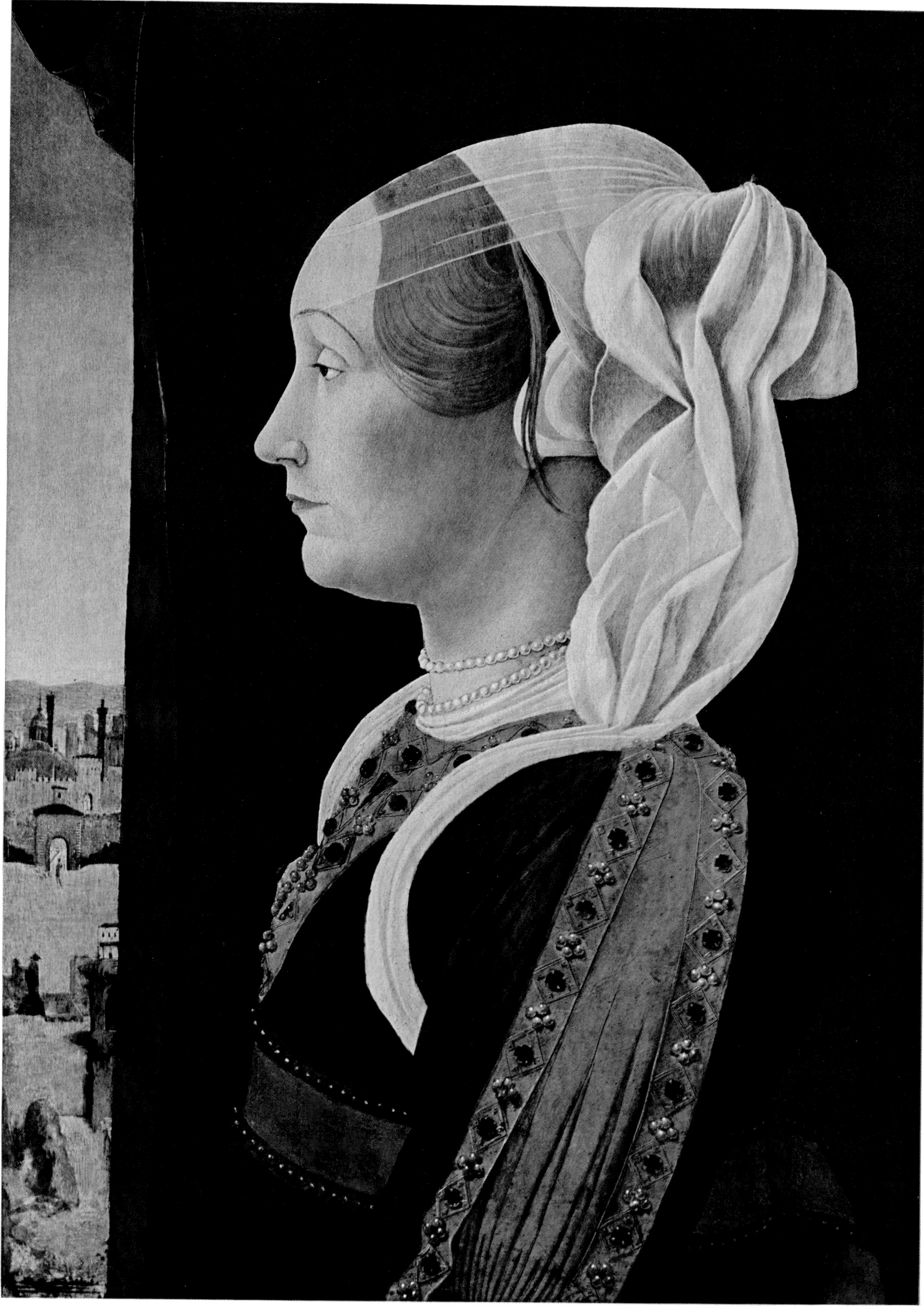

ANDREA MANTEGNA · Paduan 1431-1506

Portrait of a Man

His tendency to find expression for permanent characteristics, for those mental dispositions that are habitual and persistent, his talent for seizing with amazing certainty what is typical in the forms, for giving to his figures distinguished tranquillity and elegance of appearance, made Mantegna specially successful in portraiture. . . . He gives only what is there, without personal contribution, without bestowing upon the person portrayed anything of his own feeling. He penetrates, with the scientific seriousness of a student, into the depth of the actual character, as expressed in the features, and faithfully and honestly reproduces what he has observed without preconception. The impressive pregnancy of the forms gives to his portraits, especially at the first glance, something of an appearance of stiffness, since the movements of the body and of the muscles of the face have so little that is momentary. Let us compare, on the other hand—to remain within the same period—Donatello's portraits, especially that of Niccolò Uzzano in the Museo Nazionale at Florence. Mantegna seems to have caught his people at rest physically, yet in the most intense mental activity, in a moment of deep absorption. They seem to be quite alone and unobserved, without relation to the external world. . . .

As a portrait-painter he seems to have shared the fate of Rembrandt—he failed to please! His portraits were so true and characteristic that his models at the bottom of their hearts were almost afraid of their own likenesses. This supposition is supported not only by the circumstance that no portraits of Mantegna's later period are extant, and only very few are referred to, but also by an indirect and eminently significant opinion emanating from Isabella d'Este, the most influential personality of his circle. She was averse to sitting for her portrait at all, probably because her beauty was less a matter of form than of charm and animation; but she was pleased by the sweet expression that Leonardo da Vinci knew how to give to her face, and she was never tired of urging this capricious artist, who had only made one drawing of her, to finish the portrait. When we read how she thanked Francesco Francia, who had painted a portrait of her—without a sitting!—for having made her more beautiful by art than she was formed by nature, we can understand at once why Mantegna, for whom she otherwise had so much respect and sympathy, was not permitted to paint her likeness. And probably most people of her generation felt as she did.

Paul Kristeller
Andrea Mantegna (1901)

Its closest parallel among Mantegna's paintings is the portrait of a member of the Gonzaga family, in Naples, which is believed to date c. 1461. Collections: Ludwig Kelemen, Budapest, who is said to have acquired it from a private family in Balatonboglár, Hungary. *Samuel H. Kress Collection,* 1950. Transferred from wood to canvas. Height 9½ in.; width 7½ in. (0.243 x 0.191). Painted probably c. 1460.

ANDREA MANTEGNA · Paduan 1431-1506

Judith and Holofernes

All thoughts and emotions are inter-dependent. In the words of the dear old song,

The roses round the door
Make me love mother more.

One feeling is excited by another. Our faculties work best in a congenial emotional atmosphere. For example, Mantegna's faculty for making noble arrangements of forms was stimulated by his feelings about heroic and god-like humanity. Expressing those feelings, which he found exciting, he also expressed—and in the most perfect manner of which he was capable—his feelings about masses, surfaces, solids, and voids. "The roses round the door"—his hero worship—"made him love mother more"—made him, by stimulating his faculty for composition, paint better. If Isabella d'Este had made him paint apples, table napkins and bottles, he would have produced, being uninterested in these objects, a poor composition. And yet, from a purely formal point of view, apples, bottles and napkins are quite as interesting as human bodies and faces. But Mantegna—and with him the majority of painters—did not happen to be very passionately interested in these inanimate objects. When one is bored one becomes boring.

The apples round the door
Make me a frightful bore.

Inevitably; unless I happen to be so exclusively interested in form that I can paint anything that has a shape; or unless I happen to possess some measure of that queer pantheism, that animistic superstition which made Van Gogh regard the humblest of common objects as being divinely or devilishly alive. *"Crains dans le mur aveugle un regard qui t'épie."* If a painter can do that, he will be able, like Van Gogh, to make pictures of cabbage fields and the bedrooms of cheap hotels that shall be as wildly dramatic as a Rape of the Sabines.

Aldous Huxley
Along the Road (1925)

The theme of Judith and Holofernes was treated frequently by Mantegna and his school. Numerous drawings of this subject exist, among them one in the Uffizi, Florence, dated 1491, and another in the Samuel H. Kress Collection, National Gallery of Art. The painting reproduced may have formed part of a series of Old Testament stories, the theme of which was probably the Triumph of Woman. A grisaille showing the same subject, with the composition in reverse, is in the National Gallery, Ireland. This grisaille formed part of a series, of which two other panels, representing Samson and Delilah and the Judgment of Solomon, have been preserved. Collections: Charles I gave the panel to Lord Pembroke, in exchange for paintings by Bellini and Parmigiano. It remained in the Pembroke Collection, Wilton House, until brought to America. *Widener Collection,* 1942. Wood. Height 11⅞ in.; width 7⅛ in. (0.30 x 0.18). Inscribed on gesso surface on back of panel: AN: MANTEGNA. Painted c. 1495.

FRANCO-FLEMISH SCHOOL · Early XV Century

Profile Portrait of a Lady

Historically, the portrait, as Ruskin realized, is characteristic of certain periods which we call humanistic. In such periods man is the measure of all things, and all things are made to contribute to his awareness of his own vitality. Art is a tribute to man's own humanity. Such, no doubt, is the real basis of the popularity of portrait-painting....

The rise of the portrait corresponds fairly exactly with the rise of the novel. Portraits of Dante and others have been identified in the fresco ascribed to Giotto in the chapel of the Bargello, in Florence, which may be as late as 1337; Boccaccio wrote his first tale in 1339, and his "Decameron" nine years later. And just as at first the portrait in painting was a flat profile, so the character in the early Italian novel was somewhat restricted in depth. One must not work the comparison too far: the novel, indeed, did not attain the psychological subtlety and precision already evident in portrait painting by the end of the fifteenth century until much later—perhaps not until the seventeenth century. But the general interest in character, common to both painting and the novel, was a continuous and rapid development from the early Renaissance, and still persists....

Many portraits, however, are admittedly great works of art, so that we have to ask ourselves finally what is it that distinguishes a portrait which is a psychological document from a portrait which is a work of art? One might answer: simply the æsthetic values, meaning the formal relations of space and colour which constitute the structural organization of all works of art.

Herbert Read
The Anatomy of Art (1931)

The panel reproduced is one of the mysteries of the history of painting. Its traditional attribution to Pisanello is doubtful, for the costume seems to be of the type fashionable at the Burgundian Court around 1410, twenty years earlier than Pisanello's known activity. Yet, if the panel is French, as Richter, Hill, Degenhart, Ring, and Coletti believe, or Franco-Flemish as Sterling and Panofsky believe, then in quality and style it is unique among Northern portraits. In any case the sitter belongs to that international aristocracy which through the interweaving of dynastic marriages brought about an International style of art in the fourteenth and fifteenth centuries. Collections: De Villeroy, Paris; Mackay, Roslyn, New York. *Andrew Mellon Collection,* 1937. Wood. Height 20⅜ in.; width 14⅜ in. (0.52 x 0.365). Painted c. 1410.

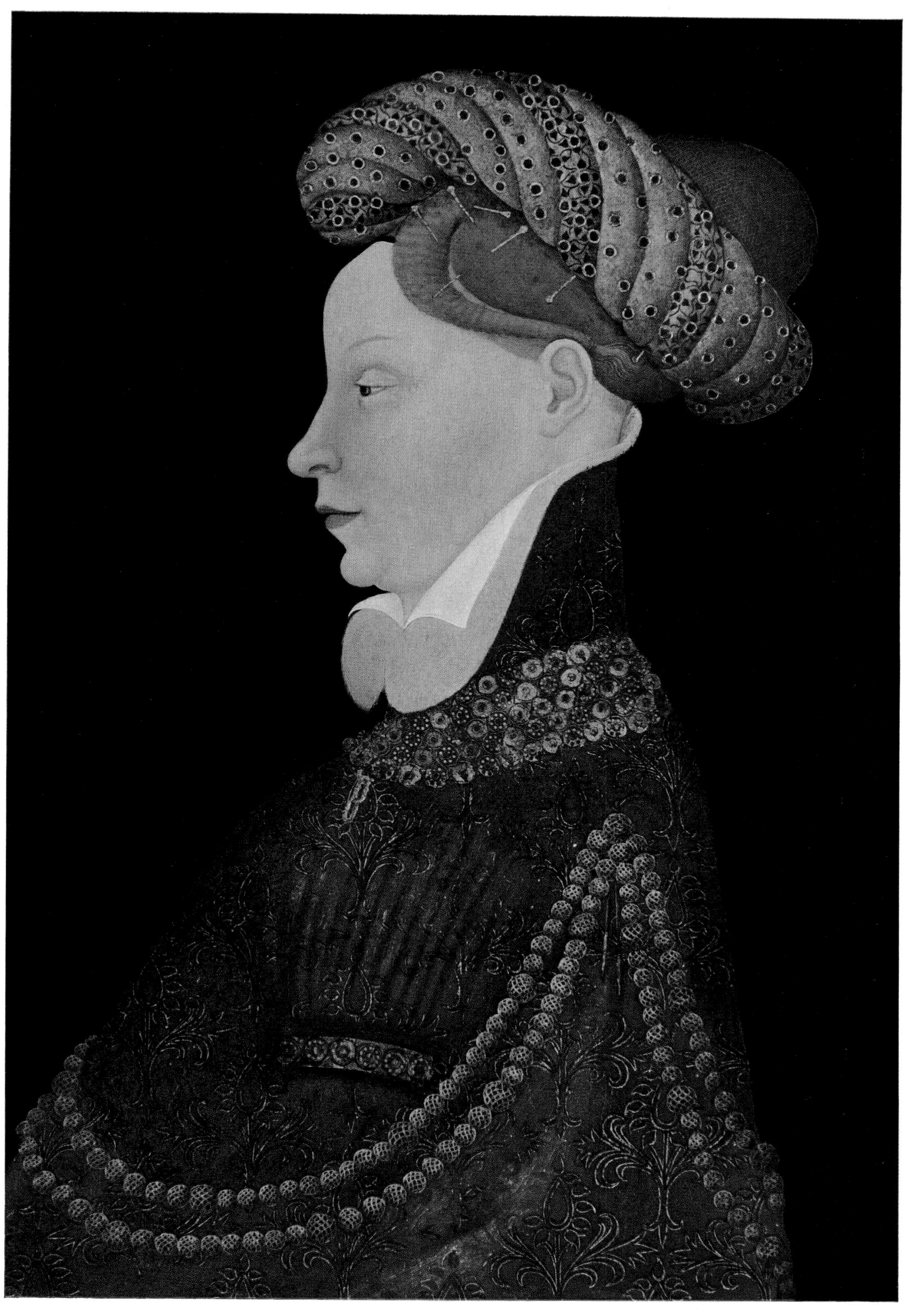

JAN VAN EYCK · Flemish 1380/1400-1441

The Annunciation

Another work of the master, which lends itself particularly to the analysis of endless detail, is the "Annunciation". . . . If the triptych of which this picture formed the right wing ever existed as a whole, it must have been a superb creation. Van Eyck here developed all the virtuosity of a master conscious of his power to overcome all difficulties. Of all his works it is the most hieratic and, at the same time, the most refined. He followed the iconographic rules of the past in using as a background for the apparition of the angel the ample space of a church and not the intimacy of a bedchamber, as he did in the altar-piece of the Lamb, where the scene is full of grace and tenderness. Here, on the contrary, the angel salutes Mary by a ceremonious bow; he is not represented with a spray of lilies and a narrow diadem; he carries a sceptre and a rich crown, and about his lips there is the stiff smile of the sculpture of Ægina. The splendour of the colours, the glitter of the pearls, the gold and the precious stones, surpass those of all the other angelic figures painted by Van Eyck. His coat is green and gold, his mantle of brocade is red and gold, his wings are covered with peacock feathers. The book of the Virgin and the cushion before her are executed with painstaking and minute care. In the church there is a profusion of anecdotal details. The tiles of the pavement are ornamented with the signs of the zodiac and scenes from the lives of Samson and of David. The wall of the apse is decorated with the figures of Isaac and of Jacob in the medallions between the arches, and that of Christ on the celestial globe between two seraphim in a window, besides other mural paintings representing the finding of the child Moses and the giving of the tables of the Law, all explained by legible inscriptions. Only the decoration of the wooden ceiling, though still discernible, remains indistinct.

This time unity and harmony are not lost in the accumulation of details. The twilight of the lofty edifice envelops all with mysterious shade, so that the eye can only with difficulty distinguish the anecdotal details.

It is the privilege of the painter that he can give the rein to his craving for endless elaboration of details (perhaps one ought to say, that he can comply with the most impossible demands of an ignorant donor) without sacrificing the general effect. The sight of this multitude of details fatigues us no more than the sight of reality itself. We only notice them if our attention has been directed to them, and we soon lose sight of them, so that they serve only to heighten effects of colouring or perspective.

Johan Huizinga
The Waning of the Middle Ages (1924)

This is probably one of the wings of a lost triptych. It seems to have been painted in the same period as the triptych in Dresden and the Ghent altarpiece, which was finished in 1432. Scenes of the Old Testament represented on the graffito floor and on the wall foretell the events of the New Testament, while the Romanesque architecture symbolizes the era before the incarnation of Christ. The building cannot be identified with an existing Flemish church, but the wall paintings and capitals reproduce with meticulous accuracy the late Romanesque style of Maastricht and Tournai. Such archaeological exactness is unique for an artist of this period. Collections: Said to have come from a church in Dijon, the painting was sold by Charles J. Nieuwenhuys of Brussels to William II, King of the Netherlands, in 1819. From his estate it was purchased by Czar Nicholas I in 1850, for the Hermitage Gallery, Leningrad. *Andrew Mellon Collection,* 1937. Transferred from wood to canvas. Height 36½ in.; width 14⅜ in. (0.93 x 0.365). Painted c. 1425/30.

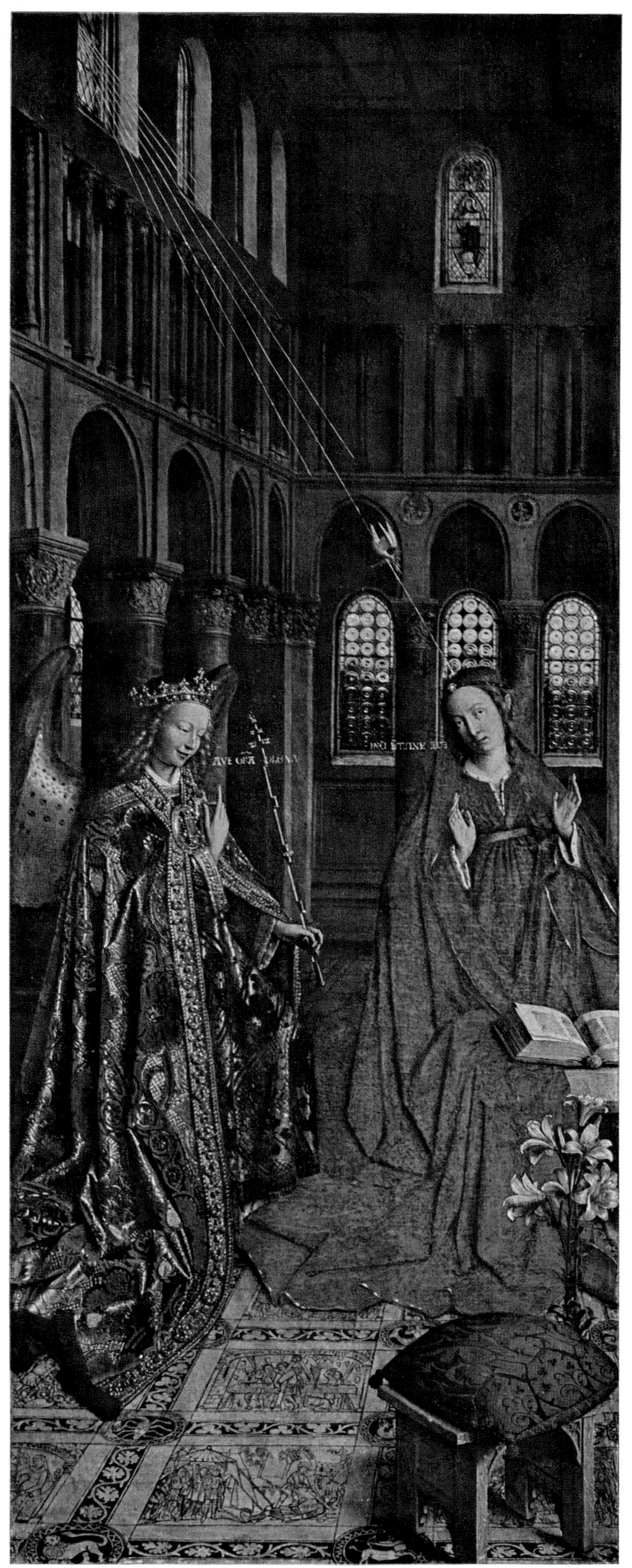
AVE GRÃ

PETRUS CHRISTUS · Flemish c. 1410-1472/73

The Nativity

The mystic insight begins with the sense of a mystery unveiled, of a hidden wisdom now suddenly become certain beyond the possibility of a doubt. The sense of certainty and revelation comes earlier than any definite belief. . . .

The first and most direct outcome of the moment of illumination is belief in the possibility of a way of knowledge which may be called revelation or insight or intuition, as contrasted with sense, reason, and analysis, which are regarded as blind guides leading to the morass of illusion. Closely connected with this belief is the conception of a Reality behind the world of appearance and utterly different from it. This Reality is regarded with an admiration often amounting to worship; it is felt to be always and everywhere close at hand, thinly veiled by the shows of sense, ready, for the receptive mind, to shine in its glory even through the apparent folly and wickedness of Man. The poet, the artist, and the lover are seekers after that glory: the haunting beauty that they pursue is the faint reflection of its sun. But the mystic lives in the full light of the vision: what others dimly seek he knows, with a knowledge beside which all other knowledge is ignorance.

Bertrand Russell
Mysticism and Logic (1914)

That "mystic insight" Bertrand Russell describes is evident in the paintings of Petrus Christus, especially in the Nativity here reproduced. But this mood of illumination, this sense of a reality just behind the world of appearance is evoked by scenes of exceptional actuality. As Roger Fry has said (*Flemish Art,* 1927): "Not only was Christus able to construct credible volumes, he pushed even further than Hubert van Eyck the possibilities of situating them in a credible space. . . . We feel the space around each of the figures and we realize fully their relatively greater or less recession from the eye. Of course, in any picture which has verisimilitude we *know* which figure is meant to be in front of which—of course, when we see a tree drawn the size of a thumbnail beside a life-sized face we know it must be a long way back, but in most Flemish primitive pictures we only know this as it were by deduction, the space and the volumes are not clearly present to the imagination as they are here." Collections: Prince Manuel Yturbe, Madrid; Duchess of Parcent, Madrid. *Andrew Mellon Collection,* 1937. Wood. Height 51¼ in.; width 38¼ in. (1.30 x 0.97). Painted c. 1445.

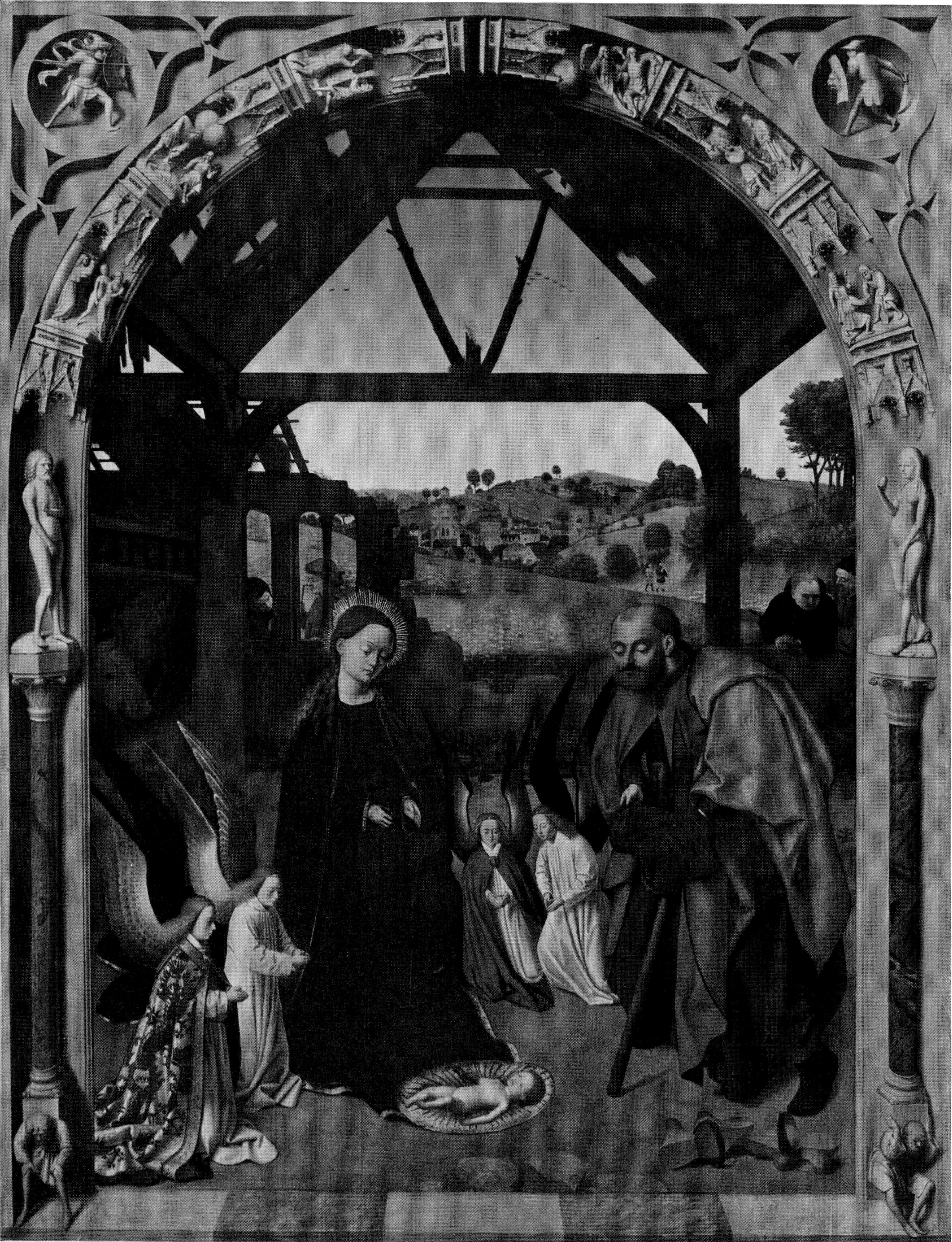

PETRUS CHRISTUS · Flemish c. 1410-1472/73

A Donor and His Wife

They [the Flemish painters] pursued resemblances with tenacity, the exact material resemblance, even to the direction, the form, and the disposition of the wrinkles, the number of the hairs and the grain of the skin, and it is this material resemblance which, through its exactitude, carries with it the moral resemblance of the individual whose needs and functions have little by little modeled the face. There are faces of merchants, eager and honest; there are faces of women resigned to their task and almost always represented as heavy with the burden of the new life. Often there are great, ugly faces with long noses, broad mouths, bony jaws, and the skin tightly drawn over the skeleton of the face or loose and falling in thick folds. They are heavy with their strength and their calmness, dense, full, material, and so nakedly truthful that one might think them carved out of the mass of the muscles, the nerves, the blood, and the bones. There is never any generalization, but also there is never a lie. Each of these beings is the one who came to seek the painter; each one is intent on living that moment of his life at which the painter found him, without a thought of the past or a thought of the future. But there are so many of these faces, donors and their wives, and nuns with clasped hands, aldermen, magistrates, and members of guilds, that finally the average type is born of the composite that forms in our memories, like the average type of the faces carved in stone by the image maker of Champagne or Picardy. It is a continuation of the Middle Ages; there is the same process of patient accumulation, wherein every element, seen close by, retains its characteristics, and wherein the ensemble, seen from a distance, forms a compact and solid whole, which it is impossible to disintegrate. Besides, their common interests gave to the artists of Flanders a common moral life.

Élie Faure
Histoire de l'art (1923)

These panels are probably the side wings of a triptych, of which the central panel is missing. The escutcheons hanging on the wall should provide clues as to the identity of the kneeling donors, but no student of heraldry has yet been able to connect the coats of arms with a specific family. We believe, however, that the lady's first name is probably Elizabeth because the woodcut attached to the wall represents Saint Elizabeth of Hungary. The saint is shown with three crowns, one on her head and one in each hand, indicating her triple sanctity, as virgin, wife, and widow. One wonders whether this is a further clue to the biography of her namesake. Collection: *Samuel H. Kress Collection,* 1961. Wood. Each panel, height 16½ in.; width 8½ in. (0.42 x 0.216). Painted c. 1455.

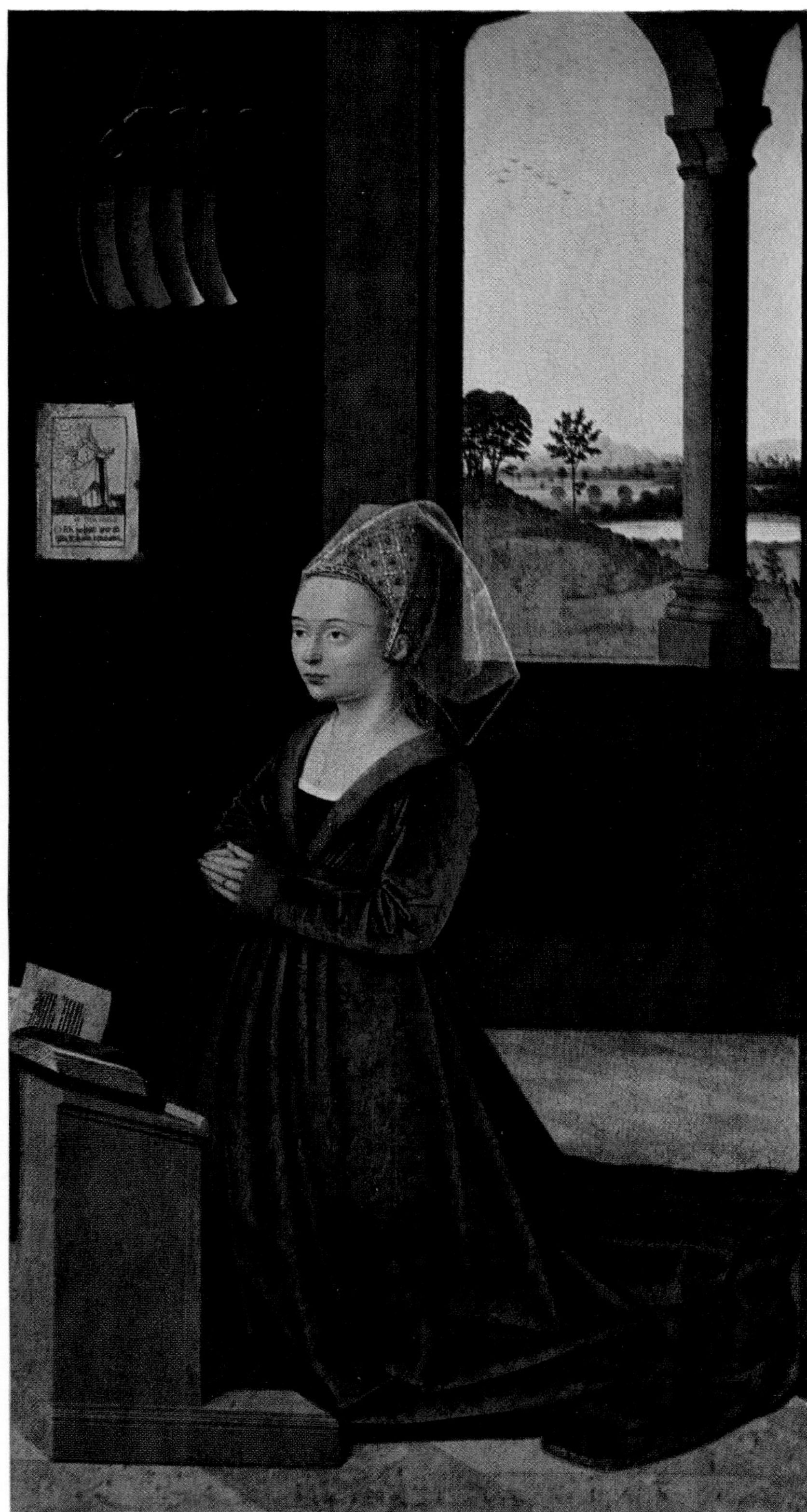

ROGIER VAN DER WEYDEN · Flemish 1399/1400-1464

Portrait of a Lady

The Flemish primitives were the greatest painters in the world, Durtal said to himself, and this Roger van der Weyden, or as others call him, this Roger de La Pasture, overwhelmed by the fame of Van Eyck and of Memling, even as, at a later date, were Gerard David, Hugo van der Goes, Justus of Ghent, Dirk Bouts, is, in my opinion, superior to all of them.

J.-K. Huysmans
La Cathédrale (1898)

The men and women out of that past are as children to us with our mechanical inventions, but we are in the same stature to them, dwarfed before their giant eminence where the poetry of the senses is concerned. Therefore, not only is antiquity sad because it is so old, ageing a little even as we think of it, but, also, its living force was something that we have missed. The massed effects and properties of those expired centuries give the illusion of something existing parallel to, but divided from, ourselves. It is the very world in which we want to live, lying near to us, but impossible to touch, or be in communion with; separated from us, so it seems, by some barrier whose nature we cannot either define, or overcome. Thus, its whole total is, in a sense, contemporary with us, and yet by no effort can we break into its area, and it is kept away from us by some infrangible rule that neither body nor mind can contradict.

It is easy enough to personify this loss. The casting for its characters need go no further than . . . a sisterhood of Ophelias, for this nunnery encloses a race, all alike, and of one pattern. The thin distention and elaboration of their form is as though they were only to be seen through a film of water, which has combed back their long, flat hair with its weedy fingers and pressed their whole symmetry into its own limpid convenience. The fine hands, pale as milk and tapering to the nail-points, seem to have been rubbed with honey from the dropped flowers floating on the stream, or from the lilies that live of their own volition upon the waters. . . . As to the mind hidden behind this chastity and its defences, the very extent of its shortcomings is an absorbing mystery, which becomes still stranger on investigation. Then, this veil between ourselves and the past is lifted a little, but only to that point of comprehension which might be reached if speech was only possible with the eyes and any understanding of the lips was still forbidden. But no further point than this is ever arrived at, and, here, only half-way into words, this communion is interrupted and can never be improved into permanence.

The body of this beautiful and strange mystery lies so close to us that we can feel the warm emanation coming from it, but our eyes, the only contact we have with it, never tell us of any change, though such lover's blindness is unwarranted and the gradual, slow decay of this ideal should be visible even to ourselves.

Sacheverell Sitwell
The Gothick North (1930)

The sitter has not been definitely identified, although the name of Marie de Valengin, illegitimate daughter of Philip the Good of Burgundy, has been suggested. Collections: Ducal House of Anhalt-Dessau, Gotisches Haus, Wörlitz. *Andrew Mellon Collection,* 1937. Wood. Height 14½ in.; width 10¾ in. (0.37 x 0.27). Painted c. 1455.

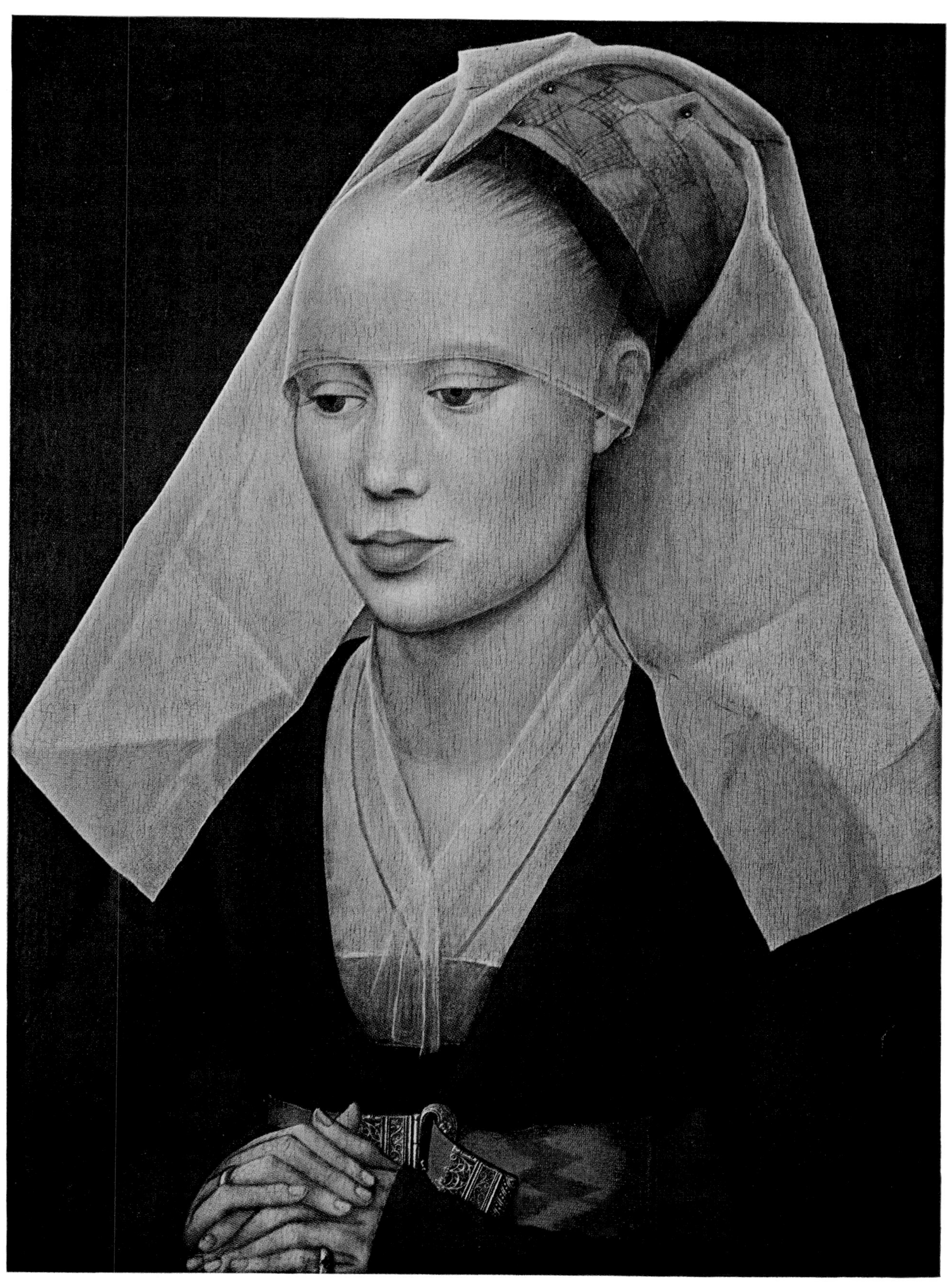

HANS MEMLING · Flemish c. 1430/35-1494

The Presentation in the Temple

Once more, ascending yet higher we maintain that It is not soul, or mind, or endowed with the faculty of imagination, conjecture, reason, or understanding; nor is It any act of reason or understanding; nor can It be described by the reason or perceived by the understanding, since It is not number, or order, or greatness, or littleness, or equality, or inequality, and since It is not immovable nor in motion, or at rest, and has no power, and is not power or light, and does not live, and is not life; nor is It personal essence, or eternity, or time; nor can It be grasped by the understanding, since It is not knowledge or truth; nor is It kingship or wisdom; nor is It one, nor is It unity, nor is It Godhead or Goodness; nor is It a Spirit, as we understand the term, since It is not Sonship or Fatherhood; nor is It any other thing such as we or any other being can have knowledge of; nor does It belong to the category of non-existence or to that of existence; nor do existent beings know It as it actually is, nor does It know them as they actually are; nor can the reason attain to It to name It or to know It; nor is it darkness nor is It light, or error, or truth; nor can any affirmation or negation apply to it; for while applying affirmations or negations to those orders of being that come next to It, we apply not unto It either affirmation or negation, inasmuch as It transcends all affirmation by being the perfect and unique Cause of all things, and transcends all negation by the pre-eminence of Its simple and absolute nature—free from every limitation and beyond them all.

Dionysius the Areopagite
De mystica theologia (6th Century A.D.)

The Christian writer and the Christian artist were both faced with problems of communication. To express truths of Christian mysticism in verbal terms Dionysius the Areopagite uses negative statements; to convey the teachings of Christian theology in visual terms Hans Memling employs symbolic devices. The church in which the Presentation of Our Lord takes place is Romanesque on the inside and Gothic on the outside. The change in architectural style indicates the change from the Old to the New Dispensation which will result from the Incarnation. The stained-glass windows in the background illustrate the fall of man, whereas the foreground prefigures his redemption. Thus in one scene the artist symbolically portrays certain basic principles of Christian doctrine. Collections: Count Johann Rudolf Czernin von Chudenitz, Vienna; Czernin Gallery, Vienna. *Samuel H. Kress Collection,* 1961. Wood. Height 23½ in.; width 19 in. (0.598 x 0.483). Painted c. 1463.

HANS MEMLING · Flemish c. 1430/35-1494

Saint Veronica

And when Tiberius Cæsar, the emperor of the Romans, was labouring under a grievous disease, and understanding that there was at Jerusalem a certain physician, Jesus by name, who by a single word cured all infirmities, he, not knowing that the Jews and Pilate had put Him to death, ordered a certain friend of his named Volusianus: Go as quickly as possible across the seas; and thou shalt tell Pilate, my servant and friend, to send me this physician, that he may restore me to my former health. And this Volusianus, having heard the emperor's command, immediately departed, and came to Pilate, as he had been commanded. And he related to the same Pilate what had been entrusted to him by Tiberius Cæsar, saying: Tiberius Cæsar, the emperor of the Romans, thy master, having heard that in this city there is a physician who by his word alone heals infirmities, begs thee earnestly to send him to him for the curing of his infirmity. Pilate, hearing this, was very much afraid, knowing that through envy he had caused Him to be put to death. Pilate answered the same messenger thus, saying: This man was a malefactor, and a man who drew to himself all the people; so a council of the wise men of the city was held, and I caused him to be crucified. And this messenger returning to his inn, met a certain woman named Veronica, who had been a friend of Jesus; and he said: O woman, a certain physician who was in this city, who cured the sick by a word alone, why have the Jews put him to death? And she began to weep, saying: Ah me! my lord, my God and my Lord, whom Pilate for envy delivered, condemned, and ordered to be crucified. Then he, being exceedingly grieved, said: I am vehemently grieved that I am unable to accomplish that for which my lord had sent me. And Veronica said to him: When my Lord was going about preaching, and I, much against my will, was deprived of His presence, I wished His picture to be painted for me, in order that, while I was deprived of His presence, the figure of His picture might at least afford me consolation. And when I was carrying the canvas to the painter to be painted, my Lord met me, and asked whither I was going. And when I had disclosed to Him the cause of my journey, He asked of me the cloth, and gave it back to me impressed with the image of His venerable face. Therefore, if thy lord will devoutly gaze upon His face, he shall obtain forthwith the benefit of health. And he said to her: Is a picture of such a sort procurable by gold or silver? She said to him: No; but by the pious influence of devotion. I shall therefore set out with thee, and shall carry the picture to be seen by Cæsar, and shall come back again.

Volusianus therefore came with Veronica to Rome, and said to Tiberius the emperor: Jesus, whom thou hast been longing for, Pilate and the Jews have delivered to an unjust death, and have through envy affixed to the gibbet of the cross. There has therefore come with me a cerain matron, bringing a picture of Jesus himself; and if thou wilt devoutly look upon it, thou shalt immediately obtain the benefit of thy health. Cæsar therefore ordered the way to be strewn with silk cloths, and the picture to be presented to him; and as soon as he had looked upon it, he regained his former health.

Apocrypha of the New Testament

Collections: Nikolay Demidov, Russian Ambassador to Florence; his descendants, San Donato, near Florence; Baron Heinrich Thyssen-Bornemisza, Lugano. *Samuel H. Kress Collection,* 1952. Wood. Height 12¼ in.; width 9½ in. (0.311 x 0.242). Painted c. 1480, probably as the right panel of a diptych.

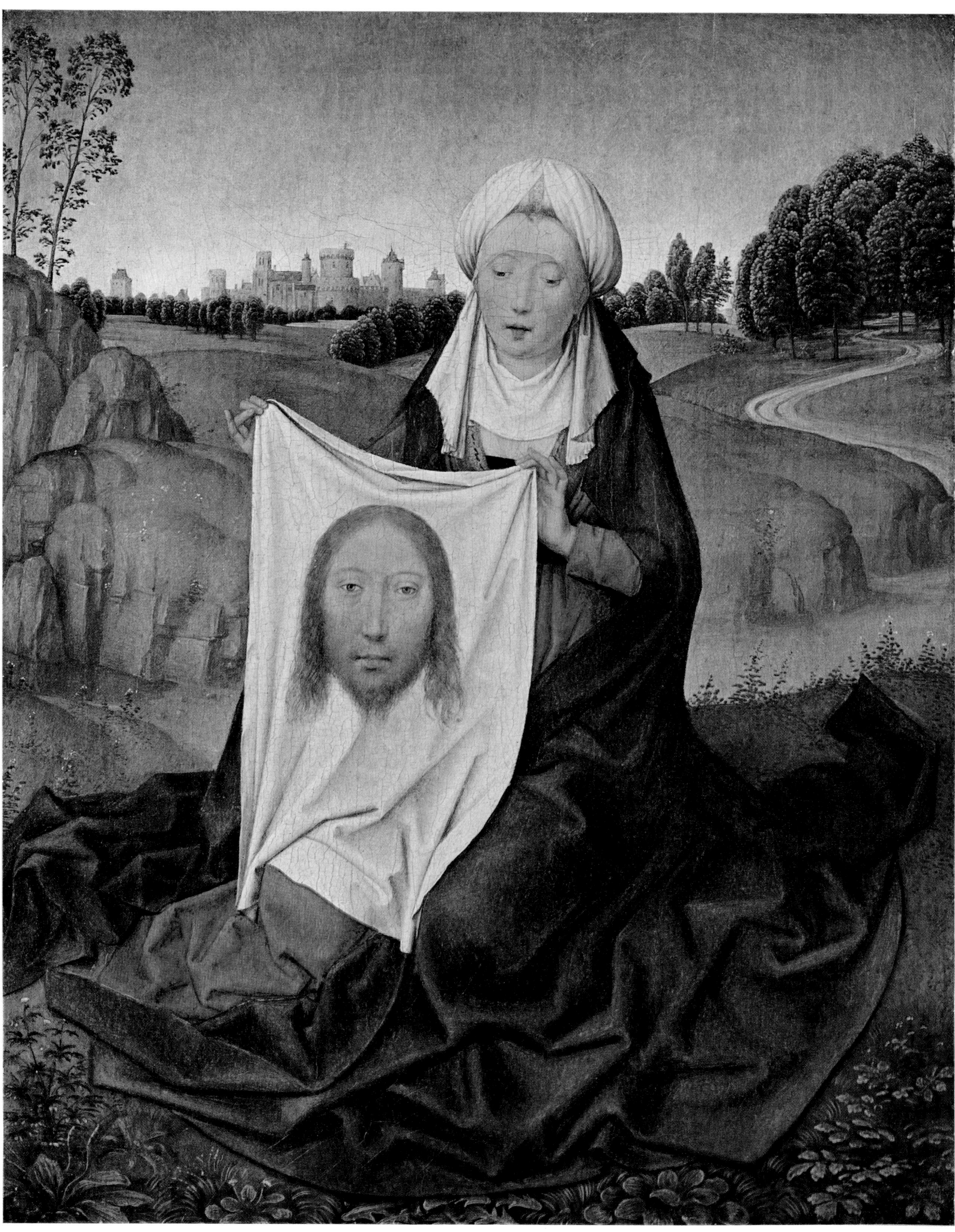

HANS MEMLING · Flemish c. 1430/35-1494

Madonna and Child with Angels

Fle we to our Lord and we shall be comforted; touch we him and we shall be made clene; cleve to him and we shall be sekir and safe fro al maner of peril. For our curtes Lord will that we ben as homley with him as herte may thinke or soule may desiren. But beware that we taken not so reklesly this homleyhede that we levyn curtesy. For our Lord himselfe is sovereyn homleyhede, and as homley as he is, as curtes he is, for he is very curtes. And the blissid creatures that shall ben in hevyn with him without end, he will have them like to himselfe in all things. And to be like our Lord perfectly, it is our very salvation and our full bliss. And if we wott not how we shall don all this, desire we of our Lord and he shal lerne us. For it is his owne likeing and his worship; blissid mot he be.

The Lady Julian of Norwich
Revelations of Divine Love (1373)

It is easy to underrate or overrate Hans Memling. The greatness of his technical gift is obvious, but so is the narrowness of his imagination. His attractiveness within his range has never needed and never lacked celebration. As the culminating figure of late Gothic painting both in a material and spiritual way he is highly important. A full generation before he was born the Van Eycks were trying to give oil painting a splendor which the Northern world had earlier seen only in stained glass and enamels. It remained for Memling to bring that splendor to a radiance beyond which no merely coloristic progress was possible. On the spiritual side Memling made for the first time visible all those tendernesses towards the Virgin and the virgin saints which the Middle Ages had expressed lyrically in Latin and vernacular poetry. After Memling, everyone could see what had been the private, chivalric ardor of a few mystics who were also poets. Others made the attempt, notably his immediate predecessors of the Cologne school, but no one struck the note so lovingly and with such richness of overtones. To have created an enduring symbolism for this exquisite phase of the beauty of holiness, is surely distinction enough for any artist.

Frank Jewett Mather, Jr.
Western European Painting of the Renaissance (1939)

Glossary: *sekir,* secure; *curtes,* courteous;
homleyhede, homeliness, intimacy; *levyn,* leave.

Fromentin (*Les Maîtres d'autrefois,* 1876) also has described the peculiar charm of Memling's paintings, especially evident in the picture reproduced. "Imagine, in the midst of the horrors of the century, a privileged spot, a sort of angelical retreat ideally silent and enclosed, where passions are quieted and troubles cease, where people pray and adore, where everything is transfigured, physical ugliness and moral ugliness, where new feelings arise, where simplicity, gentleness, and supernatural mildness grow, like lilies—and you will have an idea of the unique soul of Memling, and the miracle he works in his pictures." Collections: Gotisches Haus, Wörlitz (Ducal Collection of Anhalt-Dessau), Germany. *Andrew Mellon Collection,* 1937. Wood. Height 23⅛ in.; width 18⅞ in. (0.59 x 0.48). Painted c. 1480.

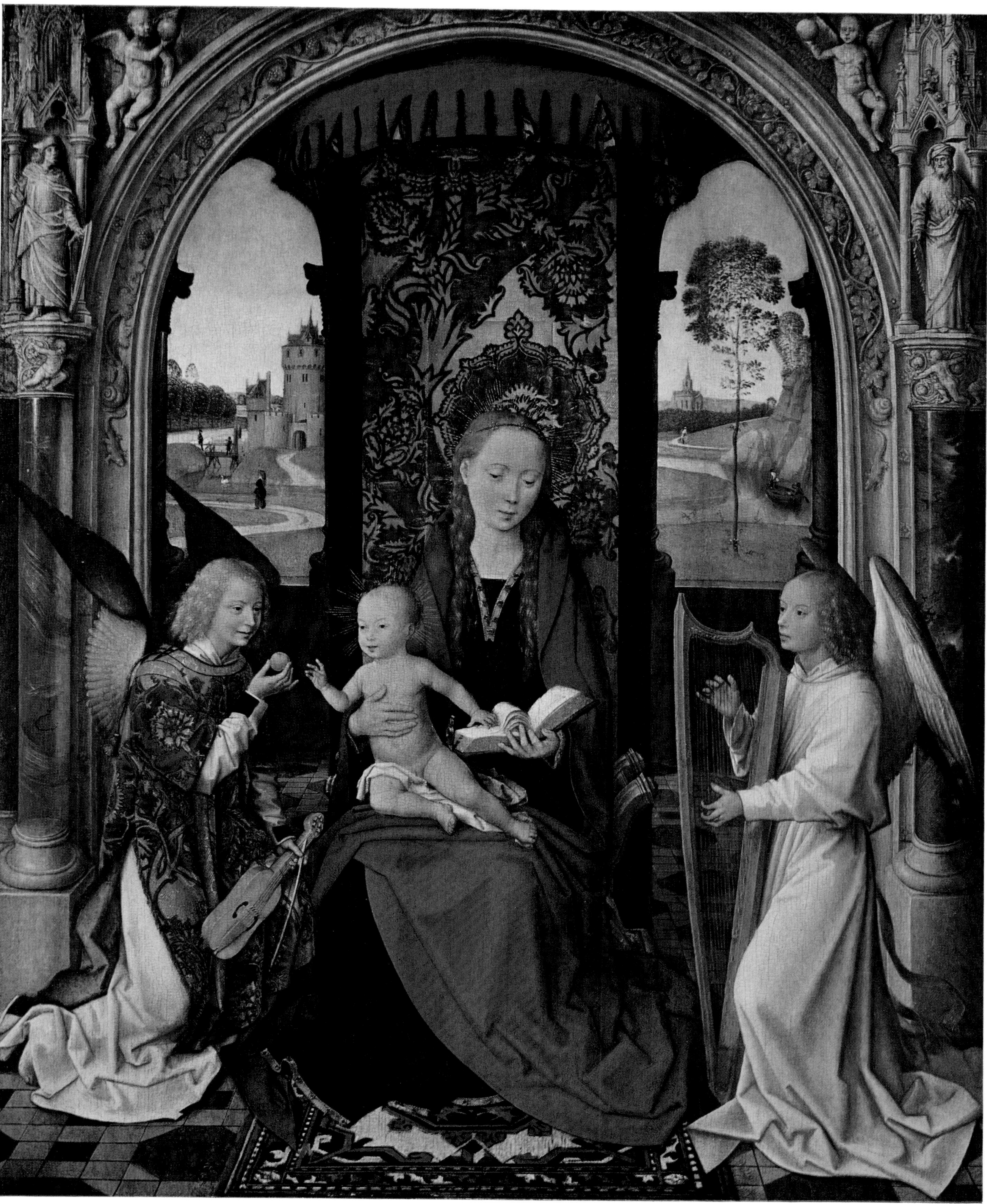

GERARD DAVID · FLEMISH c. 1460-1523

The Rest on the Flight into Egypt

He was old-fashioned, but genuinely so. It was not a pose. He was constitutionally religious. One might imagine him at home with the Brethren of the Common Life or any of the mystic fellowships whose days of vitality were coming to an end when David was born. The atmosphere of his pictures is like that of *The Imitation of Christ.* David was the only Northern artist who ever painted a St. Francis at all acceptably. The little wing picture of the Stigmatization is almost credible. The painter felt and rendered something of the ecstasy of the Saint. In face and figure he is wholly wrapt up in his vision. The contrast between him and the unfelt John the Baptist on the pendant is remarkable. The latter is a mere emblem, emotionless, meaningless. The former is intoxicated with God. David's nature seems to me to have been a deeper one than Memling's. There is much in common in the spirit of their art, but Memling, for all his dexterous and pleasant handling, is more superficial, more like a man who adapts himself, easily and naturally enough, yet still adapts himself, to the taste of the little society for whom he worked. David needed no adaptation. He painted what and how he really liked to paint. . . .

With his conservative religious tendencies, David had no temptation to devise original treatments for the round of sacred subjects he had to paint. To borrow was but to follow the good old tradition. What David did not and could not have borrowed was the reverential mood that governed his hand. Forms and details he could pick up here and there as he saw what pleased him, but his art was not in the forms. Its vitality was deep within himself. Alike in the *naïveté* of his earliest works and the complete harmony and expressiveness of the later, the spirit is the same. A single pure and simple character is behind them all. It follows that the handiwork of the man is of a piece with his nature. We need not look to him for technical innovations nor fear to be put off with a slipshod technique. There is nothing cheap about David's art. If half a hundred or more of his pictures have survived the misuse of men through half a thousand years it is because their maker was a thoroughly sound and conscientious craftsman. His methods were those of the Van Eycks, and of the best of their successors throughout the fifteenth century. All that was personal to him about them was his selection and combination of colours. His best pictures have a richness all their own.

SIR MARTIN CONWAY
The Van Eycks and Their Followers (1921)

The Christ Child with the grapes, a eucharistic symbol, is closely related to David's picture in the Museum at Rouen, painted in 1509 for the Carmelites of Sion, Bruges. The figure of Joseph beating chestnuts from a tree is derived from calendar illustrations of Flemish illuminated manuscripts. The picture must have been extremely popular, as evidenced by the many existing contemporary copies, and altered school replicas such as that by Isenbrant in the Robert Lehman Collection, New York. The motif of the wicker basket of the Virgin recurs throughout the sixteenth century, for instance, in Patinir and Jan Bruegel. Collections: Rev. Montague Taylor, London; Rudolphe Kann, Paris; J. Pierpont Morgan, New York. *Andrew Mellon Collection,* 1937. Wood. Height 17¾ in.; width 17½ in. (0.45 x 0.445). Painted c. 1510.

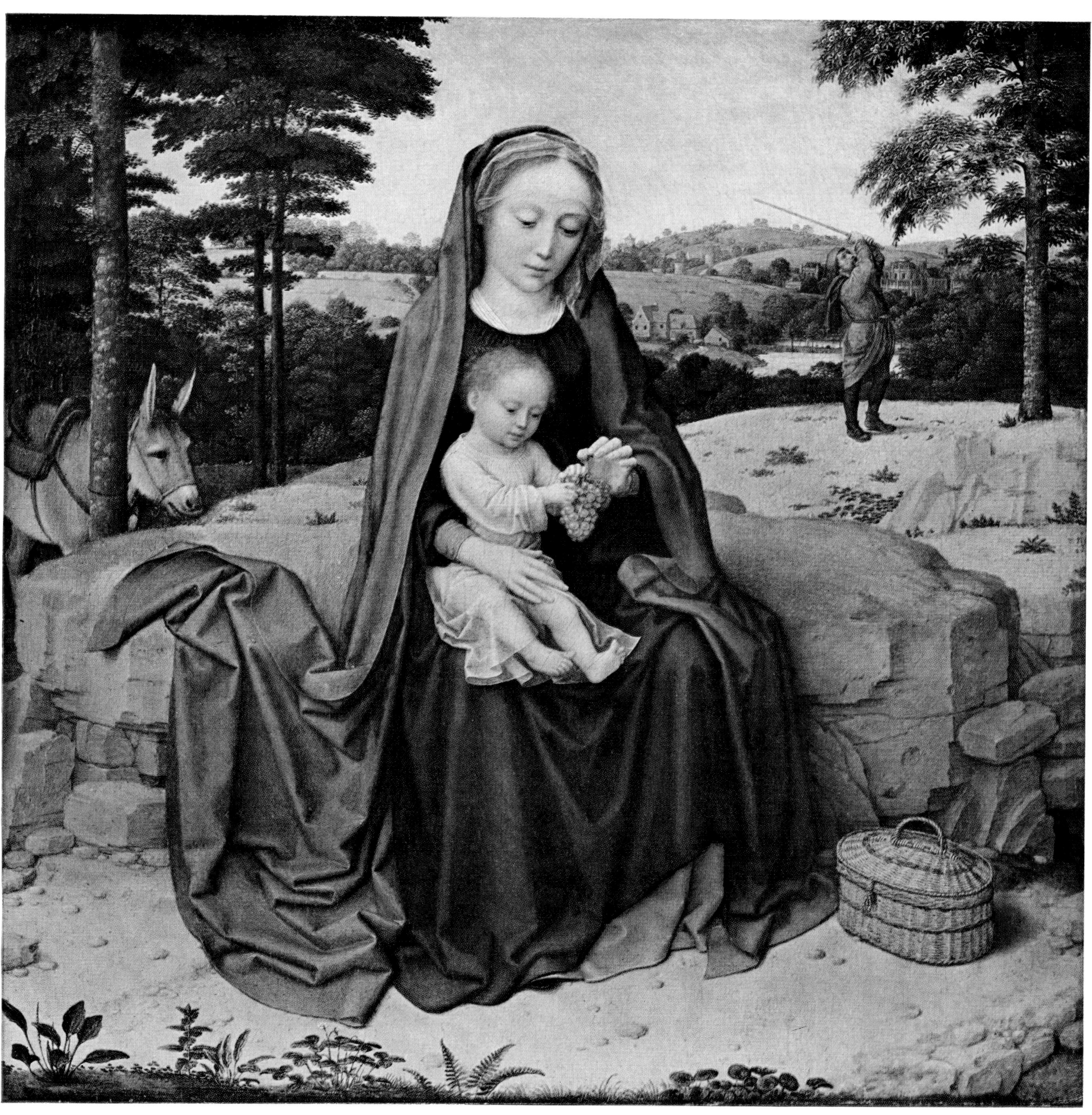

MASTER OF THE SAINT LUCY LEGEND

FLEMISH ACTIVE 1480-1489

Mary, Queen of Heaven

Ave Maria! blessèd be the hour!
    The time, the clime, the spot, where I so oft
Have felt that moment in its fullest power
    Sink o'er the earth—so beautiful and soft—
While swung the deep bell in the distant tower,
    Or the faint dying day-hymn stole aloft,
And not a breath crept through the rosy air,
And yet the forest leaves seemed stirred with prayer.

Ave Maria! 'tis the hour of prayer!
    Ave Maria! 'tis the hour of Love!
Ave Maria! may our spirits dare
    Look up to thine and to thy Son's above!
Ave Maria! oh that face so fair!
    Those downcast eyes beneath the Almighty Dove—
What though 'tis but a pictured image?—strike—
That painting is no idol,—'tis too like.

GEORGE GORDON, LORD BYRON
Don Juan (1821)

Especially interesting in this painting by a Flemish artist, who probably worked in Spain, are the magnificent brocades and the realistically represented musical instruments. Concerning the latter Emanuel Winternitz has written: "All the instruments are contemporary with the painting and depicted with the greatest exactness as if the artist had transplanted into Heaven a musical performance of his own time. Equally precise is the rendering of the finger positions, the holding of the bow, etc. Also, the organization of the two orchestras and their quantitative relation to small vocal groups is by no means fanciful; it is quite in line with contemporary practice. The music sheets are clearly legible." Collections: Convent near Burgos, Spain. *Samuel H. Kress Collection,* 1952. Wood. Height 85 in.; width 73 in. (2.159 x 1.854). Painted c. 1485.

MASTER OF SAINT GILLES · Franco-Flemish c. 1500

The Baptism of Clovis

Till the thirtieth year of his age, Clovis continued to worship the gods of his ancestors. His disbelief, or rather disregard, of Christianity might encourage him to pillage with less remorse the churches of an hostile territory; but his subjects of Gaul enjoyed the free exercise of religious worship, and the bishops entertained a more favourable hope of the idolater than of the heretics. The Merovingian prince had contracted a fortunate alliance with the fair Clotilda, the niece of the king of Burgundy, who, in the midst of an Arian court, was educated in the profession of the Catholic faith. It was her interest, as well as her duty, to achieve the conversion of a Pagan husband; and Clovis insensibly listened to the voice of love and religion. He consented (perhaps such terms had been previously stipulated) to the baptism of his eldest son; and, though the sudden death of the infant excited some superstitious fears, he was persuaded, a second time, to repeat the dangerous experiment. In the distress of the battle of Tolbiac, Clovis loudly invoked the god of Clotilda and the Christians; and victory disposed him to hear, with respectful gratitude, the eloquent Remigius, bishop of Rheims, who forcibly displayed the temporal and spiritual advantages of his conversion. The king declared himself satisfied of the truth of the Catholic faith; and the political reasons which might have suspended his public profession were removed by the devout or loyal acclamations of the Franks, who showed themselves alike prepared to follow their heroic leader to the field of battle or to the baptismal font. The important ceremony was performed in the cathedral of Rheims, with every circumstance of magnificence and solemnity that could impress an awful sense of religion on the minds of its rude proselytes. The new Constantine was immediately baptized, with three thousand of his warlike subjects; and their example was imitated by the remainder of the *gentle Barbarians,* who, in obedience to the victorious prelate, adored the cross which they had burnt, and burnt the idols which they had formerly adored.

Edward Gibbon
The History of the Decline and Fall of the Roman Empire (1781)

The Master of Saint Gilles was probably a Flemish painter who knew the works of Hugo van der Goes but spent most of his life in France. Some critics believe that this and a companion picture (also in the National Gallery of Art), placed one above the other, formed the right wing of a triptych of which the left wing was formed by the two panels, of nearly the same size, by this master in the National Gallery, London. The scene of Saint Rémy baptizing the Frankish King Clovis is shown as taking place in Sainte-Chapelle in Paris. The artist has combined the porch of the lower Sainte-Chapelle with significant details of the upper building. Through the open door, at the left, we see parts of the old Palais de Justice, now destroyed. Collections: Comte Alexandre de Lestang-Parade, Aix-en-Provence; Alexandre and Melchior Lestang-Parade; Baron E. de Beurnonville, Paris; M. Watil, Paris. *Samuel H. Kress Collection,* 1952. Wood. Height 24¼ in.; width 18⅜ in. (0.616 x 0.467). Painted c. 1500.

MIGUEL SITHIUM · FLEMISH c. 1465/70-1525

The Assumption of the Virgin

Behold! the mother bird
The Fledgling's voice hath heard!
He calls anew,
  "It was thy breast
  That warmed the nest
From whence I flew.
Upon a loftier tree
Of life I wait for thee;
Rise, mother-dove, and come;
Thy Fledgling calls thee home!"

JOHN BANISTER TABB
The Assumption (1902)

About 1500 Juan de Flandes, one of the most gifted Flemish artists working at the Spanish court, was employed in painting an "oratory" for Queen Isabella, consisting of 47 small panels depicting scenes from the life and passion of Christ. The two culminating scenes in this series, the Ascension of Christ and the Assumption of the Virgin, were not painted by Juan himself, but were entrusted to the one artist at the Spanish court who seems to have been valued even more highly, Miguel Sithium. In 1505, a few weeks after the death of Queen Isabella, the panels of the "oratory" were inventoried and offered for sale. Don Diego de Guevara, treasurer to Margaret of Austria, bought 32 of the little panels, including the two by Sithium. The panels are described in Margaret's inventories of 1516 and 1523 with more precision and elaboration than any of the other items. In both inventories they are given a separate entry, and are described as "a diptych, by the hand of Miguel, of the Assumption of Our Lord and of Our Lady, which is kept in a cypress case." In 1521 Dürer visited Margaret's collection, and she herself showed him "all her beautiful things. Among them," he writes, "I saw about 40 little panels in oil color, such as I have never seen for precision and excellence; and there I saw other good things by Jan van Eyck and Jacopo de' Barbari." Even van Eyck's great Arnolfini panel seems to have elicited less wonder from Dürer than did the "oratory" panels, among which Margaret would certainly have shown him with particular pride the two by Miguel that had been specially framed by her. What happened to the two little paintings after Margaret's death we do not know, except that they were somehow carefully preserved. In 1904 the Assumption of the Virgin was shown in an exhibition of French Primitives in Paris. It seems not to have been recognized as the picture painted by Sithium for the famous "oratory" until 1929, when Friedländer published it. This identification has been universally accepted. The other half of the diptych with the Ascension of Christ is in the collection of the Earl of Yarborough. Collections: Queen Isabella of Spain; Don Diego de Guevara; Margaret of Austria; Jules Quesnet, Paris. *Ailsa Mellon Bruce Fund,* 1965. Wood. Height 8⅜ in.; width 6½ in. (0.212 x 0.164). Painted c. 1500.

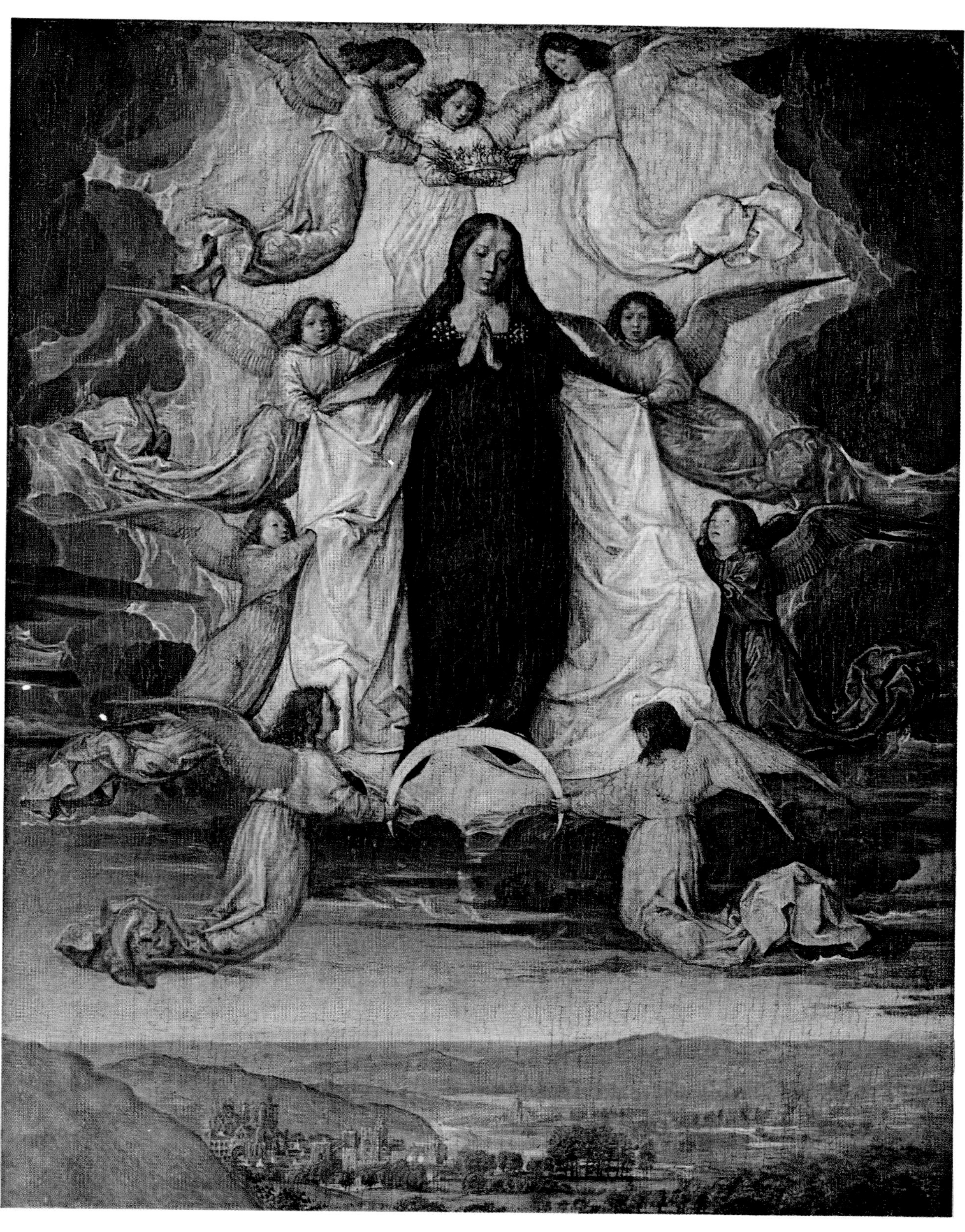

JUAN DE FLANDES · Hispano-Flemish Active 1496-c. 1519

The Adoration of the Magi

Entering the manger, and finding the Child with His mother, the Magi fell to their knees and adored Him: and opening their treasures, they offered Him gifts, gold, frankincense, and myrrh. The choice of these gifts, and the giving of them, can be explained several ways. According to Remy, among the ancients it was the custom never to present oneself before a god or a king without offering gifts; and the Wise Men, who came from the country of Persia and Chaldea, where the river Saba flows (according to the *Scholastic History*), brought the gifts which the Persians and the Chaldeans were wont to offer. Saint Bernard says that the gold was intended to give testimony of the poverty of the Blessed Virgin, the incense to purify the smell of the stable, and the myrrh to give strength to the limbs of the Child, by driving out the worms from His entrails. Moreover, these three gifts signified the royalty, the divinity, and the humanity of Christ: because gold is used for royal tribute and He was the highest King, incense for divine worship, since He was God, and myrrh for the burial of the dead, since He was a mortal man. Finally, these three gifts are symbols of what we ourselves owe to Christ: for gold is the symbol of love, incense of prayer, and myrrh of the mortification of the flesh. Or they signified three things that were in Christ: His divine nature, his pious soul, and his pure body. These three things were foreshadowed in the Ark of the Covenant. The rod which blossomed is the flesh of Christ which arose from the dead; of this the Psalm says, "And my flesh hath flourished again." The tablet on which the laws were written is the soul in which is hidden all the wisdom and knowledge of God. The manna is the divinity which has all savour and sweetness in it. The gold signifies the noble divinity, because it is more precious than all other metals; the incense signifies the pious soul, for it denotes piety and prayer, of which the Psalm says, "Let my prayer be directed as incense in thy sight"; myrrh denotes the pure body, for it protects against uncleanliness.

Jacobus de Voragine
Legenda aurea (c. 1255-66)

The personality [of Juan de Flandes] . . . is that of a charmingly sensitive and chastely imaginative northerner of the early Renaissance, who exhibits analogies to Gerard David but who was likewise familiar with the French translations of the Flemish style as they manifested themselves in such men as the Maître de Moulins. . . . Since the delicacy and illuminator's technique that Juan maintains even in his larger pictures reveal a training with the miniaturists, he should perhaps rather be compared, among French artists, to Jean Bourdichon or Jean Fouquet. He shows, moreover, a Gallic susceptibility to lovely feminine types and a Gallic feeling for solemnity and restraint in the treatment of religious themes, subduing the tonality of his color to an elegant sobriety.

Chandler Rathfon Post
A History of Spanish Painting (1933)

Collections: Parish Church of San Lázaro, Palencia. *Samuel H. Kress Collection,* 1961. Wood. Height 49⅛ in.; width 31¼ in. (1.248 x 0.794). Painted probably c. 1510 for the high altar of the Parish Church of San Lázaro, in Palencia.

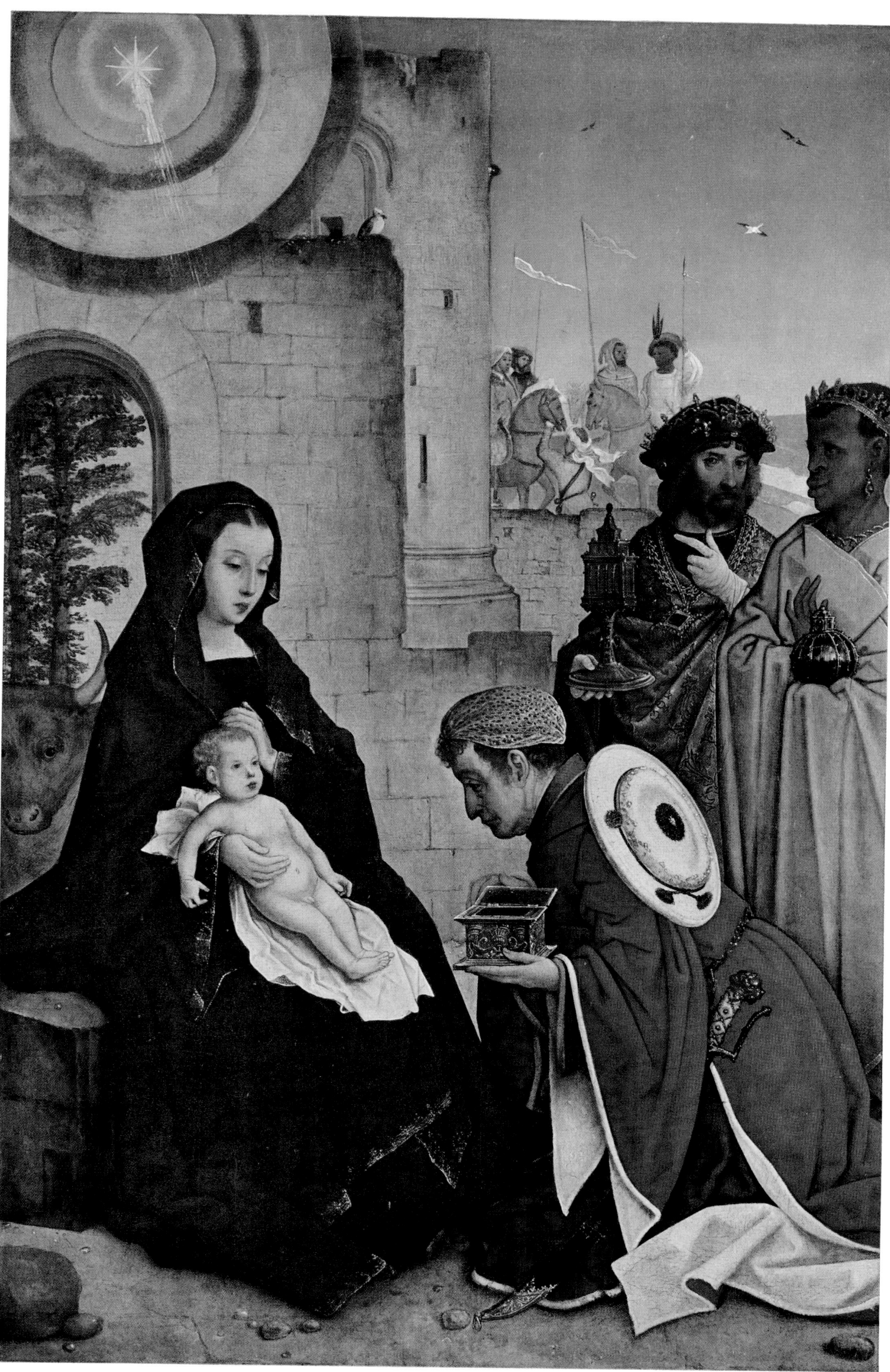

HIERONYMUS BOSCH · Flemish c. 1450-1516

Death and the Miser

The intellect of man is forced to choose
Perfection of the life, or of the work,
And if it take the second must refuse
A heavenly mansion, raging in the dark.
When all that story's finished, what's the news?
In luck or out the toil has left its mark:
That old perplexity an empty purse,
Or the day's vanity, the night's remorse.

William Butler Yeats
Collected Poems (1933)

A wicked man does know that good is lovely, and sin is of an evil and destructive nature; and when he is reproved, he is convinced; and when he is observed, he is ashamed; and when he hath done, he is unsatisfied; and when he pursues his sin, he does it in the dark. Tell him he shall dye, and he sighs deeply, but he knows it as well as you: proceed, and say that after death comes Judgement, and the poor man believes and trembles. He knows that God is angry with him; and if you tell him that for ought he knows he may be in Hell to morrow, he knows that it is an intolerable truth, but it is also undeniable. And yet after all this he runs to commit his sin with as certain an event and resolution, as if he knew no argument against it. These notices of things terrible and true passe through his understanding as an Eagle through the Air: as long as her flight lasted, the Air was shaken; but there remains no path behind her.

Jeremy Taylor
Via Intelligentiæ (1662)

Bosch has shown three stages in the life of a rich man. In his youth he has earned his money fighting with sword and spear and guarded by armor and shield. Grown older, he tries to hoard his gains, while salamanders and rats carry away his treasure. Around his waist hang the key to his strong box and his rosary, the key to his salvation. In the upper part of the picture, unaware of death, he makes his choice. Which key will he use? The *Ars Moriendi,* or treatise on the art of dying, which probably inspired this painting, suggests an optimistic outcome. But in the foreground a winged manikin, which has been identified as a self-portrait, smiles sardonically, and one feels the artist is in agreement with the conclusions of Jeremy Taylor. Collections: Baron Joseph van der Elst, Bruges. *Samuel H. Kress Collection,* 1952. Wood. Height 36⅝ in.; width 12⅛ in. (0.93 x 0.31). Probably painted c. 1490, as the outside of the left wing of an altarpiece.

PIETER BRUEGEL THE ELDER · FLEMISH c. 1525-1569

The Temptation of Saint Anthony

A little from that place toward the water of Phison is a great marvel. For there is a vale between two hills that is four mile long; and some men call it the Vale of Enchanting, some the Vale of Devils, and some the Vale Perilous. In this vale are oft-times heard many tempests and voices, ugly and hideous, both on nights and on days. And some time there is heard noise as it were of trumpets and tabors and of nakers [drums], as it were at feasts of great lords. This vale is full of devils and alway has been; and men say in that country that there is an entry to hell. In this vale is mickle gold and silver; and for to get thereof there come many men, both Christian and heathen, and enter into that vale. But there come but few out again, and namely of miscreants, for all those that go thither because of covetise are strangled with devils and foredone. In midst of the vale under a rock is showed openly the head and the visage of a devil, right hideous and dreadful to see; and there is nothing seen thereof but the head from the shoulders upward. And there is no man in this world, Christian ne other, that ne he should have great dread to behold it, it is so horrible and so foul. And he beholds ilk man so sharply and so felly, and his eyes are so fast stirring and sprinkling as fire, and he changes so oft his countenance, and out of his mouth and his nose comes so great plenty of fire of divers colours with so great stink, that no man may suffer it. But alway good Christian men, that are stable in the faith, may go into that valley without great harm, if they be clean shriven and bless them with the token of the Cross; for then shall devils not dere [harm] them. And if all they escape without harm of body, nevertheless they escape not without great dread; for fiends appear to them openly and menace them and fly up and down in the air with great thunders and lightnings and hideous tempests, that mickle dread shall they have that thereforth pass, als well good men as evil, supposing that God for their old sins will perchance take wreke on them and vengeance.

SIR JOHN MANDEVILLE
Travels (14th Century)

It is quite possible that Bruegel knew one of the many editions of Sir John Mandeville's *Travels,* a book which enjoyed great popularity in the sixteenth century. The setting of the Temptation of Saint Anthony conforms in general with Mandeville's description of the Vale of Devils. Note particularly in the center near the church, "the visage of a devil, right hideous and dreadful to see; and there is nothing seen thereof but the head from the shoulders upward . . . and out of his mouth and his nose comes so great plenty of fire of divers colours with so great stink, that no man may suffer it." Collections: Countess Montblanc, Belgium; Robert Frank, London. *Samuel H. Kress Collection,* 1952. Wood. Height 23 in.; width 33¾ in. (0.584 x 0.857). Painted probably between 1555 and 1558, this is one of the artist's earliest paintings, according to Puyvelde, Glück, and Friedländer.

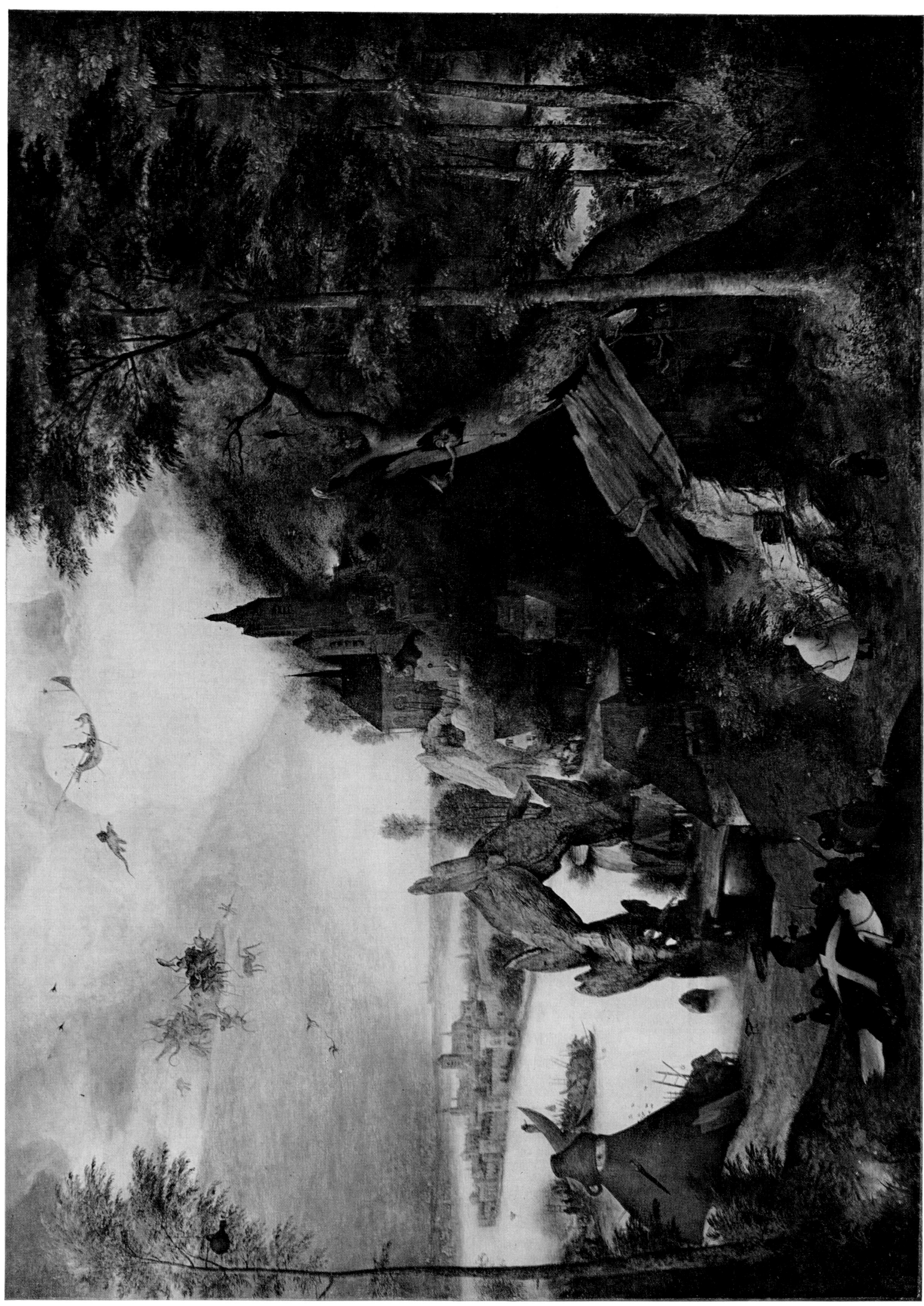

MASTER OF HEILIGENKREUZ

Franco-Austrian Early XV Century

The Death of Saint Clare

When the Tempter me pursu'th
With the sins of all my youth,
And halfe damns me with untruth;
Sweet Spirit comfort me!

When the flames and hellish cries
Fright mine eares, and fright mine eyes,
And all terrors me surprize;
Sweet Spirit comfort me!

When the Judgment is reveal'd,
And that open'd which was seal'd,
When to Thee I have appeal'd;
Sweet Spirit comfort me!

Robert Herrick
His Letanie, to the Holy Spirit (1647)

The Master of Heiligenkreuz tried to convey in this scene of Saint Clare's death the sense of the protective love of God, which Herrick seeks to communicate in words. At Clare's death, according to contemporary biographers, Christ appeared above her bed and received her soul. The Virgin, followed by crowned and garlanded virgin martyrs, bent over her and in her last moment supported her head. The martyrs with Our Lady are, from right to left: Saint Catherine of Alexandria, with her wheel; Saint Cecilia, carrying a wreath of roses; Saint Barbara, with her tower; Saint Dorothea, with a basket of flowers; and Saint Margaret, with a dragon. Saint Agnes of Rome, with her lamb, stands in the foreground. This painting once formed the right wing of a diptych; the other wing, representing the Death of the Virgin Mary, is now in the Cleveland Museum of Art. Collections: Monastery in northeast Germany; Professor Walter Schnakenberg; Dr. Carl Langbehn, Munich. *Samuel H. Kress Collection,* 1952. Wood. Height 26⅛ in.; width 21⅜ in. (0.664 x 0.545). Painted c. 1410.

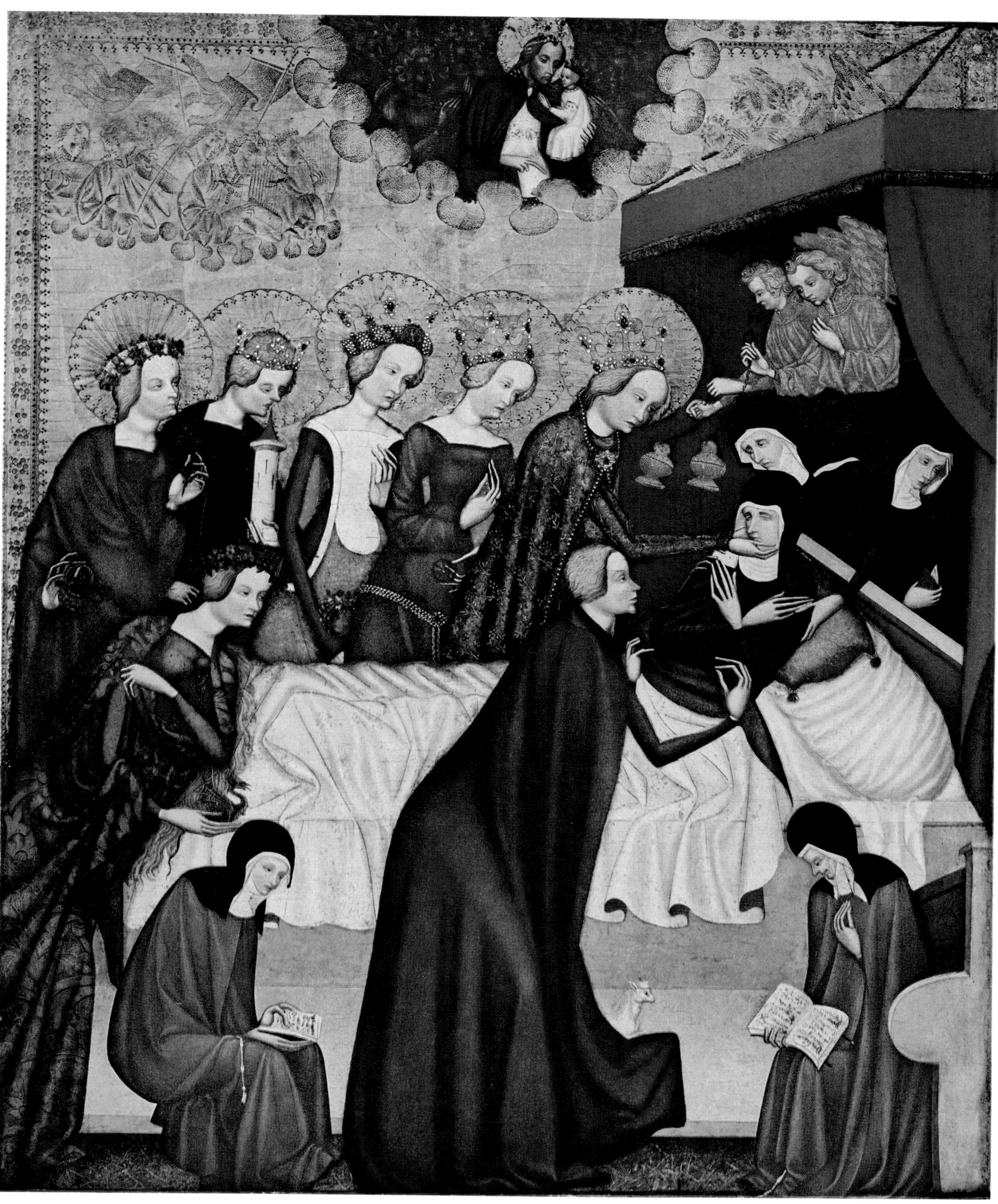

MASTER OF THE SAINT BARTHOLOMEW ALTAR

SCHOOL OF COLOGNE ACTIVE c. 1470-c. 1510

The Baptism of Christ

We cannot consider it a deficiency that the North has never adhered strictly to rules and frequently even treated them lightly; rather, this expresses a distinct and positive basic attitude indicative of the entire German relationship to nature. Germans do not *believe* in the absolute value of rules but perceive a streak of irrationality in all living things. This feeling for an irrationality that simply cannot be expressed in stable forms already conditions the style of the German primitives, a style that may appear particularly "formless" in comparison with Italian art. The great generation of sixteenth-century artists valued rules more highly than did their predecessors; yet, for it too, there was evidently a remainder that could not be carried over into the sphere of lucid order. . . .

If the Germans arrive at syntheses different from those of the Italians, it does not mean that they are unable to understand Italian form. It may even happen that, just through their awareness of the contrast, the Germans can be more appreciative of the free articulation and strict self-containment of Italian art.

HEINRICH WÖLFFLIN
Italien und das deutsche Formgefühl (1931)

It is a charming fantasy and typically northern to have the Christian martyrs see the baptism of Our Lord. In eternity historical time does not exist. The fourteen saints are, from left to right: Dorothea, Christopher, Andrew, Jerome, Catherine of Alexandria, Augustine, Agnes, Francis of Assisi, Lucy, Elizabeth of Thuringen, Mary Magdalen, Anthony Abbot, Apollonia, and George. The rich coloring of the painting, the bizarre invention, and the careful execution of details explain why the Master of the Saint Bartholomew Altarpiece has been called the Northern Crivelli. Collections: According to tradition the painting was originally in a church in Arnheim; Count Baryas, Paris; Richard von Kaufmann, Berlin; O. Henkell, Wiesbaden. *Samuel H. Kress Collection,* 1961. Wood. Height 41¾ in.; width 67⅛ in. (1.061 x 1.705). Painted c. 1500.

LUCAS VAN LEYDEN · Dutch 1494-1533

The Card Players

To those puny objectors against cards, as nurturing the bad passions, she would retort, that man is a gaming animal. He must be always trying to get the better in something or other:—that this passion can scarcely be more safely expended than upon a game at cards: that cards are a temporary illusion; in truth, a mere drama; for we do but *play* at being mightily concerned, where a few idle shillings are at stake, yet, during the illusion, we *are* as mightily concerned as those whose stake is crowns and kingdoms. They are a sort of dream-fighting; much ado; great battling, and little blood shed; mighty means for disproportioned ends; quite as diverting, and a great deal more innoxious, than many of those more serious *games* of life, which men play, without esteeming them to be such.

Charles Lamb
The Essays of Elia (1823)

I am sorry I have not learnt to play at cards. It is very useful in life: it generates kindness, and consolidates society.

Samuel Johnson
Boswell's Tour to the Hebrides (Nov. 21, 1773)

It is amazing to think this picture was painted when Raphael was still alive. For it anticipates gambling pictures of a hundred years later associated with Caravaggio. How clearly we read the minds of the players! The man with the ace of spades thinks he has won, but we feel victory will go to the lady counting out her money. The other two players look sad or disgruntled—exactly as they might appear in a poker game today. One wonders, however, whether this card game has "generated kindness, and consolidated society." Collection: *Samuel H. Kress Collection*, 1961. Wood. Height 22⅛ in.; width 24 in. (0.564 x 0.609). Painted c. 1520.

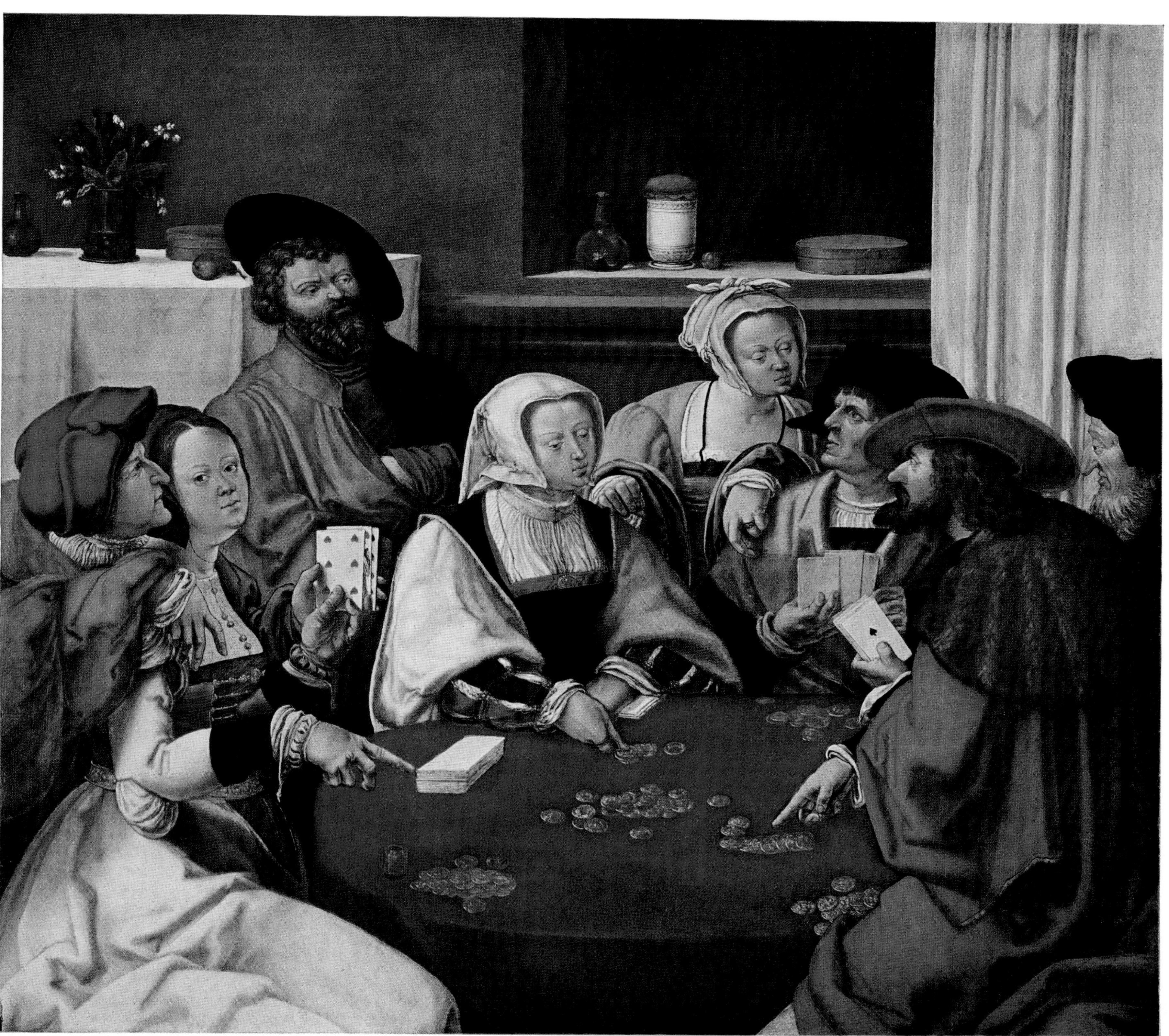

MATHIS GRÜNEWALD · German c. 1465-1528

The Small Crucifixion

Still falls the Rain—
Dark as the world of man, black as our loss—
Blind as the nineteen hundred and forty nails
Upon the Cross.

Still falls the Rain
With a sound like the pulse of the heart that is changed
    to the hammer-beat
In the Potter's Field, and the sound of the impious feet

On the Tomb
                Still falls the Rain
In the Field of Blood where the small hopes breed and the
    human brain
Nurtures its greed, that worm with the brow of Cain.

Still falls the Rain
At the feet of the Starved Man hung upon the Cross.
Christ that each day, each night, nails there, have mercy on us—
On Dives and on Lazarus:
Under the Rain the sore and the gold are as one. . . .

Still falls the Rain—
Then—O Ile leape up to my God: who pulles me doune—
See, see where Christ's blood streames in the firmament:
It flows from the Brow we nailed upon the tree
Deep to the dying, to the thirsting heart
That holds the fires of the world,—dark-smirched with pain,
As Caesar's laurel crown.
Then sounds the voice of One who like the heart of man
Was once a child who among beasts has lain—
'Still do I love, still shed my innocent light, my Blood, for thee.'

Edith Sitwell
Street Songs (1942)

Heir to the Gothic and precursor of the Baroque, Grünewald has here attained to an intensity of expression that no other artist has surpassed. Writing about this Crucifixion in the seventeenth century, Sandrart said, "Certainly it is more true to nature and reality than all Crucifixions when one contemplates it with thoughtful patience for a long time." Collections: Duke William V of Bavaria; Duke Maximilian I of Bavaria; Landrat Dr. Friedrich Schöne, Essen; Franz Wilhelm Koenigs and heirs, Haarlem. *Samuel H. Kress Collection,* 1961. Wood. Height 24¼ in.; width 18⅛ in. (0.616 x 0.46). Signed with initials. Painted c. 1510.

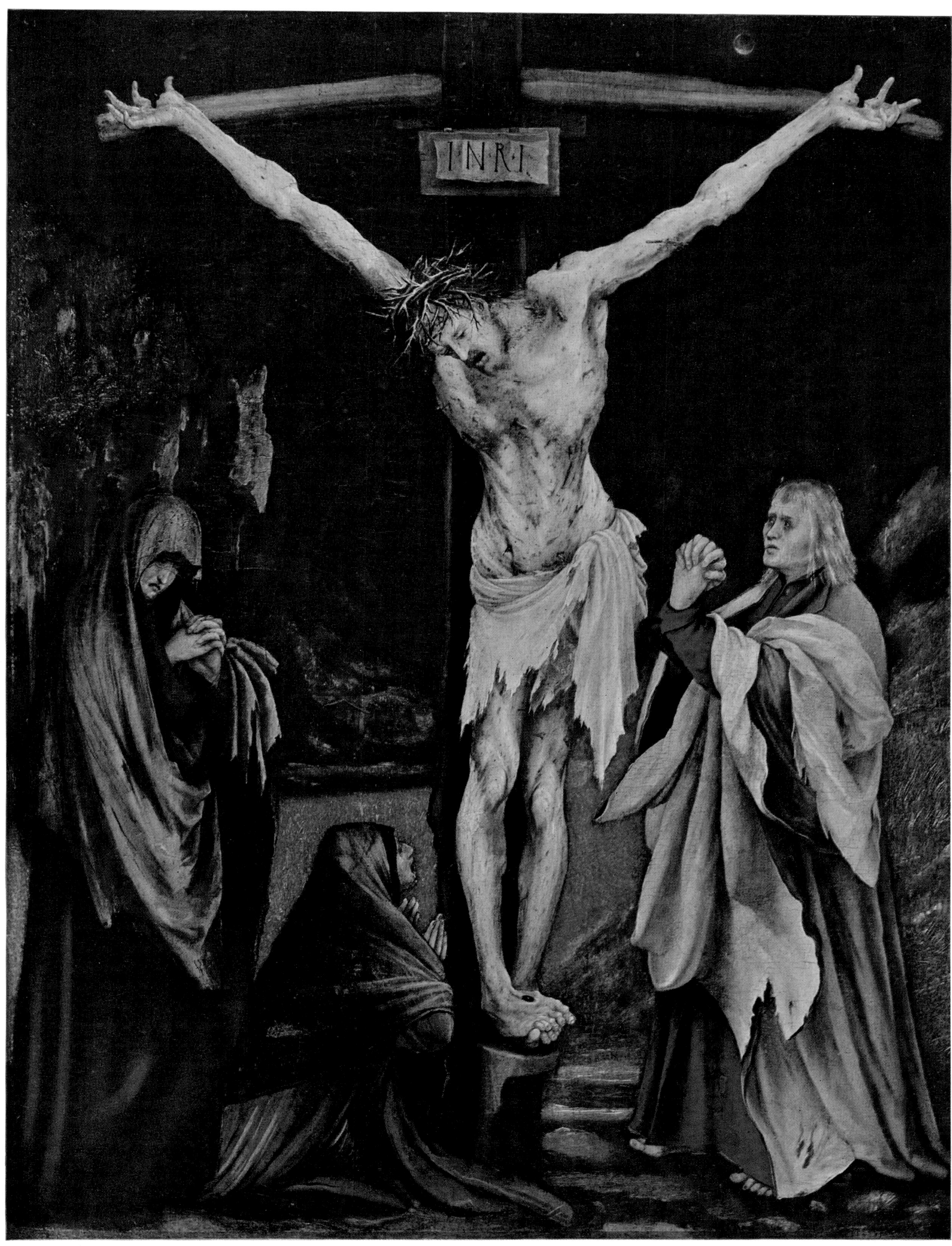
I·N·R·I·

ALBRECHT DÜRER · German 1471-1528

Madonna and Child

I wish you were here in Venice; there are so many pleasant companions amongst the Italians (*Walschen*), with whom I am becoming more and more intimate, so that it does one's heart good. There are learned men amongst them, good lute-players, pipers, some having a knowledge of painting; right honest people, who give me their friendship with the greatest kindness.

On the other hand, there are also among them the most lying, thieving rascals that ever lived on the earth; and if one was not acquainted with their ways, one would take them for the most honest men in the world. I often laugh to myself when they speak to me, for they know that all sorts of knavery is known of them, but they care nothing about it.

I have many good friends among the Italians, who warn me not to eat or drink with their painters, for many of them are my enemies, and copy my things in the church, and wherever they meet with them. And yet notwithstanding this they abuse my works, and say that they are not according to ancient art, and therefore not good. But Sanbellinus (Giovanni Bellini) has praised me highly before several noblemen, and he wishes to have something of my painting. He came himself and asked me to do something for him, saying that he would pay me well for it. And all the people here tell me what a good man he is, so that I also am greatly inclined to him. He is very old, but yet he is the best painter of them all.

Albrecht Dürer
Letter to Willibald Pirkheimer (1506)

And now, finally, to beauty! Is it not taken for granted that that which we call beautiful can be of only *one* kind? Nevertheless, the German beauty was obviously subject to numerous individual modifications. Every painter who had to create a beautiful man or a beautiful woman was permitted to say, "Beauty as *I* think of it." No one suffered more than Dürer through this disparity of taste. Throughout his entire life, he strove with everything in his power after a solution that, by providing an objective basis for beauty, would force all the purely subjective opinions together into a unity....

It is highly significant that in aesthetically divided Germany, there lived the artist, Dürer, who asked the question about the one absolute beauty, and not only asked it but pursued it fervently as a question of vital importance. But that he finally had to characterize perfect beauty as unattainable has symbolic meaning....

The Germans learned from the Italians, but they would not have sought out foreign models had a related impulse not existed in their own hearts.

Heinrich Wölfflin
Italien und das deutsche Formgefühl (1931)

The written tribute paid to Giovanni Bellini by Dürer is well known. But a still greater compliment from the northern painter to the Venetian is this Madonna, which was once thought to be by Bellini himself; so close is it to the work of that artist. Here Dürer was searching among the Italian painters for "absolute beauty," as have many other Germans. But his creation remains as essentially northern as the landscape glimpsed through the window, or the coats of arms at the lower corners, one of which has been identified as belonging to the Haller family, who came from Dürer's home town, Nuremberg. Collections: Colonel a' Court-Repington, London; Mrs. Phyllis Loder, London; Baron Heinrich Thyssen-Bornemisza, Lugano. *Samuel H. Kress Collection,* 1952. Wood. Height 19¾ in.; width 15⅝ in. (0.502 x 0.397). Painted probably between 1504 and 1507.

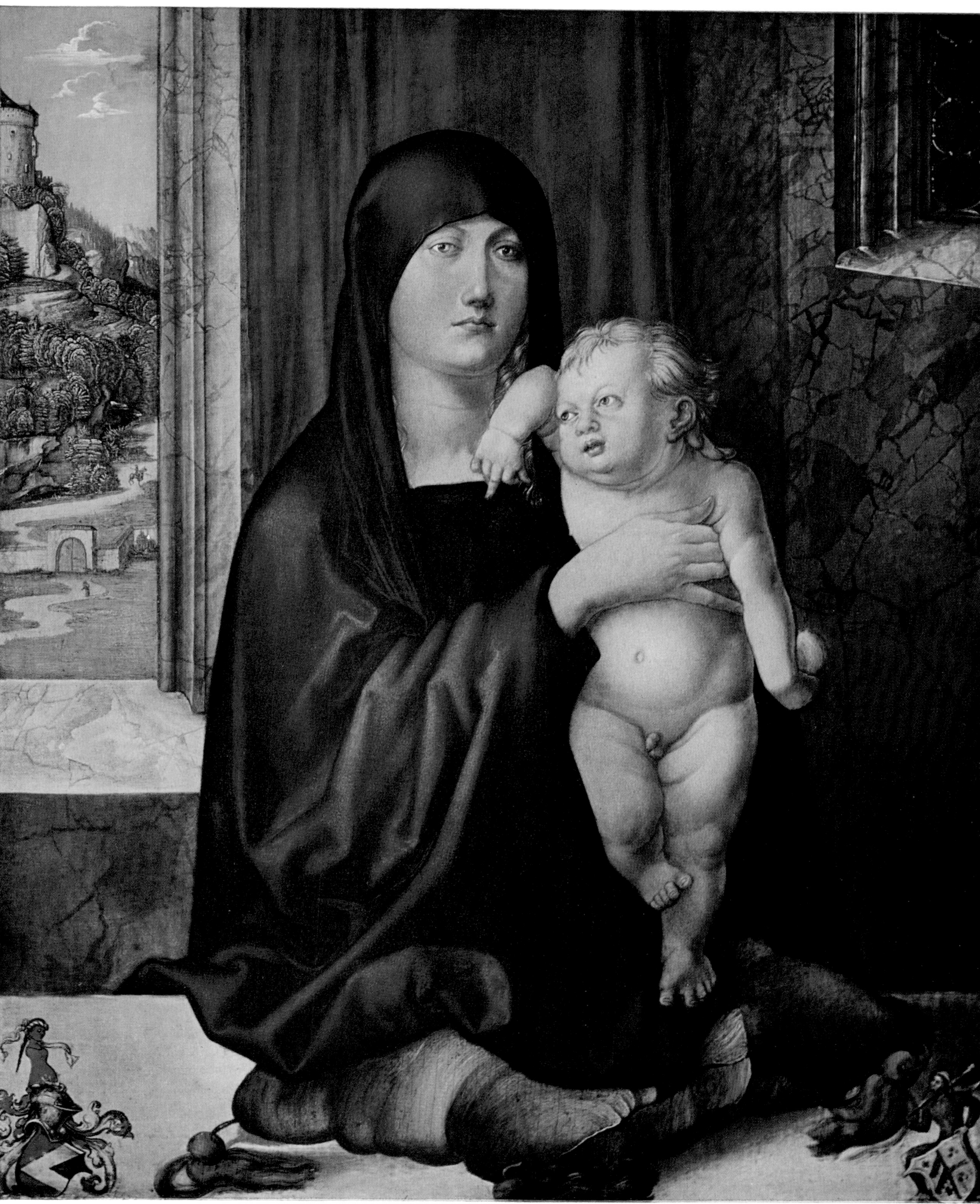

ALBRECHT DÜRER · German 1471-1528

Portrait of a Clergyman

We can, again, easily fancy it possible that the magnificent vitality of Titian might be worth more than any less healthy, though more aspiring work; and, in the same way, the majestic grace of Raphael might very probably outweigh profounder thought expressed in the coarser forms of Dürer. To speak about such different qualities relatively is as hard as to compare the commanding power of a great statesman with the more abstract ability of the philosopher; the one conveys the greater sense of power, yet in the other we recognize the higher range of thought; the best we can do is to fix on an intermediate point, where the keen eye and directing brain of the man of the world keep more abstract reflection from falling into weakness. One thing I think we can say; just as the lowest form of good art is the mere portraiture of the single, unconnected fact, with no further view beyond,—like the painting of a nosegay, for instance, with the decay, the worm, and the dew-drop set down with equal faithfulness,—so art is great in proportion as it rises above this, and the presumption is always in favor of that picture being greatest in which the lower truth of the individual is made subservient (notice, I do not say falsified or even neglected, but made subservient) to the profounder truth of the idea. Knowledge of the stains of the earth, and of the decay that accompanies all earthly life, doubtless the painter needs, but higher than this is the sight which beholds the type disguised beneath the wasting form, and higher than anything connected with the individual is the conception of the harmonious whole of a great work, and this again is great, just as its idea partakes of what is eternal. And this striving to look on types and eternal ideas, is that highest gift of the artist, which is called the ideal tendency.

Oliver Wendell Holmes, Jr.
Notes on Albert Dürer
The Harvard Magazine (1860)

When Oliver Wendell Holmes, Jr., became a lawyer America gained a great jurist, but lost perhaps a great art critic. His *Notes on Albert Dürer,* written while he was an undergraduate at Harvard, is an impressive statement of the Aristotelian concept of universality. The portrait reproduced was probably among the works by Dürer which Paul de Praun (1548-1616) bought from Wenzel Jamnitzer, who, in turn, had acquired them from Andrea Dürer, younger brother and heir of the artist. The technique, oil on parchment, is somewhat unusual, but was employed by Dürer for another painting of the same year, the Madonna in the Augsburg Gallery. Collections: Paul de Praun Cabinet, Nuremberg; Count Johann Rudolf Czernin von Chudenitz, Vienna; Czernin Gallery, Vienna. *Samuel H. Kress Collection,* 1952. Parchment on canvas. Height 16⅞ in.; width 13 in. (0.429 x 0.332). Signed with monogram, and dated 1516.

1516

LUCAS CRANACH THE ELDER · German 1472-1553

A Prince of Saxony

The child who has become aware of himself as a separate being with a sense of despair, rage and jealousy will base his whole life on the fruitless contemplation of a singularity which is formal. 'You threw me out,' he will say to his parents. 'You threw me out of the perfect whole of which I was part and condemned me to a separate existence. Well, now I'm going to turn this existence against you. If you ever wanted to get me back again, it would be impossible because I have become conscious of myself as separate from and against everybody else.' And he will say to his schoolfellows and the street urchins who persecute him: 'I'm someone else, someone different from all of you who are responsible for my sufferings. You can persecute my body, but you can't touch my "otherness".' This assertion is both a claim and a gesture of defiance. He is someone else, and because he is someone else he is out of reach and already almost revenged on his oppressors. He prefers himself to everyone else because everyone else abandons him. His preference for himself is primarily a defence-mechanism, but it is also in a sense an *ascesis* because for the child it takes the form of pure self-consciousness. It is an heroic, an aggressive choice of the abstract, a desperate stripping of oneself, at once an act of renunciation and affirmation. It has a name and its name is pride. It is a stoic pride, a metaphysical pride which owes nothing to social distinctions, to success or to any recognized form of superiority or indeed to anything at all in this world. It simply appears as an absolute event, an *a priori* choice which is entirely unmotivated and belongs to a sphere far above any of those where failure could destroy or success sustain it.

Jean-Paul Sartre
Baudelaire (1949)

It has been suggested by Friedländer and Rosenberg (1932) that the sitter in this portrait may be Prince Frederick (born 1504), the son of Duke George the Bearded. Collections: A. Salomon, Dresden. *Ralph and Mary Booth Collection,* 1947. Wood. Height 17¼ in.; width 13⅝ in. (0.437 x 0.344). Painted c. 1517.

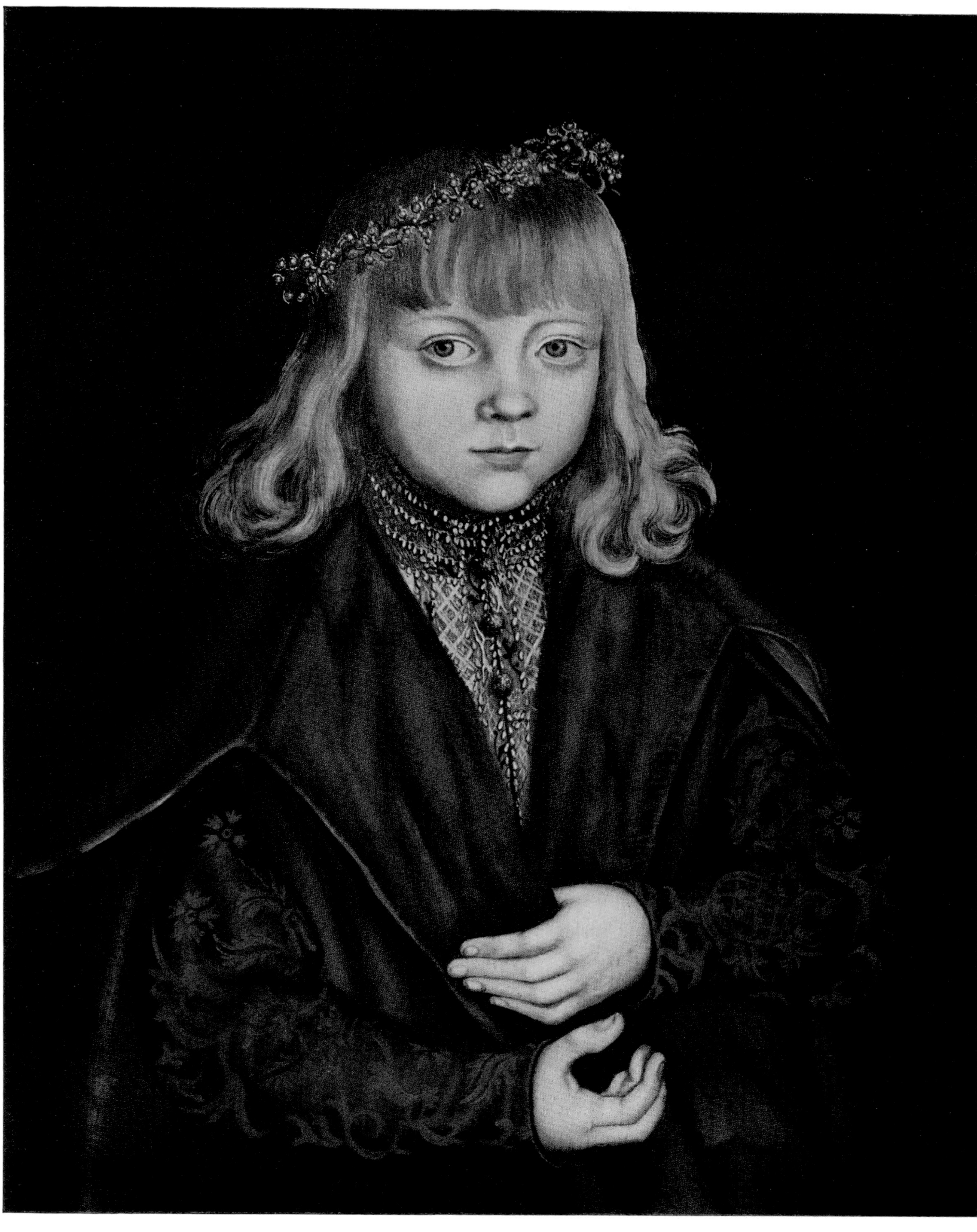

ALBRECHT ALTDORFER · German Before 1480-1538

The Fall of Man

In recompence (for such compliance bad
Such recompence best merits) from the bough
She gave him of that fair enticing Fruit
With liberal hand: he scrupl'd not to eat
Against his better knowledge, not deceav'd,
But fondly overcome with Femal charm.
Earth trembl'd from her entrails, as again
In pangs, and Nature gave a second groan,
Skie lowr'd and muttering Thunder, som sad drops
Wept at compleating of the mortal Sin
Original; while *Adam* took no thought,
Eating his fill, nor *Eve* to iterate
Her former trespass fear'd, the more to soothe
Him with her lov'd societie, that now
As with new Wine intoxicated both
They swim in mirth, and fansie that they feel
Divinitie within them breeding wings
Wherewith to scorne the Earth: but that false Fruit
Farr other operation first displaid,
Carnal desire enflaming, hee on *Eve*
Began to cast lascivious Eyes, she him
As wantonly repaid; in Lust they burne:
Till *Adam* thus 'gan *Eve* to dalliance move.

John Milton
Paradise Lost (1667)

Originally Adam and Eve now framed in the central position were each represented on an outer wing of a triptych. Thus Adam's temptation by Eve appeared only when the triptych was closed. When the triptych was opened one saw the central panel, which has disappeared, and on either side the Reign of Bacchus and the Reign of Mars. Partially preserved Latin inscriptions on these two lateral panels may be freely translated: "Bacchus confuses the senses of man with wine," and "The impious Mars upsets the world." When closed the triptych therefore illustrated the commencement of sin with Adam's fall from grace; and when opened it showed the consequences of sin, with mankind at the mercy of Bacchus, Mars, and whatever god or goddess was on the lost central panel. Paracelsus, a contemporary of Altdorfer, describes such moralizing, allegorical paintings, mixing Christian theology and astrological mythology. Collections: Professor F. van Wieser, Innsbruck; Lacher von Eiseck, Bad Tölz, Oberbayern; Baron Heinrich Thyssen-Bornemisza, Lugano. *Samuel H. Kress Collection,* 1952. Wood. Middle panel, height 15¼ in.; width 12 in. (0.387 x 0.350); side panels, each, height 15¼ in.; width 6¼ in. (0.387 x 0.159). Painted probably c. 1525, according to Friedländer; not before 1526, according to Baldass.

QVVM.BACCHIC
TVRBAT

HANS HOLBEIN THE YOUNGER · German 1497-1543

Sir Brian Tuke

Holbein, in fact, was a great Renderer. If I wanted to find a figure really akin to his I think I should go to music and speak of Bach. For in Bach you have just that peculiar Teutonic type of which Holbein is so great an example: in the musician too you have that marvellous mastery of the instrument, that composure, that want of striving. And both move one by what musicians call "absolute" means. . . .

We are, literally, in love with this arrangement of lines, of lights and of shadows. The eye is held by no object, but solely by the music of the pattern—the quality that we call "Holbein". . . .

Simplicity and severity were probably distasteful enough to him. Thus nothing could have been further from his sympathy than what is best in modern decorative art, and he had little or no idea, beyond that enforced by the exigencies of space, of adapting his design to the form of the object to be decorated or of reducing the amount of ornament further and further until the best decorated space be that which contains the least ornament. *His* dukes would never have been the worst dressed men of a House of Peers.

His is the other end of our line, in this as in so many other things, and to appreciate him thoroughly we have to make mental efforts of one kind and another. As we might put it, he was vulgar, which we are not, but he had more blood and more hope, so that he achieved the impossible so many times, and climbing in places where we are accustomed to say that climbing is wrong or hopeless, he appears on peaks more high than any of ours. That, of course, is what the master does in the realm of the arts.

Ford Madox Ford
Hans Holbein the Younger (1905)

"Holbein's heads are to the finest portraits what state-papers are to history," Hazlitt remarked. "We need hardly observe that they all have character in the extreme, so that we may be said to be acquainted with the people they represent; but then they give nothing but character, and only one part of that, *viz.* the dry, the literal, the concrete, and fixed. They want the addition of passion and beauty; but they are the finest *caput mortuums* of expression that ever were made. Hans Holbein had none of the volatile essence of genius in his composition. If portrait-painting is the prose of the art, his pictures are the prose of portrait-painting." Sir Brian Tuke was secretary to Henry VIII, in which capacity it was his business to pay Holbein's salary. He was also "governor of the king's post" and therefore to some degree responsible for founding the postal system in England. Collections: Philip Sidney, third Earl of Leicester; Sir Paul Methuen, and descendants, among whom the last owner was Paul, first Lord Methuen, Corsham Court, Chippenham, Wiltshire; Richard Sanderson, Edinburgh; Richard, second Marquess of Westminster; Lady Theodora Guest, Inwood, Templecombe, England; Watson B. Dickerman, New York. *Andrew Mellon Collection,* 1937. Wood. Height 19⅜ in.; width 15¼ in. (0.49 x 0.39). Painted c. 1527.

BRIANVS TVKE, MILES. AN° ETATIS SVÆ, LVII

. DROIT ET AVANT .

NVNQVID NON PAVCITAS DIERVM MEORVM FINIETVR BREVI ?

HANS HOLBEIN THE YOUNGER · German 1497-1543

Edward VI as a Child

There are two ways of conceiving the portrait—the historic and the romantic. The first is to render faithfully, severely, scrupulously, the contour and the modeling of the subject. This does not exclude idealization, which for the learned naturalists will consist of choosing the most characteristic attitude, that which best expresses the habits of the spirit; and furthermore, in knowing how to give each important detail a reasonable emphasis, placing in the light all that is naturally salient, accentuated and prominent, and neglecting or blending in the whole all that is insignificant, or what is the result of an accidental diminution in significance.

The second method, the one peculiar to colorists, is to make of the portrait a picture, a poem with its accessories, full of space and reverie. Here the art is more difficult, because it is more ambitious. One must know how to bathe a head in the soft vapors of a torrid atmosphere, or to make it emerge from the depths of the twilight. Here the imagination plays a greater part, and yet, just as fiction often surpasses history in truth, a subject may be more clearly defined by the facile and flowing brush of the colorist than by the pencil of the draftsman. Portraiture, apparently such a modest branch of the arts, demands immense intelligence. Unquestionably the artist must be very faithful to his model, but his insight must equal his fidelity. When I see a good portrait I think of all the efforts of the artist, who has had first to see what was evident, but also to divine what was hidden. I was just now comparing him to a historian; I might also compare him to a comedian, who of necessity feigns all characters and dons every kind of costume. Nothing, if one examines the matter well, is inconsequential in a portrait. The gesture, the grimace, the garment, even the setting—all must play a part in representing a *character*. Among great painters and excellent painters, David, both when he was but another artist of the eighteenth century and after he had become the leader of a school, and Holbein in all his portraits, tried to express with restraint but with intensity the character they undertook to paint. Others sought to do even more, or to do otherwise. Reynolds and Gérard supplied the romantic touch, always in accord with the nature of the personage; hence a stormy and tormented sky, light and airy backgrounds, poetic furnishings, a languishing attitude, an adventurous bearing. This is a dangerous procedure, which, while not to be condemned, nevertheless calls for genius. Finally, whatever the means most obviously used by the artist, whether that artist be Holbein, David, Velázquez or Lawrence, a good portrait appears to me always as a dramatized biography, or better as the human drama inherent in every man.

Charles Baudelaire
Salon de 1859
La Revue Française (1859)

Painted presumably in 1538, soon after Holbein's second arrival in England, and generally accepted as the portrait of the Prince recorded in a roll (of New Year's gifts) now in the Folger Shakespeare Library, Washington, D. C., as presented by the artist to the King on New Year's Day, 1539. The drawing which doubtless served as the study for this panel is in Windsor Castle (Woltmann, *Holbein*). The Latin inscription is a *consilium* addressed to the Prince by Sir Richard Morison, ambassador and close friend of Henry VIII: *Little one, emulate thy father and be the heir of his virtue; the world contains nothing greater. Heaven and earth could scarcely produce a son whose glory would surpass that of such a father. Do thou but equal the deeds of thy parent and men can ask no more. Shouldst thou surpass him, thou hast outstript all kings the world has revered in ages past.* Collections: From the English Royal Collection the portrait passed in the eighteenth century to the Royal and Ducal Hanoverian Collections. In 1893 it was deposited in the Provincial Museum, Hanover. *Andrew Mellon Collection,* 1937. Wood. Height 22⅜ in.; width 17⅜ in. (0.57 x 0.44).

PARVVLE PATRISSA, PATRIÆ VIRTVTIS ET HÆRES
ESTO, NIHIL MAIVS MAXIMVS ORBIS HABET.
GNATVM VIX POSSVNT COELVM ET NATVRA DEDISSE,
HVIVS QVEM PATRIS, VICTVS HONORET HONOS.
ÆQVATO TANTVM, TANTI TV FACTA PARENTIS,
VOTA HOMINVM, VIX QVO PROGRFDIANTVR, HABENT
VINCITO, VICISTI. QVOT REGES PRISCVS ADORAT
ORBIS, NEC TE QVI VINCERE POSSIT, ERIT.
Ricard. Morysini. Car.

PERUGINO · Umbrian Probably 1445-1523

The Crucifixion with the Virgin and Saints

Crucifixion! This is the word upon which we must meditate today. For is it not Good Friday?

You desire to know the art of living, my friend?
It is contained in one phrase: make use of suffering.

Will you now reject suffering as vain, useless, fierce, tyrannical, when formerly you were able to draw from it a moral and a benefit? To damn it is easier than to bless it, but it means falling back into the point of view of earthly, carnal, natural man. How else did Christianity conquer the world but by the deification of grief, by the glorious transmutation of anguish into triumph, of the crown of thorns into a crown of glory, and of a gallows into a symbol of salvation? What signifies the apotheosis of the cross, if not the death of death, the destruction of sin, the beatification of the martyr, the raising to heaven of voluntary sacrifice, the defiance of pain?

"O Death, where is thy sting? O Grave, where is thy victory?" From a long contemplation of this theme—the agony of the Just, peace in the midst of agony, and glory in such peace—mankind came to understand that a new religion had been born, that is, a new way of explaining life and of understanding suffering. . . .

Crucify the ungovernable self, mortify yourself wholly, offer up everything to God, and peace which is not of this world will descend upon you. For eighteen centuries no greater word has been spoken, and although men seek an ever more exact, more complete application of justice, yet secretly they put their faith in pardon only, for only pardon conciliates the inviolable purity of perfection with the infinite pity for weakness.

Henri Frédéric Amiel
Journal intime (April 15, 1870)

Few paintings convey more clearly than this the concepts of "peace in the midst of agony," "the inviolable purity of perfection," and "the infinite pity for weakness." Though Vasari said Perugino was a person of little religion and disbelieved in the immortality of the soul, to an extraordinary degree he makes us vibrate to the emotions of the religious themes he illustrates. The present triptych was formerly ascribed to Perugino's greater pupil, Raphael, but as we know that it was given to the Church of San Domenico at San Gimignano by Bartolommeo Bartoli, who died in 1497, when Raphael was only fourteen, we can be certain that this attribution was incorrect. The picture is now unanimously attributed to Perugino. Collections: Church of San Domenico, San Gimignano; Antonio Moggi; Dr. Buzzi; Prince Alexander Galitzin; Prince Theodore Galitzin; Galitzin Museum; Hermitage Gallery, Leningrad. *Andrew Mellon Collection,* 1937. Transferred from wood to canvas. Center panel, height 39⅞ in.; width 22¼ in. (1.013 x 0.565). Each side panel, height 37½ in.; width 12 in. (0.952 x 0.305). Painted c. 1485.

RAPHAEL · UMBRIAN 1483-1520

Saint George and the Dragon

This wonderful art can take us away from ourselves and give us, while we are under its spell, the feeling of being identified with the universe, perhaps even of being the soul of the universe. The feeling may be so conscious that it remains an artistic sensation—the most artistic of all; or it may transport one into the raptures of mysticism; but for those of us who are neither idolaters nor suppliants, this sense of identification with the universe is of the very essence of the religious emotion.

BERNARD BERENSON
The Italian Painters of the Renaissance (1930)

Men's curiosity searches past and future
And clings to that dimension. But to apprehend
The point of intersection of the timeless
With time, is an occupation for the saint—
No occupation either, but something given
And taken, in a lifetime's death in love,
Ardour and selflessness and self-surrender.
For most of us, there is only the unattended
Moment, the moment in and out of time,
The distraction fit, lost in a shaft of sunlight,
The wild thyme unseen, or the winter lightning
Or the waterfall, or music heard so deeply
That it is not heard at all, but you are the music
While the music lasts. These are only hints and guesses,
Hints followed by guesses; and the rest
Is prayer, observance, discipline, thought and action.
The hint half guessed, the gift half understood, is
   Incarnation.
Here the impossible union
Of spheres of existence is actual,
Here the past and future
Are conquered, and reconciled,
Where action were otherwise movement
Of that which is only moved
And has in it no source of movement—
Driven by daemonic, chthonic
Powers. And right action is freedom
From past and future also.
For most of us, this is the aim
Never here to be realised;
Who are only undefeated
Because we have gone on trying;
We, content at the last
If our temporal reversion nourish
(Not too far from the yew-tree)
The life of significant soil.

T. S. ELIOT
Four Quartets (1943)

This is one of the most beautifully preserved of all Raphael's paintings on panel. It was commissioned by Duke Guidobaldo da Montefeltro, the ruler of Urbino, and taken as a gift to Henry VII of England by his Ambassador, Baldassare Castiglione, author of *The Courtier* (see quotation, page 64). Raphael has depicted Saint George wearing the insignia of the Order of the Garter to commemorate the bestowal of this honor on Duke Guidobaldo. On the horse's harness can be seen the signature of the artist, Raphello V,—the V standing for the first letter of the name of Raphael's birthplace, Urbino. The pen-and-ink drawing used originally as a tracing for the painting is in the Uffizi, Florence. Collections: From the English Royal Collection the panel passed into the possession of the Earl of Pembroke, and was engraved by L. Vosterman. Later it formed part of the collection of Charles I, and was reproduced in tapestry at the royal factory at Mortlake. After the execution of Charles I the panel was taken to France, and was acquired from the Crozat Collection by Catherine the Great for the Hermitage Gallery, Leningrad. *Andrew Mellon Collection,* 1937. Wood. Height 11⅛ in.; width 8⅜ in. (0.285 x 0.215). Signed. Painted 1504-06.

RAPHAEL · UMBRIAN 1483-1520

The Small Cowper Madonna

Raphael was aiming at beauty as much as were Alberti and Politian, and he tried as far as he could to keep his faces serene and quiet and free from the agitations of active feeling, so that his figures are epic rather than dramatic. That indefinable sense of quietude, of being deeply and truly satisfied, which we feel in the *Stanze* of Politian, which brings us nearer to the repose of Nature than the agitations of the human face, the "tranquil peace, without anything to trouble it," is what distinguished this ideal of lovely form—except that this peace of Raphael's is not "like unto that which is absorbed in God"; it is not a musical ideal, like Beatrice and Laura, but comes from the closest study of the real in its smallest details. We feel that the painter had a model before him, a model that sank into his imagination and fulfilled itself there, and acquired that purity and repose of form which he called "a certain idea." It is true that in this "certain idea" there is something of the classical, of the conventional, of the schools, but it is barely noticeable in these works of genius, sprung from a true inspiration, in which the feeling for beauty and the study of the real predominate. So the Madonnas of this century were born, Madonnas in whose faces there is nothing of the tremor, the abstraction, the ecstasy, of the saint, but only the simple and idyllic quietude of virginity and innocence. This type of face became more and more realistic, until in the Venetian imagination of Titian it took a form that is almost voluptuous.

· · · ·

The positive side of this movement is the ideal of form: form loved and studied as form, apart from content; and its negative side is precisely this indifference to content. With some of the men of the day it was a sort of eclecticism, as with Raphael, Leonardo da Vinci, Michelangelo, Ficino, Pico, who embraced all the contents, on the principle that all are a part of culture, of art, of thought—an eclecticism that in others was mixed with a gay satirizing, without acrimony, of the principles and forms and customs of the past that were still in good repute among the lower classes. The divine in this movement is the ideal of form, or, to put it differently, is culture taken by itself and deified. And even its comic and negative side is nothing more than a revelation of culture.

FRANCESCO DE SANCTIS
Storia della letteratura italiana (1870)

Painted probably about the same time as the Granduca Madonna in the Pitti, Florence, the present panel was considered by Morelli (*Italian Masters in German Galleries*), as "perhaps the most lovely of all Raphael's Madonnas." A drawing showing the whole composition in reverse is in the Uffizi, Florence; but whether this is a preliminary sketch or a contemporary copy after the painting remains in doubt. The building in the background is probably San Bernardino, a small church on the outskirts of Urbino, from which town this Madonna is said to have come. Collections: Purchased in Florence by Earl Cowper about 1780, the present painting remained in the possession of his family at Panshanger, Hertfordshire, until 1913. *Widener Collection,* 1942. Wood. Height 23⅜ in.; width 17⅜ in. (0.595 x 0.44). Painted c. 1505.

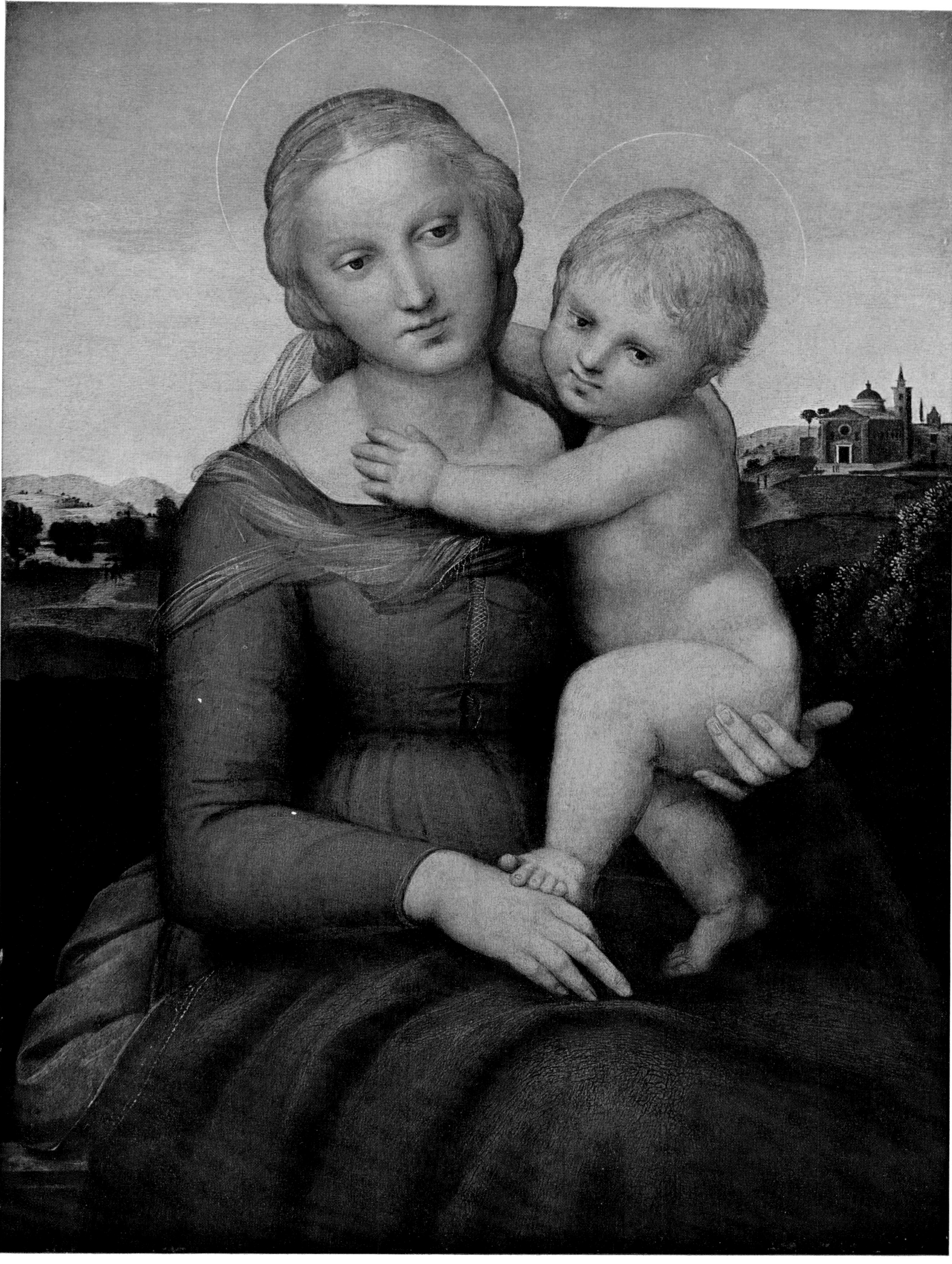

RAPHAEL · Umbrian 1483-1520

The Niccolini-Cowper Madonna

"Beauty is a thing severe and unapproachable, never to be won by a languid lover. You must lie in wait for her coming and take her unawares, press her hard and clasp her in a tight embrace, and force her to yield. Form is a Proteus more intangible and more manifold than the Proteus of the legend; compelled, only after long wrestling, to stand forth manifest in his true aspect. Some of you are satisfied with the first shape, or at most by the second or the third that appears. Not thus wrestle the victors, the unvanquished painters who never suffer themselves to be deluded by all those treacherous shadow-shapes; they persevere till nature at the last stands bare to their gaze, and her very soul is revealed.

"In this manner worked Raphael," said the old man, taking off his cap to express his reverence for the King of Art. "His transcendent greatness came from the intimate sense that, in him, seems as if it would shatter external form. Form in his figures (as with us) is a symbol, a means of communicating sensations, ideas, the vast imaginings of a poet. Every face is a whole world."

Honoré de Balzac
Le Chef-d'œuvre inconnu (1831)

Great curiosity had been excited amongst the artists to see Zoffany's picture of the *Florentine Gallery,* which had been much spoken of by such of the English noblemen and gentlemen as (returned from abroad) had visited Florence in their continental tour. . . .

The painter in this piece . . . . has not neglected to introduce his own portrait . . . . He is exhibiting, to a group of *virtuosi,* a Madonna, by Raffael, which is introduced by way of episode, and a profitable one it turned out to the artist. The picture did not belong to the gallery—it was picked up by accident by Zoffany, and for a small sum. He was wont to ask all English comers to Florence, "Have you seen my Raffael?—Ah! den you must see it." He is herein submitting it to the admiring group, Sir John Dick, the Earl of Plymouth, Mr. Stevenson, the Earl of Dartmouth, and last, though the first *par eminence,* the late Earl Cowper, who, charmed with its *gusto,* purchased it, and brought it to England. It is now in the collection of the present worthy earl.

The picture is considered an original Raffael, and a treasure of art. His lordship paid down a certain liberal sum, and granted, by way of residue, an annuity of a hundred pounds, which the fortunate painter, (who lived, as is said and pretty generally believed, to be between ninety and a hundred,) enjoyed to the last. Hence this Madonna, perhaps, whatever may be its merits, is the dearest Raffael that ever was purchased, even by a travelling English lord!

The London Literary Gazette (July 15, 1826)

Collections: Casa Niccolini, Florence; John Zoffany, Florence; Earl Cowper and descendants, Panshanger, Hertfordshire. *Andrew Mellon Collection,* 1937. Wood. Height 31¾ in.; width 22⅝ in. (0.81 x 0.57). Signed with initials, and dated 1508.

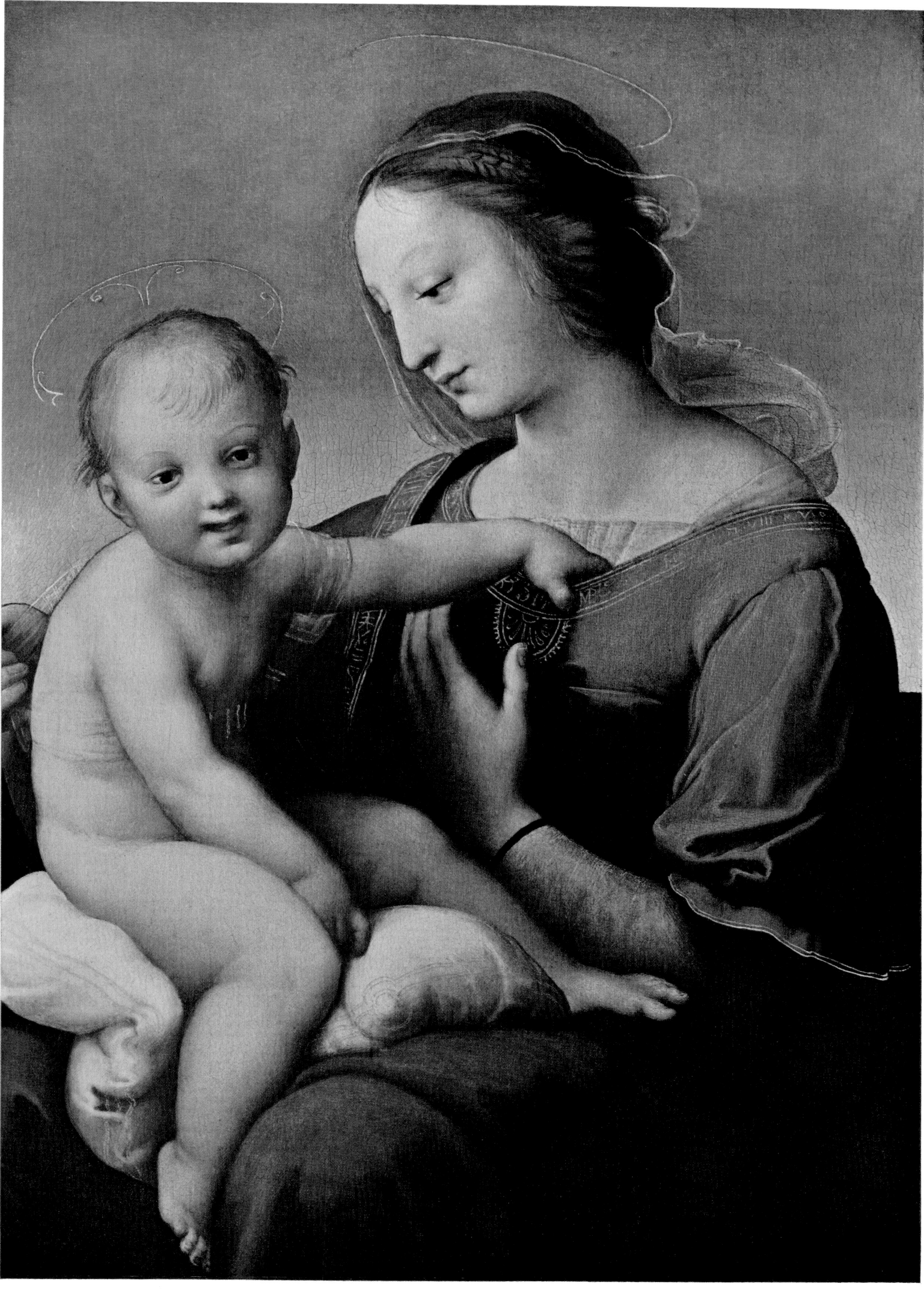

RAPHAEL · Umbrian 1483-1520

The Alba Madonna

As in ancient Greece, so also in Renaissance Italy, the fine arts assumed the first place in the intellectual culture of the nation. But the thought and feeling of the modern world required an æsthetic medium more capable of expressing emotion in its intensity, variety, and subtlety than sculpture. Therefore painting was the art of arts for Italy. Yet even painting, notwithstanding the range and wealth of its resources, could not deal with the motives of Christianity so successfully as sculpture with the myths of Paganism. The religion it interpreted transcended the actual conditions of humanity, while art is bound down by its nature to the limitations of the world we live in. The Church imagined art would help her; and within a certain sphere of subjects, by vividly depicting Scripture histories and the lives of saints, by creating new types of serene beauty and pure joy, by giving form to angelic beings, by interpreting Mariolatry in all its charm and pathos, and by rousing deep sympathy with our Lord in His Passion, painting lent efficient aid to piety. Yet painting had to omit the very pith and kernel of Christianity as conceived by devout, uncompromising purists. Nor did it do what the Church would have desired. Instead of riveting the fetters of ecclesiastical authority, instead of enforcing mysticism and asceticism, it really restored to humanity the sense of its own dignity and beauty, and helped to prove the untenability of the mediæval standpoint; for art is essentially and uncontrollably free, and, what is more, is free precisely in that realm of sensuous delightfulness from which cloistral religion turns aside to seek her own ecstatic liberty of contemplation.

The first step in the emancipation of the modern mind was taken thus by art, proclaiming to men the glad tidings of their goodliness and greatness in a world of manifold enjoyment created for their use. Whatever painting touched, became by that touch human; piety, at the lure of art, folded her soaring wings and rested on the genial earth. This the Church had not foreseen. Because the freedom of the human spirit expressed itself in painting only under visible images, and not, like heresy, in abstract sentences; because this art sufficed for Mariolatry and confirmed the cult of local saints; because its sensuousness was not at variance with a creed that had been deeply sensualised —the painters were allowed to run their course unchecked.

John Addington Symonds
Renaissance in Italy (1897)

Preliminary drawings for the tondo are in the Lille Museum. The painting was given, probably in 1528, to the Church of Monte Oliveto at Nocera de' Pagani. Taken to Spain at the end of the seventeenth century, it remained in the possession of the Dukes of Alba for more than a hundred years. Collections: Church of Monte Oliveto, Nocera de' Pagani near Naples; Don Gasparo Méndez de Haro y Guzmán, Naples; the Dukes of Alba, Madrid; Don Manuel Godoy, Príncipe de la Paz; Count Edmond de Bourke, Danish Ambassador to Spain; W. G. Coesvelt, London; Hermitage Gallery, Leningrad. *Andrew Mellon Collection,* 1937. Transferred from wood to canvas. Diameter 37¼ in. (0.945). Painted c. 1510 when Raphael, having just come to Rome, was beginning to show the influence of Michelangelo.

RAPHAEL · Umbrian 1483-1520

Bindo Altoviti

The ancients excelled in beauty of form; Michael Angelo in grandeur of conception; Raphael in expression. In Raphael's faces, particularly his women, the expression is very superior to the form; in the ancient statues, the form is the principal thing. The interest which the latter excite, is in a manner external; it depends on a certain grace and lightness of appearance, joined with exquisite symmetry and refined susceptibility to voluptuous emotions; but there is in general a want of pathos. In their looks, we do not read the workings of the heart; by their beauty they seem raised above the sufferings of humanity, by their beauty they are deified. The pathos which they exhibit is rather that of present and physical distress, than of deep internal sentiment. What has been remarked of Leonardo da Vinci, is also true of Raphael, that there is an angelic sweetness and tenderness in his faces, in which human frailty and passion are purified by the sanctity of religion. The ancient statues are finer objects for the eye to contemplate; they represent a more perfect race of physical beings, but we have little sympathy with them. In Raphael, all our natural sensibilities are heightened and refined by the sentiments of faith and hope, pointing mysteriously to the interests of another world. The same intensity of passion appears also to distinguish Raphael from Michael Angelo. Michael Angelo's forms are grander, but they are not so informed with expression. Raphael's, however ordinary in themselves, are full of expression, "even to o'erflowing;" every nerve and muscle is impregnated with feeling,—bursting with meaning. In Michael Angelo, on the contrary, the powers of body and mind appear superior to any events that can happen to them; the capacity of thought and feeling is never full, never strained or tasked to the extremity of what it will bear. All is in a lofty repose and solitary grandeur, which no human interest can shake or disturb. It has been said, that Michael Angelo painted *man,* and Raphael *men;* that the one was an epic, the other a dramatic painter. But the distinction we have stated is, perhaps, truer and more intelligible, *viz.* that the one gave greater dignity of form, and the other greater force and refinement of expression.

William Hazlitt
Fine Arts (1817)

Bindo Altoviti was a Florentine banker, born in 1490, who lived for some time in Rome. He commissioned Raphael, according to Vasari, to paint two works, a religious picture, the Madonna dell' Impannata, now in the Pitti, Florence, and the portrait reproduced. A bust of Bindo Altoviti as an older man, by Benvenuto Cellini, is in the Isabella Stewart Gardner Museum, Boston. Collections: The portrait remained in the Altoviti Palace, Rome, until shortly before 1790, and in the Altoviti Palace, Florence, until 1808, when it was bought by Ludwig of Bavaria, later King Ludwig I, who presented it to the Alte Pinakothek in Munich. *Samuel H. Kress Collection,* 1943. Wood. Height 23½ in.; width 17¼ in. (0.60 x 0.44). Painted c. 1515.

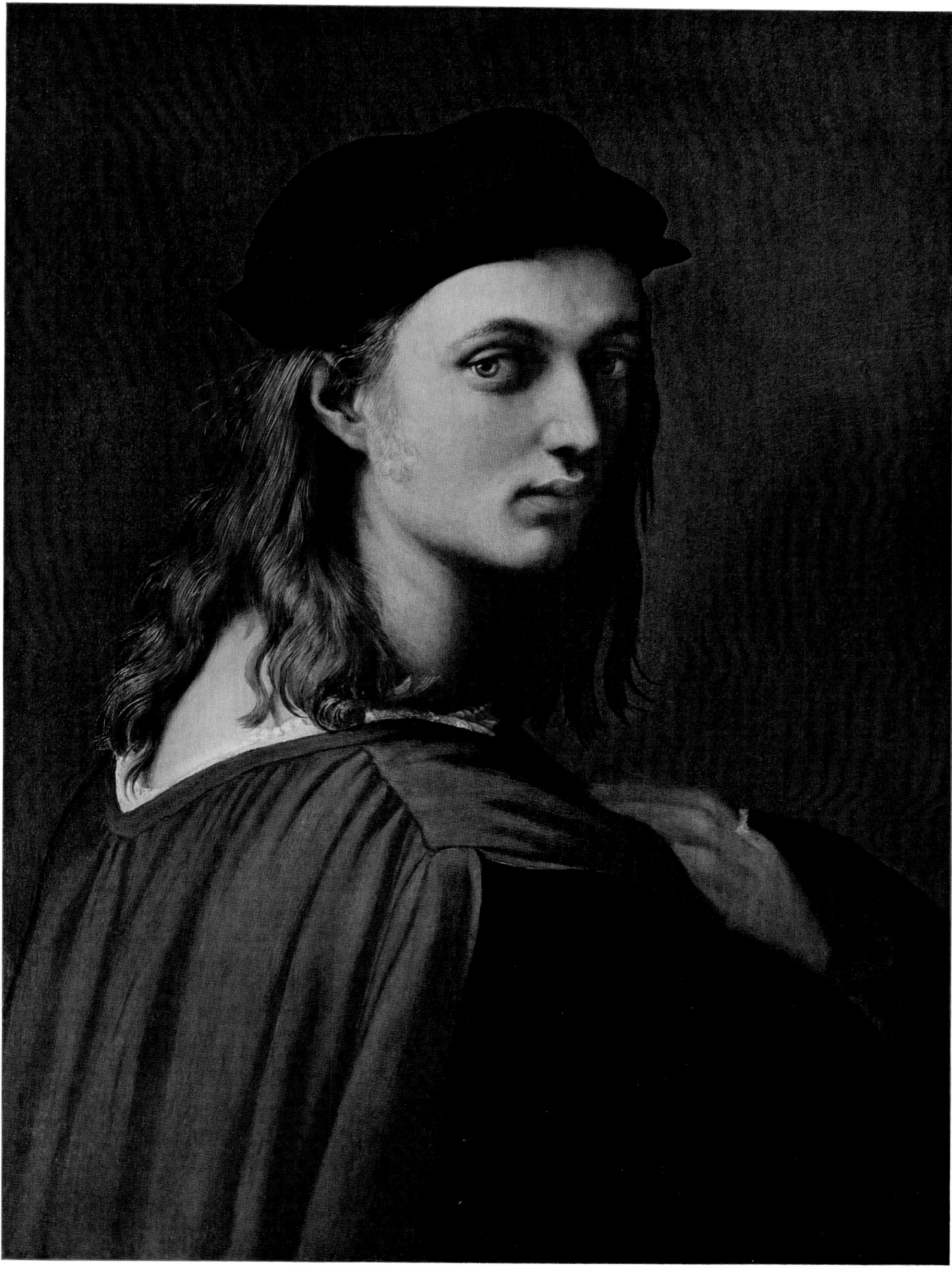

ANDREA DEL SARTO · Florentine 1486-1530

Charity

Though I speak with the tongues of men and of angels, and have not charity, I am become as sounding brass, or a tinkling cymbal. And though I have the gift of prophecy, and understand all mysteries, and all knowledge; and though I have all faith, so that I could remove mountains, and have not charity, I am nothing. And though I bestow all my goods to feed the poor, and though I give my body to be burned, and have not charity, it profiteth me nothing. Charity suffereth long, and is kind; charity envieth not; charity vaunteth not itself, is not puffed up, doth not behave itself unseemly, seeketh not her own, is not easily provoked, thinketh no evil; rejoiceth not in iniquity, but rejoiceth in the truth; beareth all things, believeth all things, hopeth all things, endureth all things. Charity never faileth: but whether there be prophecies, they shall fail; whether there be tongues, they shall cease; whether there be knowledge, it shall vanish away. For we know in part, and we prophesy in part. But when that which is perfect is come, then that which is in part shall be done away. When I was a child, I spoke as a child, I understood as a child, I thought as a child: but when I became a man, I put away childish things. For now we see through a glass, darkly; but then face to face: now I know in part; but then shall I know even as also I am known. And now abideth faith, hope, charity, these three; but the greatest of these is charity.

Saint Paul of Tarsus
First Letter to the Corinthians (50-70 A.D.)

Vasari wrote that this picture was commissioned by the agent of the King of France, Giovanni Battista della Palla. But following the capture of Florence in 1530 by Imperial troops, the king's agent was imprisoned and the painting remained unsold. Andrea's widow finally disposed of it to another painter and pupil of her husband's, Domenico Conti. He in turn sold it to Niccolò Antinori, who owned it in Vasari's day and "valued it as the rare thing that it truly is." Collections: Domenico Conti, Florence; Niccolò Antinori, Florence; Bastiano Antinori, Florence; Prince Rospigliosi Gallery, Rome; John Proctor Anderdon, Farley Hall, Berkshire; H. A. J. Munro of Novar, England; T. Ward, Cheltenham, Gloucestershire. *Samuel H. Kress Collection,* 1957. Wood. Height 47½ in.; width 36½ in. (1.20 x 0.927). Painted shortly before 1530.

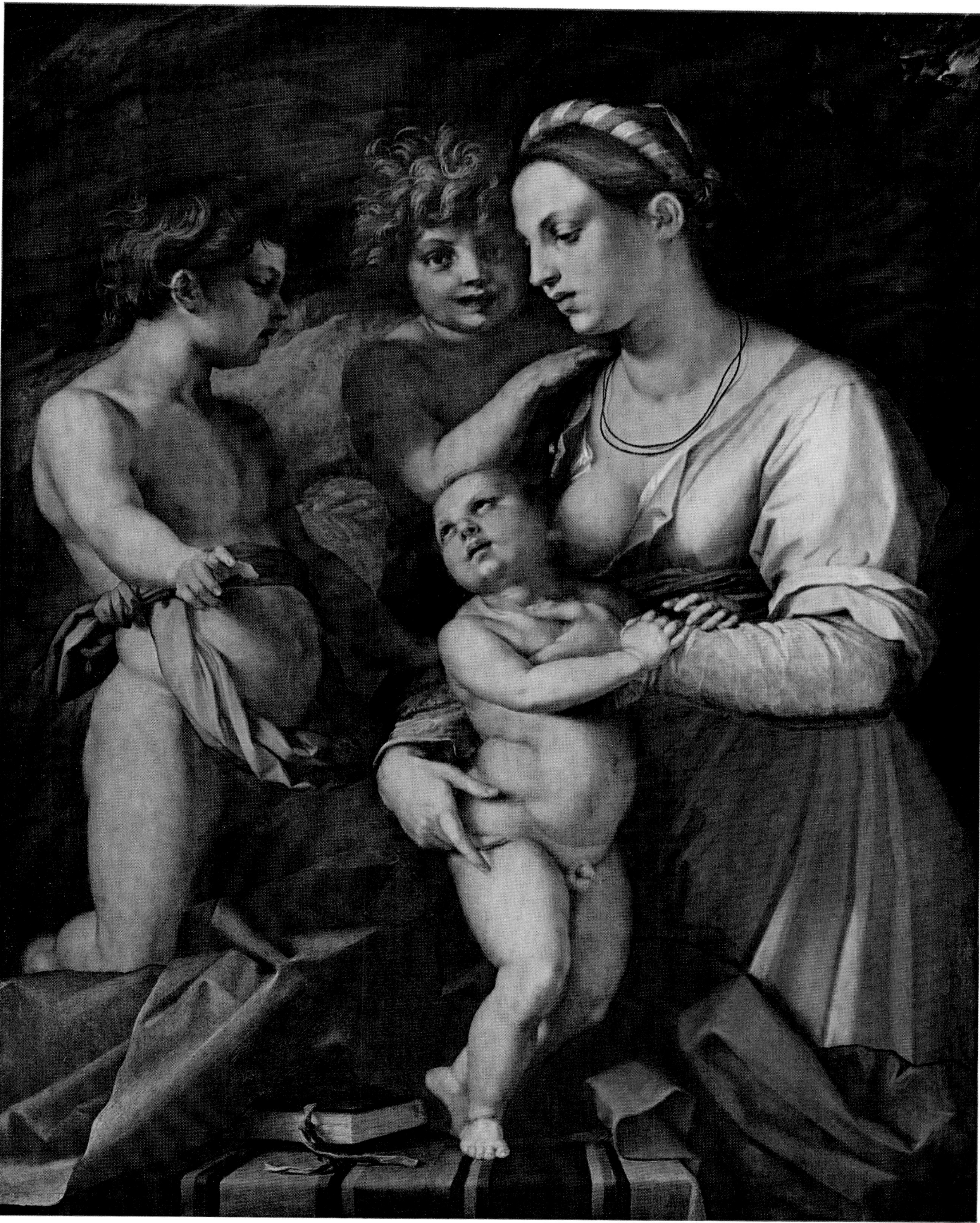

PONTORMO · Florentine 1494-c. 1556

Monsignor della Casa

A man should dress according to convention, in order not to appear to censure others and correct them, which in most cases would conflict with their wishes, since they look for approval. But it would also offend against the good taste of people who appreciate such things, because clothes which belong to another age do not suit a person who belongs to this one. It is equally wrong to dress like an old clothes man, whose garments fit him so badly that his doublet is obviously at odds with his hose. . . .

A man must therefore not be content to do things well, but must also aim to do them gracefully. Gracefulness is like a light which shines in things which are fit and proper for their purpose because they are well ordered and arranged both in relation to each other and as a whole. Without it even goodness has no beauty and beauty has no charm. However healthy and nourishing it might be, guests would not like food which had a nasty taste or no taste at all. In the same way manners which are quite harmless in themselves may sometimes be, as it were, insipid and unpalatable unless they are flavoured with something to sweeten them. This, I believe, is what we mean by grace and charm. . . .

Polite people ought therefore to be mindful of the need for restraint such as I have described in their manner of walking, standing, or sitting, and in all that they do, in their gestures and in their dress, when they speak and when they are silent, when they are at rest and when they are at work. This is why a man ought not to embellish himself like a woman, for the adornments would be out of keeping with his sex. Yet I sometimes see men whose hair and beards are curled with hot tongs and whose faces, necks, and hands have been smoothed and titivated more than any young wench would allow, or even any harlot who is more anxious to hawk her wares and sell them at a good price.

Giovanni della Casa
Il Galateo, ovvero de' costumi (1558)

Grace and charm, the two qualities della Casa stresses, were the twin goals of Florentine artists of the generation of Pontormo. Without gracefulness they felt "goodness has no beauty and beauty has no charm." Giovanni della Casa, a man of letters, was a functionary at the papal court and resided also in Bologna, Florence, and Venice. Pontormo's portrait closely resembles a lost Titian, of which a copy is preserved in the Uffizi. Collections: Marchese Bargagli, Florence (of the same family as Monsignor della Casa). *Samuel H. Kress Collection,* 1961. Wood. Height 40⅛ in.; width 31 in. (1.021 x 0.788). Painted probably between 1541 and 1544.

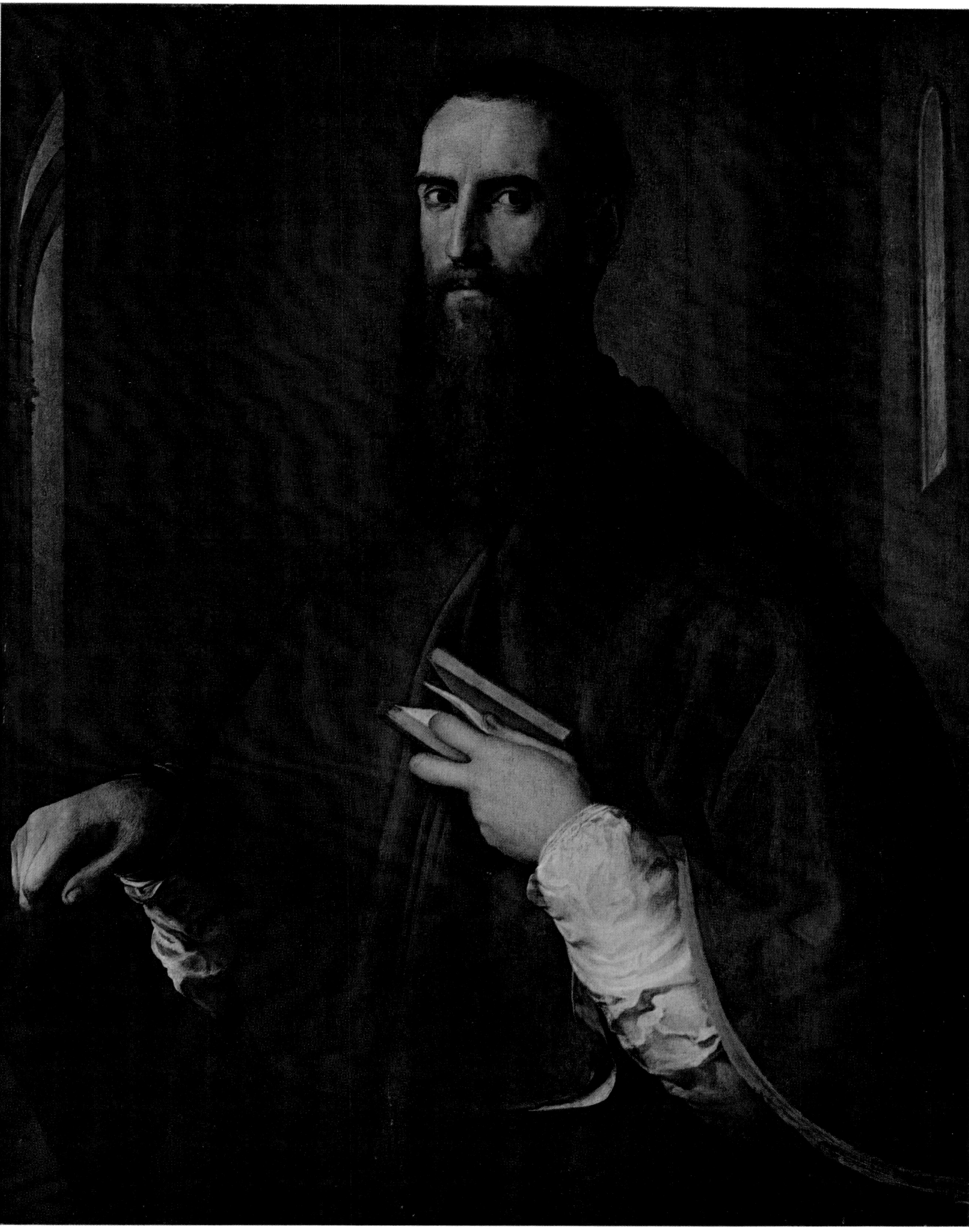

AGNOLO BRONZINO · Florentine 1503-1572

A Young Woman and Her Little Boy

Bronzino could also portray the aristocratic demeanor of a noblewoman. At the beginning of the 15th century the feminine ideal is the elegance of simplicity, but soon foreign fashions bring a greater variety to dress; little by little the low-cut neck disappears, and there comes a fondness for luxury, for materials and jewels of great richness. A curious dialogue, entitled "Of the Proper Education of Women", which dates from 1538, reveals to us the general characteristics of these new customs. One of the speakers, Raffaella, cannot imagine that a woman could dress herself without the most meticulous attention; "men and women should dress opulently, with grace and taste; women, especially, because they are delicate, and because they were created to help us bear the misfortunes of this world more easily; the pure beauty of dress suits their refined and exquisite nature better than the harsh and somewhat rough character of men." The elegant woman of that period is fond of variety and originality in attire. How can one recognize beautiful apparel? By its richness and cut. Richness comes not only from the ornaments and embroideries, but above all from the splendor of the cloth itself. It should be the concern of a princess and a great lady to clothe herself in the finest brocades, which should be adorned with "pearls, diamonds, rubies, and other such things." Raffaella dwells long on the choice of materials, which is one of the most difficult aspects of the art of dressing well; it is especially important that their colors harmonize with the complexion and the "portatura", that is to say the bearing, of the individual.

Jean Alazard
Le Portrait florentin (1938)

The "refined and exquisite nature" of women which Raffaella mentions is stressed in Bronzino's paintings where he portrays figures of Florentine society sitting still and unmoved, sure of themselves, and of their position in the world, the gestures of their thin hands with their long, tapering fingers formal and unnatural, their hair carefully arranged in chiseled waves. The cool beauty of the lady in the Widener portrait already hints at that glacial style of Bronzino's later works, a style which was to become the fashion throughout Italy. Here we see Florentine painting on the verge of its ice age. Collections: Princesse de Sagan, Paris. *Widener Collection,* 1942. Wood. Height 39⅛ in; width 29⅞ in. (0.995 x 0.760). Painted c. 1540, according to McComb.

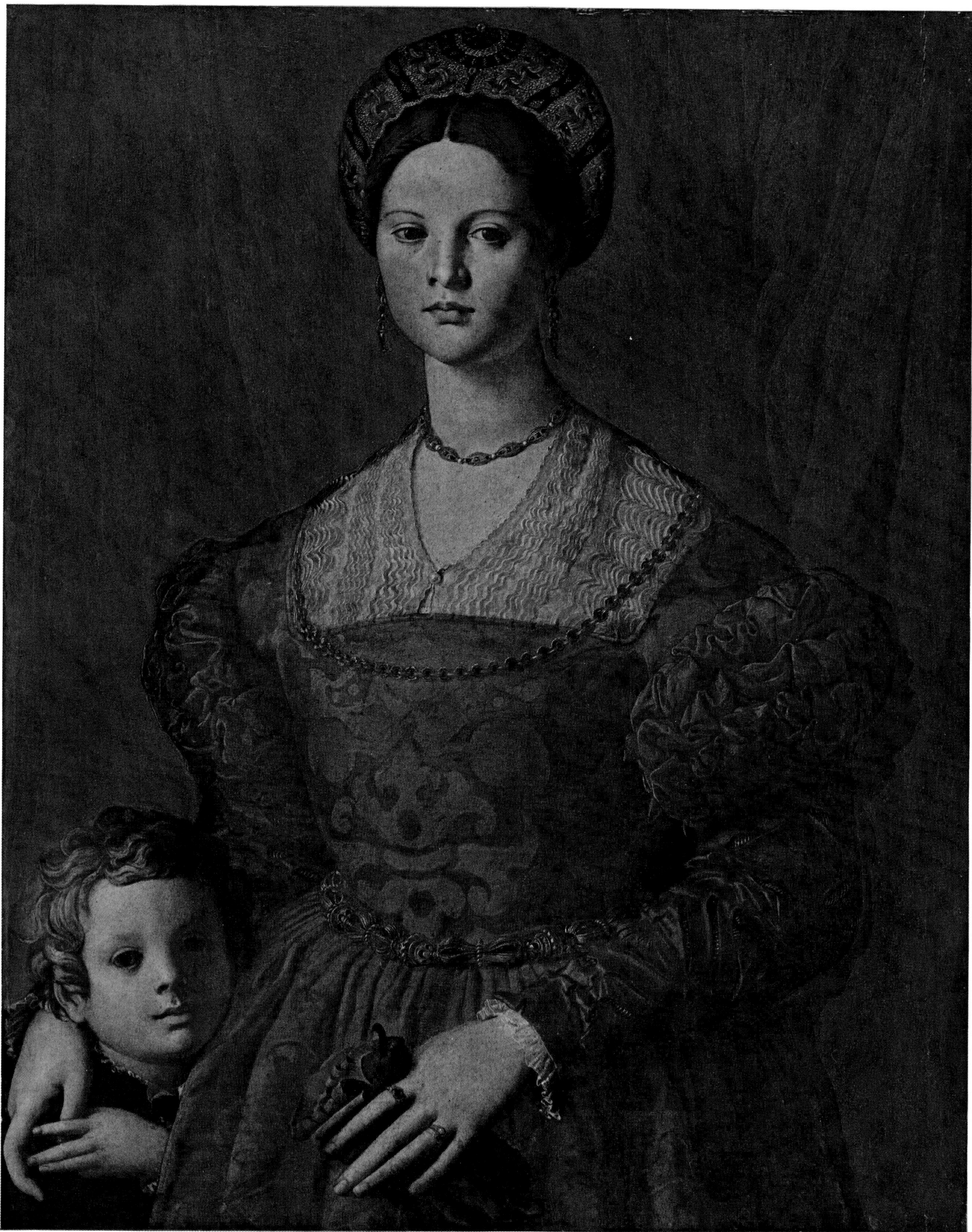

BOLTRAFFIO · Milanese 1467-1516

Portrait of a Youth

He was destined to learn his own wisdom apart from others or to learn the wisdom of others himself wandering among the snares of the world. The snares of the world were its ways of sin. He would fall. He had not yet fallen but he would fall silently, in an instant. Not to fall was too hard, too hard: and he felt the silent lapse of his soul, as it would be at some instant to come, falling, falling, but not yet fallen, still unfallen, but about to fall.... He drew forth a phrase from his treasure and spoke it softly to himself:

—A day of dappled seaborne clouds.—

....Where was his boyhood now? Where was the soul that had hung back from her destiny, to brood alone upon the shame of her wounds and in her house of squalor and subterfuge to queen it in faded cerements and in wreaths that withered at the touch? Or, where was he. He was alone. He was unheeded, happy, and near to the wild heart of life. He was alone and young and wilful and wild-hearted, alone amid a waste of wild air and brackish waters and the seaharvest of shells and tangle and veiled grey sunlight and gayclad lightclad figures of children and girls and voices childish and girlish in the air.

James Joyce
A Portrait of the Artist as a Young Man (1916)

Whoever is delighted with his own picture must derive his pleasure from the pleasure of another. Every man is always present to himself, and has, therefore, little need of his own resemblance, nor can desire it, but for the sake of those whom he loves, and by whom he hopes to be remembered. This use of the art is a natural and reasonable consequence of affection; and though, like other human actions, it is often complicated with pride, yet even such pride is more laudable than that by which palaces are covered with pictures, that, however excellent, neither imply the owner's virtue, nor excite it.

Samuel Johnson
The Idler (Feb. 24, 1759)

The portrait has sometimes been thought to be of the poet Girolamo Casio; but when Casio was the age of this boy, about twelve, the artist was only nine. The identity of the sitter will probably remain a mystery, but there is a curious clue. He apparently has lost one arm, for the artist is at some pains to show his empty right sleeve. Was this loss suffered in some heroic act of which his parents wished to be reminded? Was the prominence given to this mutilation "a natural and reasonable consequence of affection"? Perhaps in a forgotten archive in Lombardy lies buried the explanation of this strange effigy, so far as we know the unique representation in the Renaissance of a child with only one arm. The haunting quality of this painting, however, does not arise from an empty sleeve, touching as is this note of verisimilitude, but rather from the portrayal of that moment of transition between boyhood and adolescence which Joyce so sensitively describes. Collections: Baron Gustave de Rothschild, Paris; Sir Philip Sassoon, London. *Ralph and Mary Booth Collection,* 1947. Wood. Height 18¾ in.; width 13¾ in. (0.467 x 0.35). Painted shortly before 1500.

BERNARDINO LUINI · Milanese c. 1480-1532

The Illusion of Cephalus

Because Leonardo made models of machines, dug canals, built fortifications, and dissipated half his art-power in capricious ingenuities, we have many anecdotes of him;—but no picture of importance on canvas, and only a few withered stains of one upon a wall. But because his pupil, or reputed pupil, Luini, laboured in constant and successful simplicity, we have no anecdotes of him; —only hundreds of noble works. Luini is, perhaps, the best central type of the highly-trained Italian painter. He is the only man who entirely united the religious temper which was the spirit-life of art, with the physical power which was its bodily life. He joins the purity and passion of Angelico to the strength of Veronese: the two elements, poised in perfect balance, are so calmed and restrained, each by the other, that most of us lose the sense of both. The artist does not see the strength, by reason of the chastened spirit in which it is used; and the religious visionary does not recognize the passion, by reason of the frank human truth with which it is rendered. He is a man ten times greater than Leonardo;—a mighty colourist, while Leonardo was only a fine draughtsman in black, staining the chiaroscuro drawing, like a coloured print: he perceived and rendered the delicatest types of human beauty that had been painted since the days of the Greeks, while Leonardo depraved his finer instincts by caricature, and remained to the end of his days the slave of an archaic smile: and he is a designer as frank, instinctive, and exhaustless as Tintoret, while Leonardo's design is only an agony of science, admired chiefly because it is painful, and capable of analysis in its best accomplishment. Luini has left nothing behind him that is not lovely; but of his life I believe hardly anything is known beyond remnants of tradition which murmur about Lugano and Saronno, and which remain ungleaned. This only is certain, that he was born in the loveliest district of North Italy, where hills, and streams, and air, meet in softest harmonies. Child of the Alps, and of their divinest lake, he is taught, without doubt or dismay, a lofty religious creed, and a sufficient law of life, and of its mechanical arts. Whether lessoned by Leonardo himself, or merely one of many, disciplined in the system of the Milanese school, he learns unerringly to draw, unerringly and enduringly to paint. His tasks are set him without question day by day, by men who are justly satisfied with his work, and who accept it without any harmful praise, or senseless blame. Place, scale, and subject are determined for him on the cloister wall or the church dome; as he is required, and for sufficient daily bread, and little more, he paints what he has been taught to design wisely, and has passion to realize gloriously: every touch he lays is eternal, every thought he conceives is beautiful and pure: his hand moves always in radiance of blessing; from day to day his life enlarges in power and peace; it passes away cloudlessly, the starry twilight remaining arched far against the night.

John Ruskin
The Queen of the Air (1869)

This painting, in which Cephalus is described as haunted by apparitions of his murdered wife and her dog, Laelaps, is the sixth scene in a series of nine frescoes depicting the story of Cephalus and Procris, now in the National Gallery of Art, Samuel H. Kress Collection. They were painted about 1520, as part of the decorations of the Casa Rabia, Piazza San Sepolcro, Milan. Vasari, who saw the frescoes in 1560, states that Luini painted "the house of Signor Gian Francesco Rabbia—that is, the façade, loggie, halls, and apartments—depicting there many of the Metamorphoses of Ovid and other fables, with good and beautiful figures, executed with much delicacy." The remains of these frescoes are now scattered among a number of other museums: the Brera, Milan; Louvre, Paris; Berlin Museum; and in several private collections. Collections: Casa Rabia, Piazza San Sepolcro, Milan; Michele Cavalieri, Milan; Henri Cernuschi, Paris; Rodolphe Kann, Paris. *Samuel H. Kress Collection,* 1943. Fresco transferred to canvas. Height 89¾ in.; width 49 in. (2.28 x 1.245).

BERNARDINO LUINI · Milanese c. 1480-1532

Portrait of a Lady

With education, the individuality of women in the upper classes was developed in the same way as that of men. Till the time of the Reformation, the personality of women out of Italy, even of the highest rank, comes forward but little. Exceptions like Isabella of Bavaria, Margaret of Anjou, and Isabella of Castille, are the forced result of very unusual circumstances. In Italy, throughout the whole of the fifteenth century, the wives of the rulers, and still more those of the Condottieri, have nearly all a distinct, recognizable personality, and take their share of notoriety and glory. To these came gradually to be added a crowd of famous women of the most varied kind; among them those whose distinction consisted in the fact that their beauty, disposition, education, virtue, and piety, combined to render them harmonious human beings. There was no question of 'woman's rights' or female emancipation, simply because the thing itself was a matter of course. The educated woman, no less than the man, strove naturally after a characteristic and complete individuality. The same intellectual and emotional development which perfected the man, was demanded for the perfection of the woman. Active literary work, nevertheless, was not expected from her, and if she were a poet, some powerful utterance of feeling, rather than the confidences of the novel or the diary, was looked for. These women had no thought of the public; their function was to influence distinguished men, and to moderate male impulse and caprice. . . .

Women of this stamp could listen to novels like those of Bandello, without social intercourse suffering from it. The ruling genius of society was not, as now, womanhood, or the respect for certain presuppositions, mysteries, and susceptibilities, but the consciousness of energy, of beauty, and of a social state full of danger and opportunity. And for this reason we find, side by side with the most measured and polished social forms, something our age would call immodesty, forgetting that by which it was corrected and counterbalanced—the powerful characters of the women who were exposed to it.

Jakob Burckhardt
Die Cultur der Renaissance in Italien (1860)

In order to paint a beautiful woman, I should need to see many of them, and have your Lordship's assistance in selecting the fairest. But since there is a dearth both of good judges and of beautiful women, I make use of a certain ideal that is in my mind. Whether it possesses any artistic excellence I do not know; but I try hard to see that it does.

Raphael
Letter to Baldassare Castiglione (1514)

There are few portraits by Luini and the present one is the most important of those on panel. In the light and shadow and in the smile, it shows the influence of Leonardo da Vinci, to whom some of Luini's works were formerly attributed. All the character and individuality that Burckhardt describes in the women of the period are here displayed with exceptional skill. Collections: Frederick Richards Leyland, London; Charles Fairfax Murray, Florence; Robert H. and Evelyn Benson, London. *Andrew Mellon Collection,* 1937. Wood. Height 30⅜ in.; width 22½ in. (0.77 x 0.575). Painted c. 1525.

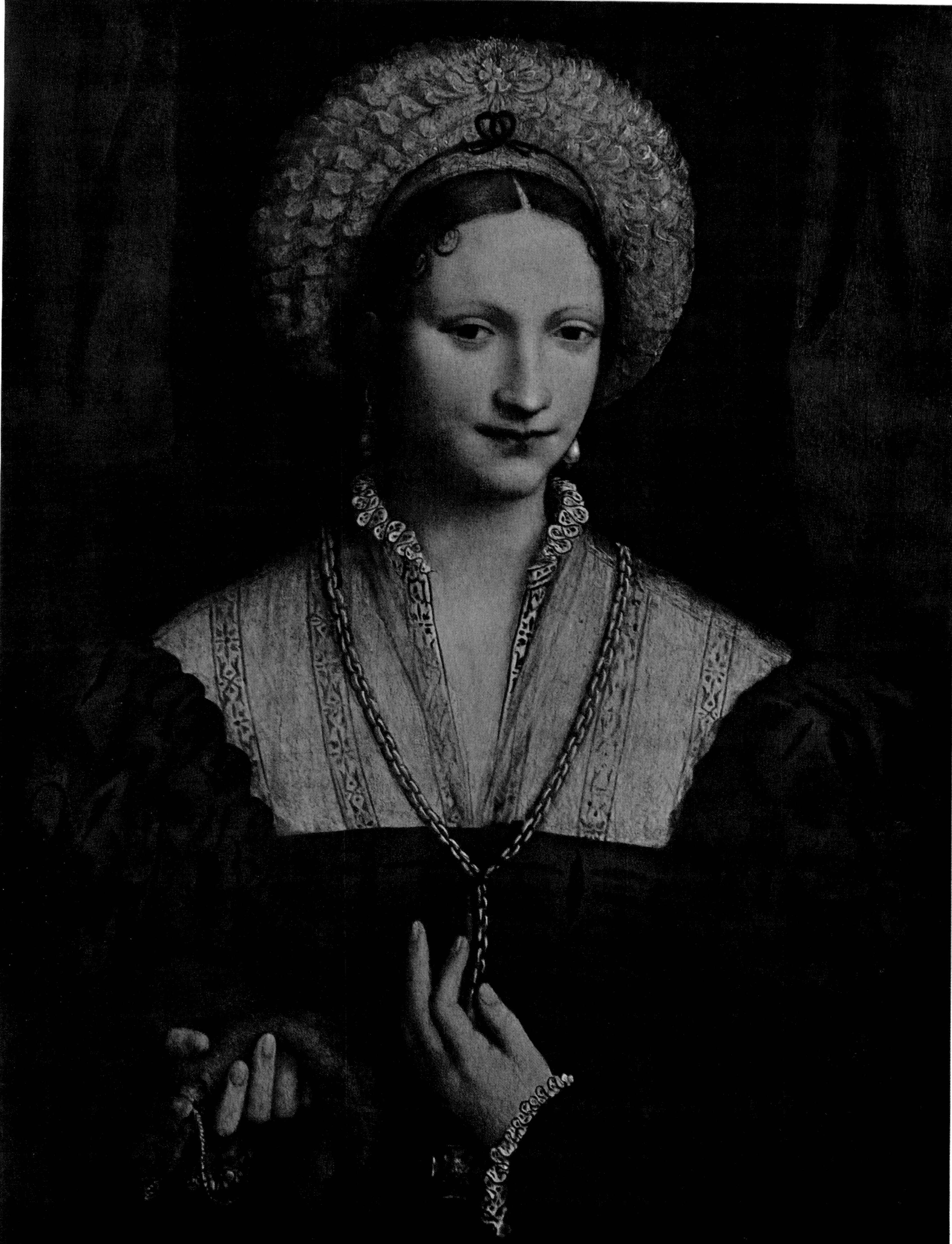

SODOMA · Sienese 1477-1549

Saint George and the Dragon

Worship of a Hero is transcendent admiration of a Great Man. I say great men are still admirable; I say there is, at bottom, nothing else admirable! No nobler feeling than this of admiration for one higher than himself dwells in the breast of man. It is to this hour, and at all hours, the vivifying influence in man's life. Religion I find stand upon it; not Paganism only, but far higher and truer religions,—all religion hitherto known. Hero-worship, heartfelt prostrate admiration, submission, burning, boundless, for a noblest godlike Form of Man,—is not that the germ of Christianity itself? The greatest of all Heroes is One—whom we do not name here! Let sacred silence meditate that sacred matter; you will find it the ultimate perfection of a principle extant throughout man's whole history on earth.

Or coming into lower, less *un*speakable provinces, is not all Loyalty akin to religious Faith also? Faith is loyalty to some inspired Teacher, some spiritual Hero. And what therefore is loyalty proper, the life-breath of all society, but an effluence of Hero-worship, submissive admiration for the truly great? Society is founded on Hero-worship. All dignities of rank, on which human association rests, are what we may call a *Hero*archy (Government of Heroes),—or a Hierarchy, for it is 'sacred' enough withal! The Duke means *Dux,* Leader; King is *Kön-ning, Kan-ning,* Man that *knows* or *cans.* Society everywhere is some representation, not *in*supportably inaccurate, of a graduated Worship of Heroes;—reverence and obedience done to men really great and wise.

Thomas Carlyle
On Heroes, Hero-Worship, and the Heroic in History (1840)

One feels that Carlyle took heroism more seriously than Sodoma. There is something deliciously comic in Saint George's incipient header, in the ferocious bite his steed is about to deliver, in the operatic gesture of the Princess Cleodolinda, and in the angel in the sky who, like a referee at a prize fight, seems about to count ten over the dragon. The picture was probably painted for Alfonso I d'Este, the famous Duke of Ferrara, husband of Lucretia Borgia and brother of Isabella d'Este. In his small principality Alfonso was a great man, and Saint George was not only his city's patron saint but also his hero. Collections: Seventeenth Earl of Shrewsbury, Alton Towers, Staffordshire; Cook, Doughty House, Richmond, Surrey. *Samuel H. Kress Collection,* 1952. Wood. Height 55½ in.; width 38⅜ in. (1.378 x 0.976). Painted probably 1518.

CARLO CRIVELLI · Venetian Active 1457-c. 1493

Madonna and Child Enthroned with Donor

Wherfor in laude, as I best can or may,
Of thee, and of the whyte lily flour
Which that thee bar, and is a mayde alway,
To telle a storie I wol do my labour;
Not that I may encresen hir honour;
For she hir-self is honour, and the rote
Of bountee, next hir sone, and soules bote.—

O moder mayde! o mayde moder free!
O bush unbrent, brenninge in Moyses sighte,
That ravisedest doun fro the deitee,
Thurgh thyn humblesse, the goost that in th'alighte,
Of whos vertu, whan he thyn herte lighte,
Conceived was the fadres sapience,
Help me to telle it in thy reverence!

Lady! thy bountee, thy magnificence,
Thy vertu, and thy grete humilitee
Ther may no tonge expresse in no science;
For som-tyme, lady, er men praye to thee,
Thou goost biforn of thy benignitee,
And getest us the light, thurgh thy preyere,
To gyden us un-to thy sone so dere.

My conning is so wayk, o blisful quene,
For to declare thy grete worthinesse,
That I ne may the weighte nat sustene,
But as a child of twelf monthe old, or lesse,
That can unnethes any word expresse,
Right so fare I, and therfor I yow preye,
Gydeth my song that I shal of yow seye.

Geoffrey Chaucer
The Canterbury Tales (c. 1387)

Glossary: *bote,* salvation; *moder,* mother; *unbrent,* unburnt; *brenninge,* burning; *fadres,* parents; *biforn,* before; *unnethes,* scarcely.

Not only in stone, but also in simulated stone, religious art of the quattrocento teems with marine motifs. Their first use, of course, is decorative, but there is also a theological meaning. In the ancient world, the dolphin was thought to carry the soul to the Isles of the Blessed. Later the Greek word for fish, *ichthus,* came to stand as an anagram for Jesus Christ, God's Son, Saviour. Jonah's liberation from the inside of a fish was also considered a prefiguration of the Resurrection. The shells are emblems of pilgrimage (see Friedmann, *Gazette des Beaux-Arts,* 1947). Above the Madonna is written the plaintive cry of the tiny donor. "Remember me, O Mother of God. O Queen of Heaven, rejoice!"—a plea which is the implied refrain of Chaucer's poem. Longhi believes the painting formed the central panel of the polyptych executed c. 1470 for the church at Porto San Giorgio. The best general estimate of Crivelli's style is given by Berenson (*Venetian Painters,* 1894): "He takes rank with the most genuine artists of all times and countries, and does not weary even when 'great masters' grow tedious. He expresses with the freedom and spirit of Japanese design a piety as wild and tender as Jacopo da Todi's, a sweetness of emotion as sincere and dainty as of a Virgin and Child carved in ivory by a French craftsman of the fourteenth century. The mystic beauty of Simone Martini, the agonized compassion of the young Bellini, are embodied by Crivelli in forms which have the strength of line and the metallic lustre of old Satsuma or lacquer, and which are no less tempting to the touch." Collections: Earl of Dudley, Himley Hall, Dudley; Cook, Doughty House, Richmond, Surrey. *Samuel H. Kress Collection,* 1952. Wood. Height 51 in.; width 21⅜ in. (1.295 x 0.545). Painted c. 1470.

MEMENTO·MEI·MATER·DEI·REGINA·CELI·LETARE

GIOVANNI BELLINI · Venetian c. 1430-1516

Portrait of a Young Man in Red

The artist must imitate that which is within the thing, that which is active through form and figure, and discourses to us by symbols—the *Natur-geist,* or spirit of nature, as we unconsciously imitate those whom we love; for so only can he hope to produce any work truly natural in the object and truly human in the effect. The idea which puts the form together cannot itself be the form. It is above form, and is its essence, the universal in the individual, or the individuality itself,—the glance and the exponent of the indwelling power. . . .

Hence a good portrait is the abstract of the personal; it is not the likeness for actual comparison, but for recollection. This explains why the likeness of a very good portrait is not always recognized; because some persons never abstract, and amongst these are especially to be numbered the near relations and friends of the subject, in consequence of the constant pressure and check exercised on their minds by the actual presence of the original.

Samuel Taylor Coleridge
Biographia Literaria (1817)

The quotation above defines the problem of portraiture. In the Renaissance, "near relations and friends" seem to have accepted more readily than today "the abstract of the personal." Consequently, from that period we have received a series of great portraits which show "the universal in the individual," but which remain, because of their abstractions, difficult to identify, even when it seems likely that they represent famous personages. Borenius (*Burlington Magazine,* 1932) has pointed out that the present picture resembles a seventeenth-century drawing of a portrait once in the Vendramin Collection, Venice. The sitter was perhaps a member of that celebrated Venetian family. Collections: Von Ingenheim, Ober-Rengersdorf, Germany. *Andrew Mellon Collection,* 1937. Wood. Height 12½ in.; width 10¾ in. (0.32 x 0.265). Painted c. 1480.

GIOVANNI BELLINI · Venetian c. 1430-1516

Portrait of a Condottiere

War being an occupation by which a man cannot support himself with honour at all times, ought not to be followed as a business by any but princes or governors of commonwealths; and if they are wise men they will not suffer any of their subjects or citizens to make that their only profession. Indeed no good man ever did; for surely he cannot be called a good man, who exercises an employment that obliges him to be rapacious, fraudulent and cruel, at all times, in order to support himself; as all those must be of course, of what rank soever they are, who make a trade of war, because it will not maintain them in time of peace; upon which account, they are under a necessity either of endeavouring to prevent a peace, or of taking all means to make such provisions for themselves in time of war, that they may not want sustenance when it is over. But neither of these courses is consistent with common honesty; for whoever resolves to heap as much in time of war as will support him for ever after, must be guilty of robbery, murder, and many other acts of violence upon his friends as well as his enemies; and in endeavouring to prevent a peace, commanders must have recourse to many pitiful tricks and artifices to deceive those that employ them. But if they fail in their designs, and find they cannot prevent a peace, as soon as their pay is stopped, and they can live no longer in the licentious manner they used to do, they set up for soldiers of fortune, and having got a parcel of their disbanded men together, make no scruple of plundering a whole country without mercy or distinction. You must have heard that when the late wars were over in Italy, and the country full of disbanded soldiers, they formed themselves into several bands, and went about plundering some towns and laying others under contribution. You must likewise have read how the Carthaginian soldiers (after the first war was ended in which they had been engaged with the Romans) assembled together under the banners of Matho and Spendius (two officers whom they had chosen in a tumultuary manner to command them) and made a more dangerous war upon their own country, than that which had been just concluded.... Such evils, and others of the like nature, are owing to men who make war their only occupation; according to the proverb, *war makes thieves, and peace hangs them;* for those that know not how to get their bread any other way, when they are disbanded, finding nobody that has occasion for their service, and disdaining the thoughts of living in poverty and obscurity, are forced to have recourse to such ways of supporting themselves as generally bring them to the gallows.

Niccolò Machiavelli
Arte della guerra (1520)

The traditional identification of the sitter in this austere portrait is the Venetian condottiere, Colleoni, whose statue by Verrocchio is well known. Colleoni, however, died in 1475, and the present painting can scarcely be earlier than 1480, which is the approximate date given to it by Gronau (*Giovanni Bellini*). Von Hadeln (*Burlington Magazine,* 1927) believes it to be not earlier than 1500. The military air of the sitter is unmistakable, and it is entirely possible that another Venetian leader is here represented. Gronau tentatively suggests that the present picture may be identified with a small portrait by Giovanni Bellini of Giacomo Marcello, Captain-General of the Army, which Michiel (the Anonimo Morelliano) saw in the Marcello Palace, Venice, in the sixteenth century. Tietze (1947) upholds Gronau's tentative identification. But T. Bertelè (1950) supports the Colleoni identification, while Suida (1950) suggests an identification of the sitter as the condottiere Bartolomeo d' Alviano, of whom, according to Vasari, Bellini is known to have painted a portrait. Collections: The painting was bought in Venice in 1786 by Sir Abraham Hume and passed through his descendants to the collection of Earl Brownlow, Ashridge, Berkhamsted, England. *Samuel H. Kress Collection,* 1939. Wood. Height 19¼ in.; width 13⅞ in. (0.49 x 0.35). Painted c. 1500.

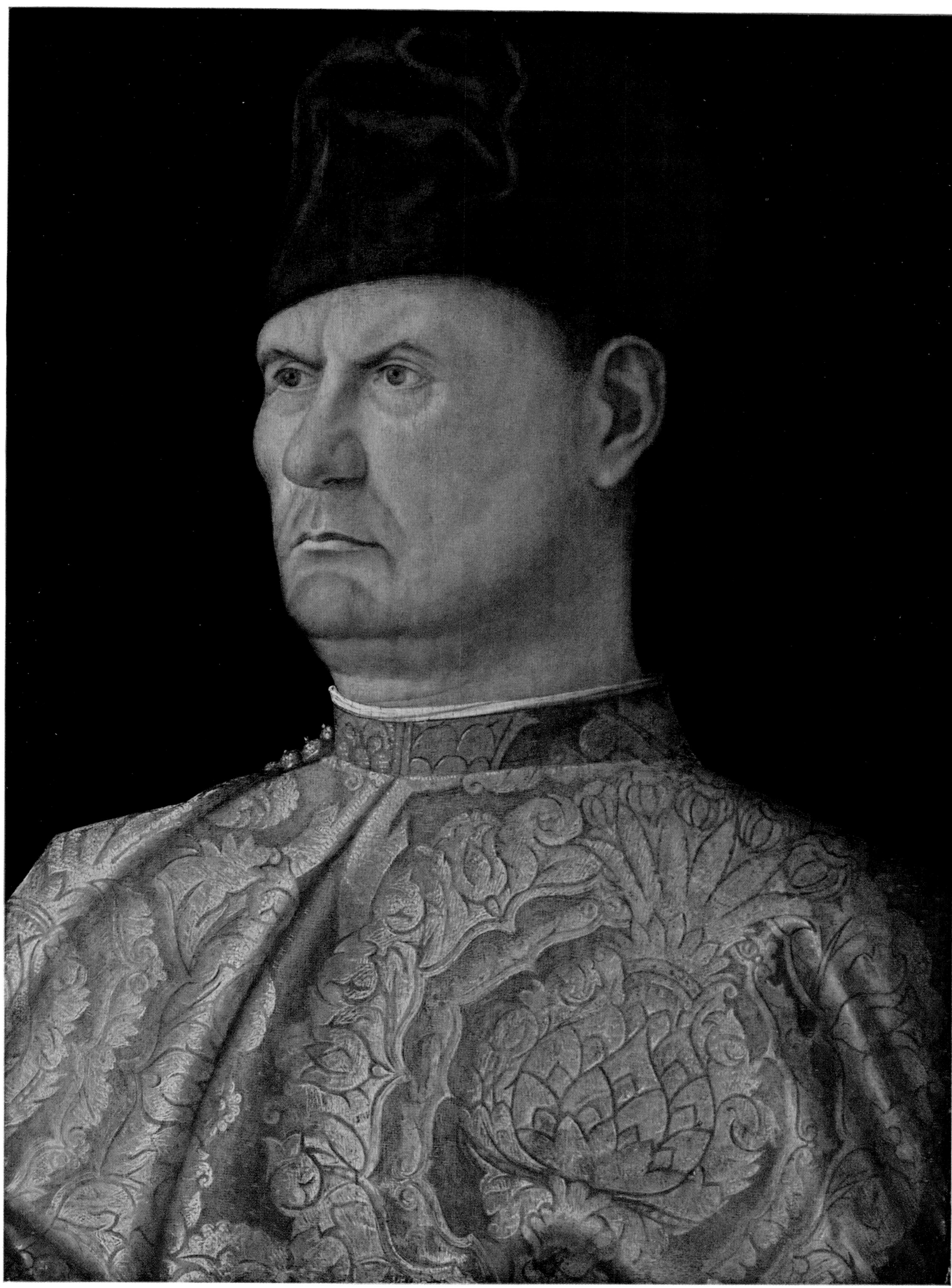

GIOVANNI BELLINI · Venetian c. 1430-1516

The Feast of the Gods

Turrigera frontem Cybele redimita corona
  convocat aeternos ad sua festa deos.
convocat et satyros et, rustica numina, nymphas;
  Silenus, quamvis nemo vocarat, adest.
nec licet et longum est epulas narrare deorum:
  in multo nox est pervigilata mero.
hi temere errabant in opacae vallibus Idae,
  pars iacet et molli gramine membra levat,
hi ludunt, hos somnus habet, pars brachia nectit
  et viridem celeri ter pede pulsat humum.
Vesta iacet placidamque capit secura quietem,
  sicut erat, positum caespite fulta caput.

Cybele, with her brow crowned with turrets, invites to her feast the eternal Gods. She invites, too, the Satyrs and the Nymphs, Deities of the country. Silenus comes, *too,* though no one had invited him. It is not lawful, 'twere tedious, too, to relate the banquet of the Gods; a sleepless night is spent over copious draughts of wine. Some are carelessly wandering in the vales of the shady Ida; some are lying down, and resting their limbs on the soft herbage. Some are disporting: upon some, Sleep lays her hand: some join hands, and then with active foot they beat the ground. Vesta is lying down, and, free from fear, she enjoys quiet repose, supporting her head, reclining just as it was, on a tuft of grass.

Ovid
Fasti (c. 7 A.D.)

In the year 1514 Duke Alfonso of Ferrara had caused a little chamber to be decorated, and had commissioned Dosso . . . . and he desired that there should also be there pictures by the hand of Gian Bellini. Bellini painted on another wall a vat of red wine with some Bacchanals around it, and Satyrs, musicians, and other men and women, all drunk with wine, and near them a nude and very beautiful Silenus, riding on his ass, with figures about him that have the hands full of fruits and grapes; which work was in truth executed and coloured with great diligence, insomuch that it is one of the most beautiful pictures that Gian Bellini ever painted. . . . On that vat Gian Bellini wrote these words: JOANNES BELLINUS VENETUS, P. 1514. That work he was not able to finish completely, because he was old, and Tiziano, as the most excellent of all the others, was sent for to the end that he might finish it.

Giorgio Vasari
Le Vite de' piv eccellenti pittori, scvltori, e architettori (1568)

The connoisseurship of paintings offers, from time to time, investigations as fascinating and complex as a detective story. The Feast of the Gods, for example, is signed by Giovanni Bellini. Yet Titian, according to Vasari, brought it to completion. A composite X-ray of the painting made recently indicates that the picture has had three backgrounds. There is evidence that the first alteration, and perhaps the earlier changes as well, are due to Titian. As far as one can tell his motives were mixed; but the impelling reason seems to have been that the original design did not harmonize with the other pictures in the same room in the Castle of Ferrara which Alfonso d'Este asked him to paint: Bacchus and Ariadne now in the National Gallery, London, and the Venus Worship and the Andrians, now in the Prado in Madrid (John Walker, *Bellini and Titian at Ferrara,* 1956). A century after it was painted, Nicolas Poussin was so impressed by the Feast of Gods that he made the famous copy now in the National Gallery of Scotland. Collections: Duke Alfonso I d'Este, Ferrara; Cardinal Pietro Aldobrandini, Rome; Vincenzo Camuccini, Rome; Duke of Northumberland, Alnwick Castle. *Widener Collection,* 1942. Canvas. Height 67 in.; width 74 in. (1.70 x 1.88). Signed, and dated 1514.

GIOVANNI BELLINI · Venetian c. 1430-1516

Orpheus

Orpheus with his Lute made Trees,
And the Mountaine tops that freeze,
Bow themselues when he did sing.
To his Musicke, Plants and Flowers
Euer sprung, as Sunne and Showers,
There had made a lasting Spring.
Euery thing that heard him play,
Euen the Billowes of the Sea,
Hung their heads, & then lay by.
In sweet Musicke is such Art,
Killing care, & griefe of heart,
Fall asleepe, or hearing dye.

William Shakespeare
The Life of King Henry the Eight (1623)

The old masters taught, not because they liked teaching, nor yet from any idea of serving the cause of art, nor yet because they were paid to teach by the parents of their pupils. The parents probably paid no money at first. The masters took pupils and taught them because they had more work to do than they could get through and wanted some one to help them. They sold the pupil's work as their own, just as people do now who take apprentices. When people can sell a pupil's work, they will teach the pupil all they know and will see he learns it. This is the secret of the whole matter.

The modern schoolmaster does not aim at learning from his pupils, he hardly can, but the old masters did. See how Giovanni Bellini learned from Titian and Giorgione who both came to him in the same year, as boys, when Bellini was 63 years old. What a day for painting was that! All Bellini's best work was done thenceforward. I know nothing in the history of art so touching as this. [1883.]

P.S. I have changed my mind about Titian. I don't like him. [1897.]

Samuel Butler
Note-Books (1912)

The subject would seem to be allegorical, but no satisfactory interpretation has yet been offered: the figures are tentatively identified as Orpheus, Circe with her wand, and Pan tempting Luna with white wool. The apprentice system described by Samuel Butler is well illustrated by the difficulty of attributing this particular painting. Generally ascribed to Bellini, it has also been given to Giorgione, to Titian, to Basaiti, and to some unidentified follower of Bellini, possibly Giulio Campagnola. Collections: Hugo Bardini, Paris. *Widener Collection,* 1942. Transferred from wood to canvas. Height 18⅝ in.; width 32 in. (0.395 x 0.81). Painted c. 1515.

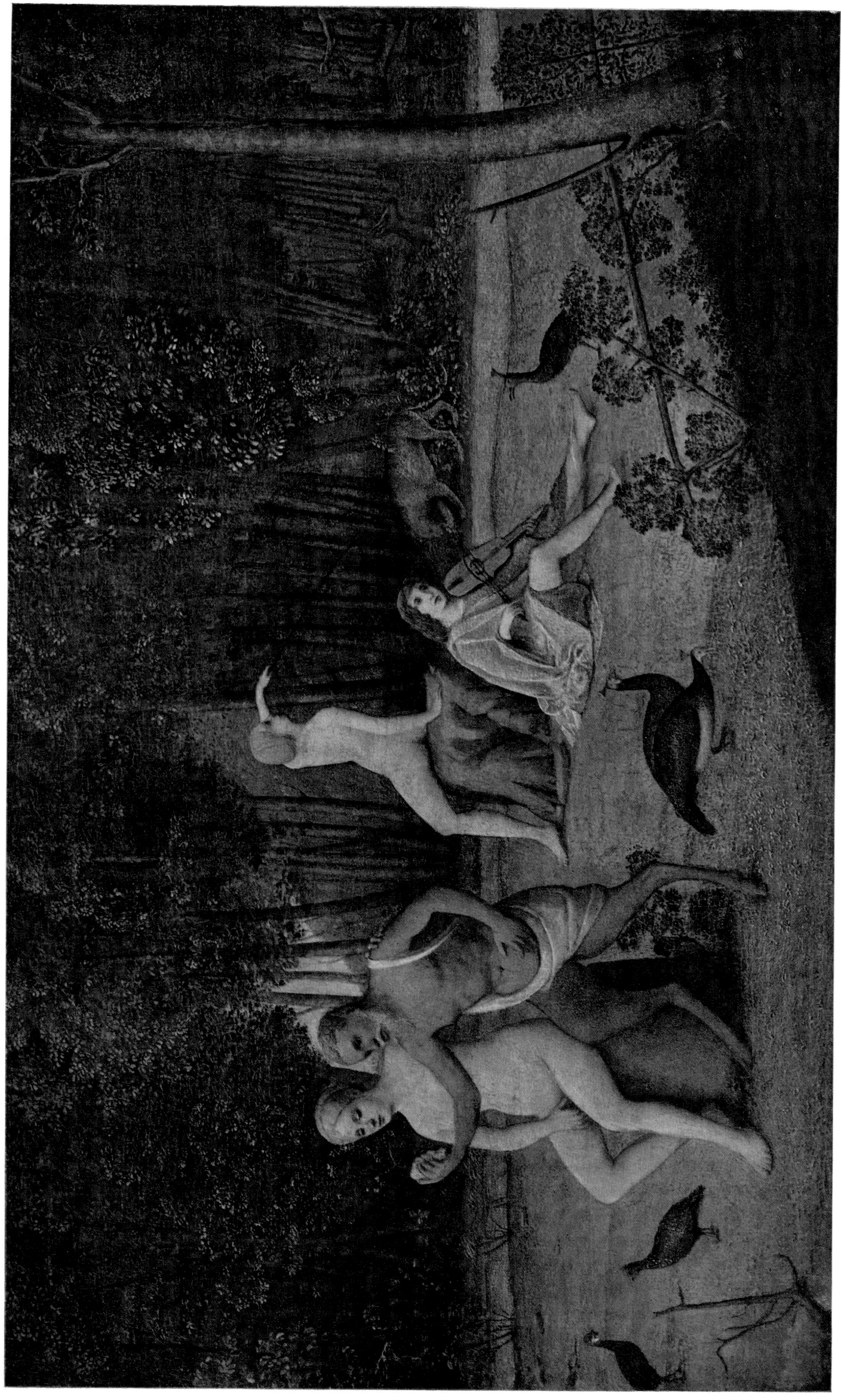

GIORGIONE · Venetian c. 1478-1510

The Holy Family

Little Jesus, wast Thou shy
Once, and just so small as I?
And what did it feel like to be
Out of Heaven, and just like me?
Didst Thou sometimes think of *there,*
And ask where all the angels were?
I should think that I would cry
For my house all made of sky;
I would look about the air,
And wonder where my angels were;
And at waking 'twould distress me—
Not an angel there to dress me!
Hadst Thou ever any toys,
Like us little girls and boys?
And didst Thou play in Heaven with all
The angels that were not too tall,
With stars for marbles? Did the things
Play *Can you see me?* through their wings?
And did Thy Mother let Thee spoil
Thy robes, with playing on *our* soil?
How nice to have them always new
In Heaven, because 'twas quite clean blue!

Francis Thompson
Ex Ore Infantium (1893)

Just as the influence of Verrocchio permeated Florentine style around 1470, as illustrated in the painting on page 57, so Giorgione dominated the art of Venice in the first decade of the sixteenth century. When a personality is so strong that other artists feel compelled to imitate his way of painting, then the attribution of pictures becomes extremely difficult. The present panel has been ascribed to Cariani and to Catena, but critical opinion in recent years has tended strongly toward an attribution to Giorgione himself, including such critics as G. M. Richter, Gronau, Morassi, and Berenson. Collections: Possibly Allard van Everdingen; Henry Willett, Brighton; Robert H. and Evelyn Benson, London. *Samuel H. Kress Collection,* 1952. Wood. Height 14⅝ in.; width 17⅞ in. (0.373 x 0.456). Painted probably c. 1500.

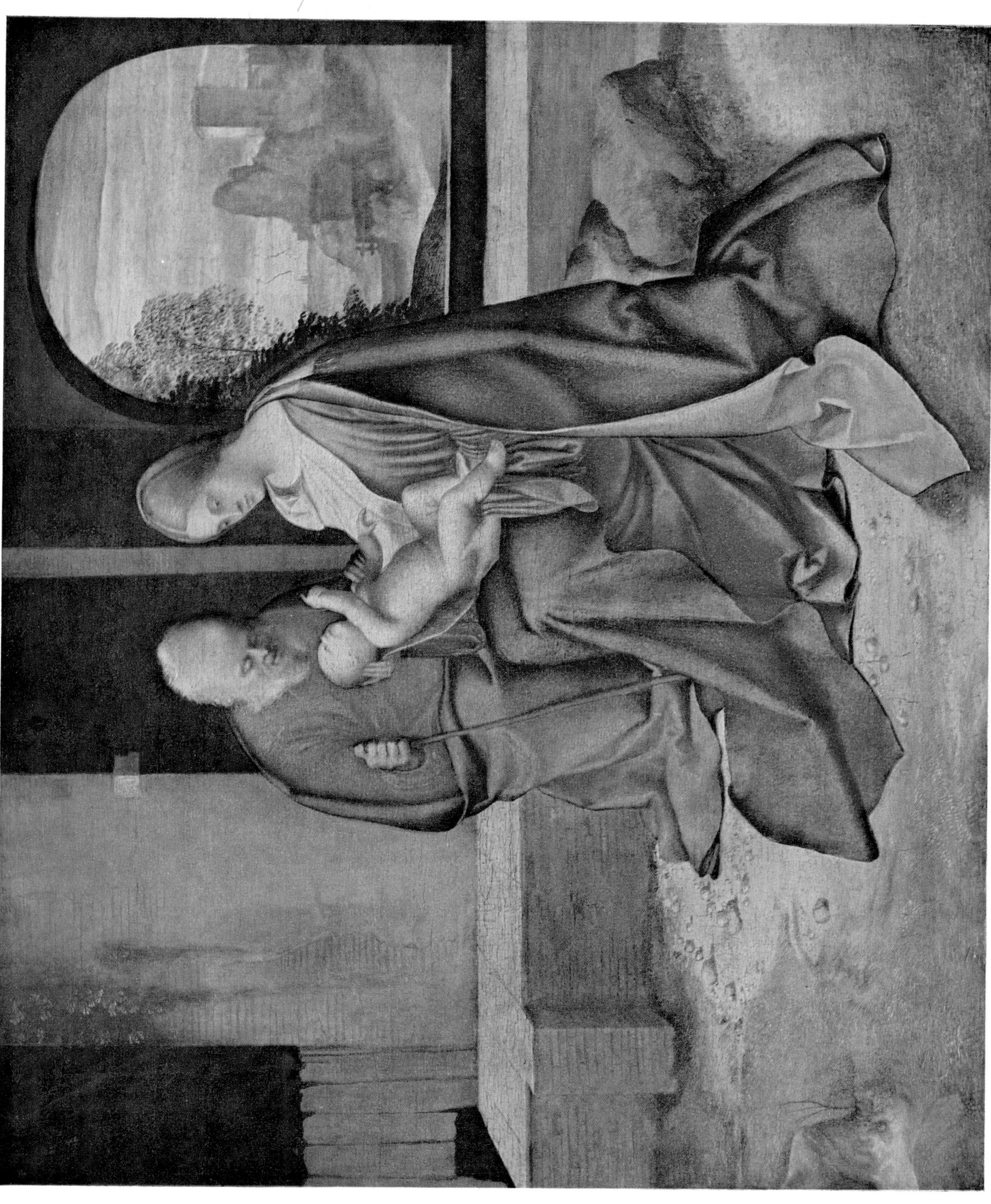

GIORGIONE · Venetian c. 1478-1510

The Adoration of the Shepherds

'And now try, she said, to give me all your mind.

'He who has been instructed so far in the mystery of love, and who has learned to see the beautiful correctly and in due order, when he comes toward the end will suddenly perceive a wondrous beauty (and this, Socrates, is the final cause of all our former toils). It is eternal, uncreated, indestructible, subject neither to increase or decay; not like other things partly beautiful, partly ugly; not beautiful at one time or in one relation or in one place, and deformed in other times, other relations, other places; not beautiful in the opinion of some and ugly in the opinion of others. It is not to be imagined as a beautiful face or form or any part of the body, or in the likeness of speech or knowledge: it does not have its being in any living thing or in the sky or the earth or any other place. It is Beauty absolute, separate, simple, and everlasting, which without diminution, and without increase, or any change, is imparted to the ever-growing and perishing beauties of all other things. If a man ascends from these under the influence of the right love of a friend, and begins to perceive that beauty, he may reach his goal. And the true order of approaching the mystery of love is to begin from the beauties of earth and mount upwards for the sake of that other beauty, using these as steps only, and from one going on to two, and from two to all beautiful forms, and from beautiful forms to beauty of conduct, and from beauty of conduct to beauty of knowledge, until from this we arrive at the knowledge of absolute beauty, and at last know what the essence of beauty is. . . . But what if man had eyes to see the true beauty—the divine beauty, I mean, pure and clear and unalloyed, not clogged with the pollutions of mortality and all the colours and vanities of human life—gazing on it, in communion with the true beauty simple and divine? Remember how in that communion only, beholding beauty with the eye of the mind, he will be able to bring forth, not shadows of beauty, but its truth, because it is no shadow that he grasps, but the truth; and he will give birth to true virtue and nourish it and become the friend of God and be immortal as far as mortal man may. Would that be an ignoble life?'

Such, Phaedrus, were the words of Diotima; and I am convinced of their truth.

Plato
Symposium (385-371 B.C.)

The quotation from the *Symposium* is basic in Neo-Platonism, the most influential element in Renaissance aesthetics. Isabella d'Este, who was familiar with such theories, may have known the picture reproduced and referred to it in her correspondence with Taddeo Albano in 1510, where she discusses two paintings representing "una Nocte" (i.e. a Nativity or Adoration). It is also possible that the present Adoration is mentioned in Bordone's appraisal of the Grimani Collection in 1563 and in the catalogue of the English Royal Collection by Bathoe in 1758. However, the first certain mention is in 1841, as belonging to the collection of Cardinal Fesch in Rome. A drawing in Windsor closely related to the painting is reproduced by Von Hadeln. Collections: Cardinal Fesch, Rome; Claudius Tarral, Paris; Thomas Wentworth Beaumont and thence by inheritance to Lord Allendale, London. *Samuel H. Kress Collection,* 1939. Wood. Height 35¾ in.; width 43½ in. (0.91 x 1.11). Painted c. 1510.

GIORGIONE AND TITIAN

VENETIAN c. 1478-1510 AND c. 1477-1576

Portrait of a Venetian Gentleman

Giorgione forged the link between his teacher Giovanni Bellini and his illustrious pupil Titian. More significant however than his acknowledged historical achievement in connecting two epochs of expert painting is the truth that he remained independent of both. It was his destiny to make a unique aesthetic contribution. He invented the painted lyric. As in the more abstract art of music the meaning reaches us subtly, through the senses, and the subject is almost inseparable from the picture form. Such a conception of art was far from general acceptance even in Giorgione's enlightened day.... The broken parapet of the portrait.... has functional purpose in the pattern. Its reflecting surfaces and its angles are repeated in the open window thru which one can look across the Grand Canal to Palaces opposite and to a distant bridge. Amusingly its curve seems to repeat in its arch of light over dark water the prominent arched eyeball of the dark man portrayed. His expression is baffling—perhaps because he himself is baffled. We would like to know what troubles him. In his abstracted gaze we seem to see his determination to be resolute about something which is not yet satisfactorily settled in his own mind. His unseeing stare relates to the clenched fist on the closed book and perhaps even to the distant bridge at the Rialto. Thus a compact functioning of the lines is also contributory in every detail to the portrait's purpose of characterizing more than a man, of standing for a state of mind which the artist has known in himself and as a universally difficult moment of dangerous doubt and abrupt need for decision.

DUNCAN PHILLIPS
The Leadership of Giorgione (1937)

This picture appears to date from a period when Titian and Giorgione were closely associated and frequently working in collaboration. Burroughs (*Art Criticism from a Laboratory*, 1938) has stated that the X-ray evidence indicates that the underpainting of the head resembles Giorgione's manner. The X-ray also shows that the hand originally grasped a sword, the hilt cutting across the space now occupied by the book; then the sword was repainted as a scroll; and finally, as a handkerchief. Possibly this painting is to be identified with "*A Man with a Sword,* by Giorgione" listed as at Somerset House in the inventory made of the Collection of King Charles I of England at the time of the sale of this collection (1649-1653). Collections: Henry Doetsch, London; Colonel George Kemp, Lord Rochdale, Beechwood Hall, England; Henry Goldman, New York. *Samuel H. Kress Collection,* 1939. Canvas. Height 30 in.; width 25 in. (0.76 x 0.64). Painted c. 1510.

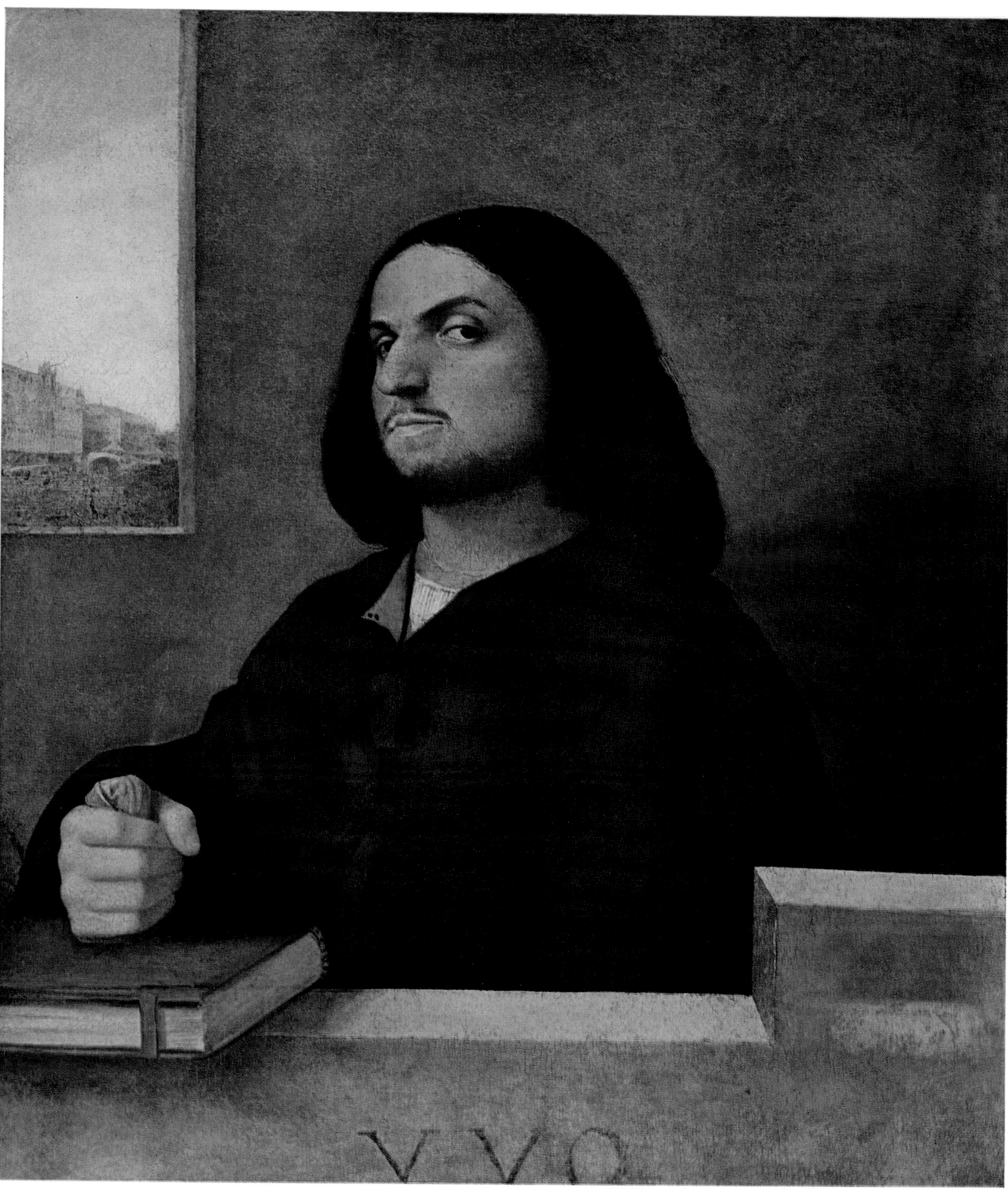
VVO

DOSSO DOSSI · Ferrarese c. 1479-c. 1542

Circe and Her Lovers in a Landscape

There are paintings which, like "huge cloudy symbols of a high romance," never cease to challenge the imagination, to promise the revelation of some hidden secret. In the canvas by Dosso Dossi (c. 1479-c. 1542) from the Kress Collection in the National Gallery of Art, a nude woman, seated in an idyllic landscape, is surrounded by birds and beasts. Who is she and why does she point, like one of Michelangelo's Sibyls, toward an inscribed tablet? The scene fits the legend of Circe, who turned men into animals; but absent are those wolves, lions and swine Ulysses saw when he encountered that "awful Goddess of the luxuriant tresses, own sister to the wizard Aeëtes." A transformation in the story has taken place. The animals are now the most charming and gentle of beasts and even the lioness is more heraldic than savage. Nature seems under a spell, so that the spoonbill and the owl do not fear the falcon, nor the stag and the doe the dogs. It is a scene of sorcery based on the legend of Circe, but transformed from the Olympian realm of the *Odyssey* into the fairy world of *A Midsummer Night's Dream.*

There is a clue to this change. In the court of Ferrara, where this picture was probably painted, Ariosto had composed his famous *Orlando Furioso,* setting forth a new version of the Circean myth. In his romantic epic, Alcina is the perfect example of the beautiful and seductive woman. Like Circe, she changes her lovers into animals; but instead of doing this with the touch of a wand, as Homer describes the transformation of the followers of Ulysses, she uses esoteric incantations. These in Dosso Dossi's canvas are symbolized by the tablet and the cabalistic book with which Alcina—for the nude figure is probably she—holds her court of wild creatures spellbound.

And here there is perhaps a parallel to the human admirers who were enthralled by Dosso Dossi's patroness, Lucrezia Borgia, then Duchess of Ferrara. For she, too, wove a spell over her lovers, whether poets, courtiers or princes. One wonders whether she may have felt some instinctive sympathy for the seductress in *Orlando Furioso.* Does this perhaps explain why the witch in Dosso Dossi's picture is portrayed in such an appealing way, with a look of innocent expectancy? It is easy to speculate, to imagine that Lucrezia Borgia, considering herself a victim of the sinister forces aroused by her beauty, may have identified herself with the wistful enchantress depicted by her court painter, Dosso Dossi, as she may have considered herself eulogized in the tribute to Alcina composed by her court poet, Ariosto:

> Her matchless person every charm combin'd,
> Form'd in th' idea of a painter's mind.

John Walker
Circe and Her Lovers in a Landscape (1949)

Painted about 1514 or 1516, at a time when—according to Vasari—Duke Alfonso I of Ferrara had caused a little chamber to be decorated with pictures by Dosso Dossi, Bellini, and Titian. In his *Orlando Furioso,* Ariosto, court poet of Alfonso, places Dosso, who was court painter at that time, on a level with Mantegna, Leonardo, Bellini, Michelangelo, and Raphael. The influence of Ariosto's poem can be detected in the present picture. The various beasts recall Pisanello's animal sketches, and the greyhound seems to be based on Dürer's engraving of Saint Eustace. Collections: William Graham, London; Robert H. and Evelyn Benson, London. *Samuel H. Kress Collection,* 1943. Canvas. Height 39⅝ in.; width 53½ in. (1.008 x 1.361).

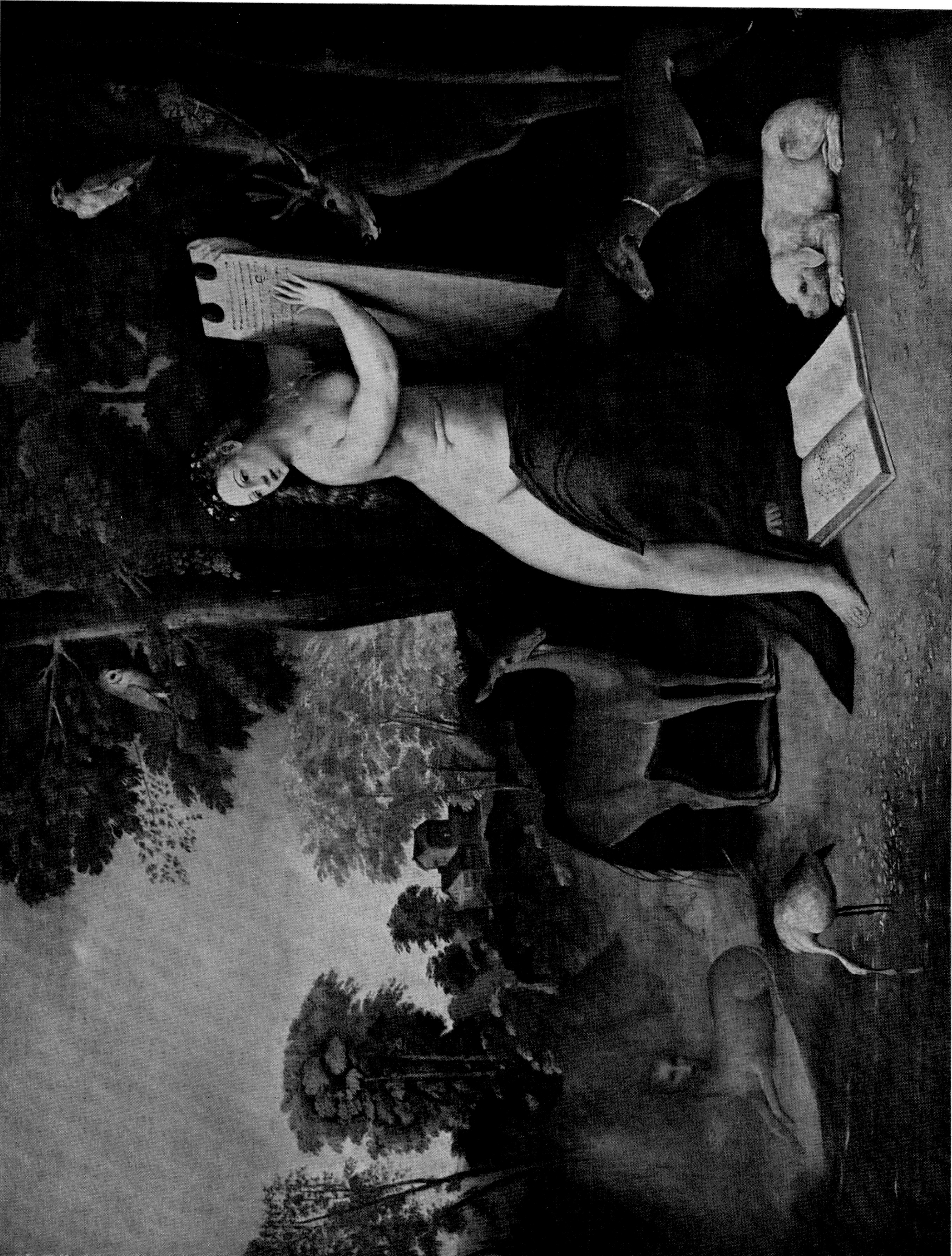

VITTORE CARPACCIO · Venetian c. 1460/65-1523/26

The Virgin Reading

Like the good primitive that he still was, Carpaccio told all that he knew in each one of his canvases. It is true that he knew much. One may love him for his anecdotes, for he is a wonderful storyteller. But the anecdote, always transfigured and magnified, always a motive for painted decorations and transpositions, is lost in the poetic sentiment which lifts up and frees everything. The sea is covered with boats and with ships. The city is as exact and new as that which Bellini paints, but more somber harmonies announce its maturity. Through their high arcades, the palaces permit us to see masts with pennants flying from them, the multicolored pavements of the great docks where merchants and promenaders come and go before the vessels at anchor. We see also leprous houses, dirty clothes hung from one façade to the other across the plague-ridden canals, and the incredible swarm of beggars, boatmen, jugglers, and ruffians. There are people everywhere: in the streets, on the staircases, on the bridges, and on the terraces. Lords and ladies file by, people are chatting, people are parading, people bend the knee before princes who receive in the open air. Palm trees grow in solitary squares, an unexpected camel is seen outlined at the corner of a dock, and the lion of Saint Jerome actually treads the pavement of the Piazetta dragged along by a black lion-tamer around whom the street boys dance gayly. Carpaccio mingles with the crowd, he listens, he gossips, he is out of doors all day long. The violins and the brass instruments of the showmen creak and snore; the showman's nasal patter excites jest and laughter. The good painter is in the very first rank. Everything amuses him, but if one keeps one's eye upon him one sees why his face becomes serious at times. In some corner he has seen a strange isolated figure which holds his attention. . . . He becomes pensive and turns aside, the sound of the music dies away.

Élie Faure
Histoire de l'art (1921)

It is such isolated figures as this in Carpaccio's crowded scenes that elevate his paintings above the prose of genre. In the present case there is evidence that the picture is a fragment of a larger composition. While the painting was in the Benson Collection, a small arm and foot, corresponding to those of a Christ Child, were visible against the cushion to the left, and slight traces of these details can still be seen. The same seated figure appears in the guise of a midwife in the Birth of the Virgin ascribed to Carpaccio and assistants, in the Carrara Academy, Bergamo. Collections: Marquis of Exeter, Burghley House, Stamford, Lincolnshire; Robert H. and Evelyn Benson, London. *Samuel H. Kress Collection,* 1939. Wood. Height 30¾ in.; width 20 in. (0.78 x 0.51). Painted c. 1505.

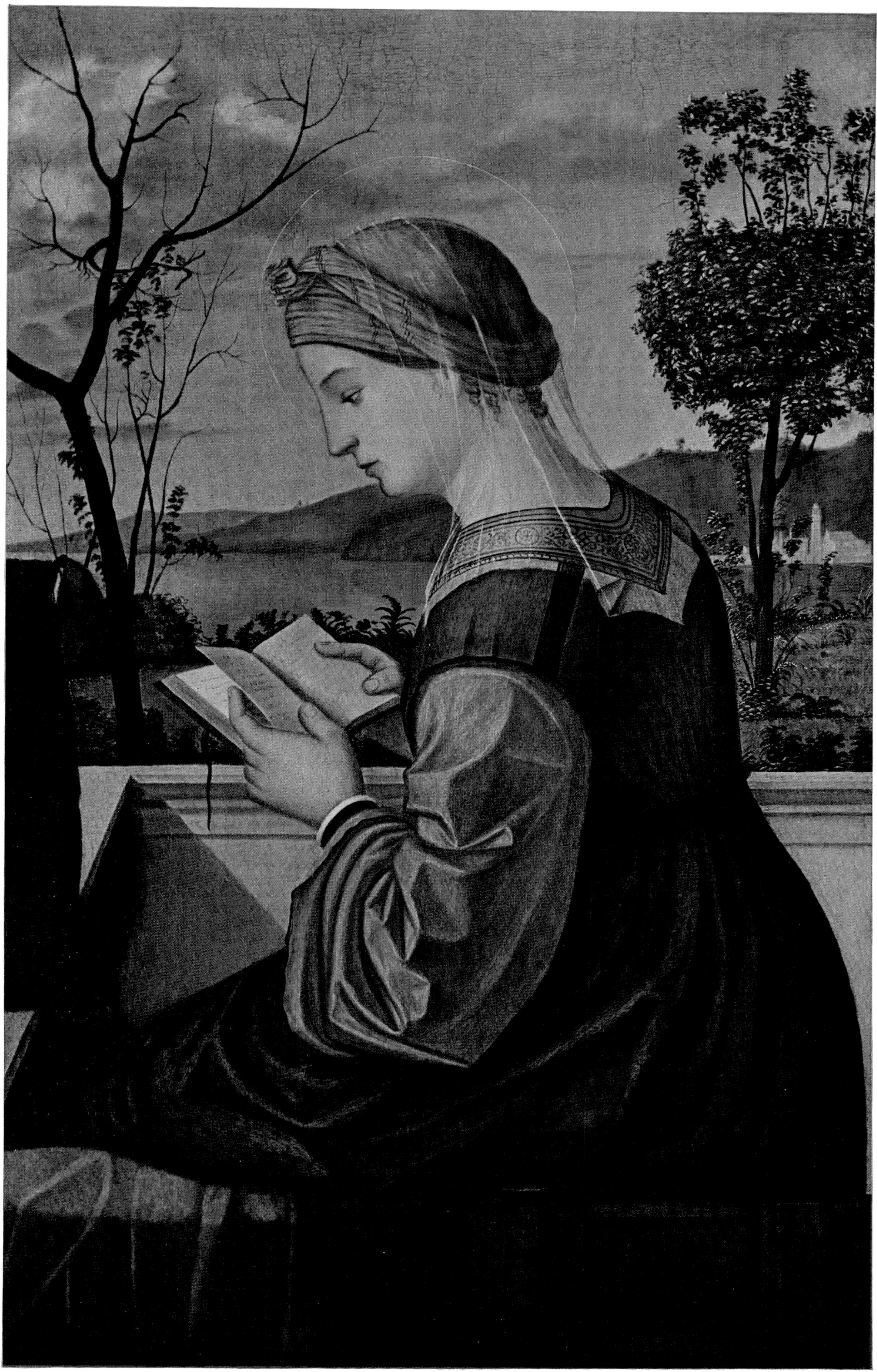

LORENZO LOTTO · Venetian c. 1480-1556

A Maiden's Dream

Already in the fifteenth century artists began to feel that landscape had become too tame and domesticated, and they set about exploring the mysterious and the unsubdued. These artists came from and worked for an urban population which had long since learnt to control natural forces. They therefore could view the old menaces of flood and forest with a kind of detachment. They could use them consciously to excite a pleasing horror. To this extent they may justifiably be called romantic. But it would be a mistake to suppose that they were similar to the Gothic novelists or the men of 1830. Horace Walpole wrote from the absolute security of Twickenham; to Grünewald, Altdorfer and Bosch the menaces of life were still real.... They knew that the human mind was full of darkness, twisted and fiery, and they painted an aspect of nature which expressed these dark convolutions of the spirit, just as the backgrounds of Piero della Francesca had expressed the clarity of the intellect. In doing so they no doubt made a conscious use of certain disturbing shapes and symbols. They are what we now call 'expressionist' artists, a term which is not as worthless as it sounds, because, in fact, the symbols of expressionism are remarkably consistent, and we find in the work of these early sixteenth-century landscape painters not only the same spirit but the same shapes and iconographical motives which recur in the work of such recent expressionists as van Gogh, Max Ernst, Graham Sutherland and Walt Disney....

There is no doubt that Lotto was directly in touch with German painters. In his earliest painting, the *Maiden's Dream* in the National Gallery, Washington, which dates from about 1498, the trees and their relation to the distant landscape show unmistakably the influence of Dürer, who was in Venice in 1494-95, and foreshadow the forest landscapes which, in the next five years were to excite the imaginations of Altdorfer and Cranach. The *St. Jerome* in the Louvre, dated 1500, contains rocks and trees remarkably similar to the drawings which Dürer did on his journey home from Italy in 1495.

Kenneth Clark
Landscape into Art (1949)

The resemblance between figures in Lotto's early altarpieces and the Saint Sebastian painted by Grünewald for the altar at Isenheim is further evidence of the connection between Lotto and German art, as Sir Kenneth Clark points out. Also the fact that Lotto painted portraits of Martin Luther and his wife suggests that he may have been in touch with the leaders of the Protestant Reformation. The subject of the painting reproduced has been considered by many critics to be a free interpretation of the Danaë myth. It seems more likely, however, to be Plutus dropping a shower of gold (in the semblance of flowers) upon the nymph Rhodos. Collections: Lord Conway, Maidstone, England. *Samuel H. Kress Collection,* 1939. Wood. Height 16⅞ in.; width 13¼ in. (0.43 x 0.34). Painted c. 1505.

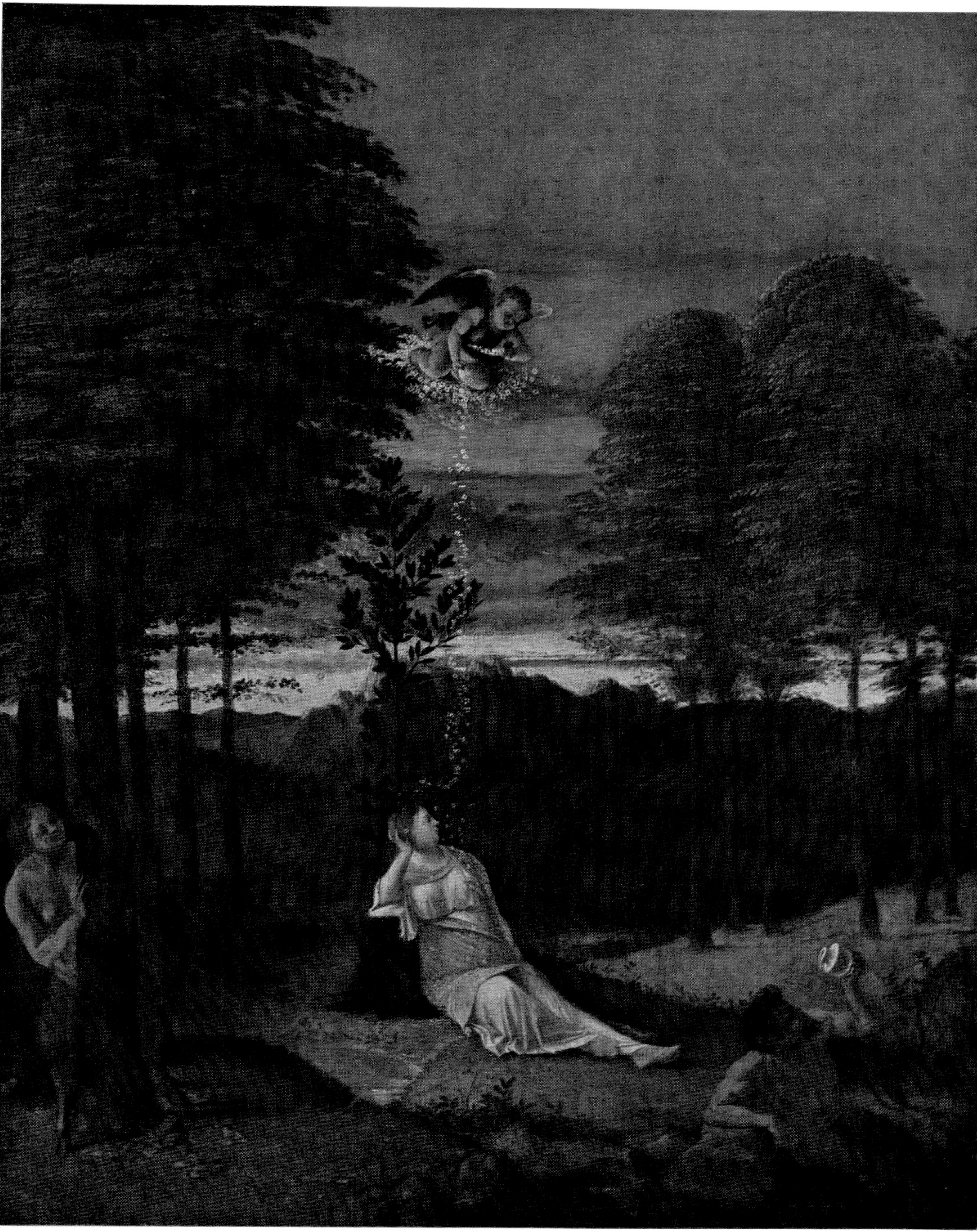

LORENZO LOTTO · VENETIAN c. 1480-1556

Allegory

Michael Angelo here paused for breath, and Zapata began. . . .

Pray, Signor Michael . . . . explain a doubt of mine about the art of painting: why is it that artists sometimes, as we see in many parts of this city, paint a thousand monsters and animals, some of them with a woman's face and the lower parts and tail of a fish, others with the arms of tigers and with wings, or with a man's face; anything in fact that delights the painter's fancy and has never existed.

I shall be glad, said Michael, to tell you why it is the custom to paint things that have never existed and how reasonable is this licence and how it accords with the truth; for some critics, not understanding the matter, are wont to say that Horace, the lyric poet, wrote those lines in dispraise of painters:

Pictoribus atque poetis
Quidlibet audendi semper fuit aequa potestas:
Scimus, et hanc veniam petimusque damusque vicissim.

And in this sentence he does in nowise blame painters but praises and favours them, since he says that poets and painters have licence to dare, that is to dare do what they choose. And this insight and power they have always had; for whenever (as very rarely happens) a great painter makes a work which seems to be artificial and false, this falseness is truth; and greater truth in that place would be a lie. For he will not paint anything that cannot exist according to its nature; he will not paint a man's hand with ten fingers, nor paint a horse with the ears of a bull or a camel's hump . . . . for all such things are most false. But if, in order to observe what is proper to a time and place, he exchange the parts or limbs (as in grotesque work which would otherwise be very false and insipid) and convert a griffin or a deer downwards into a dolphin or upwards into any shape he may choose, putting wings in place of arms, and cutting away the arms if wings are more suitable, this converted limb, of lion or horse or bird, will be most perfect according to its nature; and this may seem false but can really only be called ingenious or monstrous. And sometimes it is more in accordance with reason to paint a monstrosity (to vary and relax the senses and the object presented to men's eyes, since sometimes they desire to see what they have never seen and think cannot exist) rather than the ordinary figure, admirable though it be, of man or animals. And . . . . it may be really great work if it is made by a skilful artist.

FRANCISCO DE HOLLANDA
Quatro Dialogos sobre a pintura (1548)

This panel is a cover for the portrait of Bishop Bernardo Rossi of Treviso, now in the Naples Museum. The content of the painting reflects an aspect of Renaissance humanistic thought. The left half, where a cupid examines evidences of intellectual pursuits, possibly may be taken to represent the contemplative side of life, while the right half, where a satyr drinks from a silver ewer, may symbolize the sensual side. In the background, a winged figure climbs a steep path, perhaps denoting the spirit ascending to the light of reason. The lines quoted above from Horace may be translated: "Painters and poets always have enjoyed unlimited license; we know this and we claim for ourselves the same liberty, and grant it to others." Collections: Antonio Bertoli, Parma; Giacomo Gritti, Bergamo, Italy. *Samuel H. Kress Collection,* 1939. Wood. Height 22¼ in.; width 17 in. (0.565 x 0.432). Painted 1505.

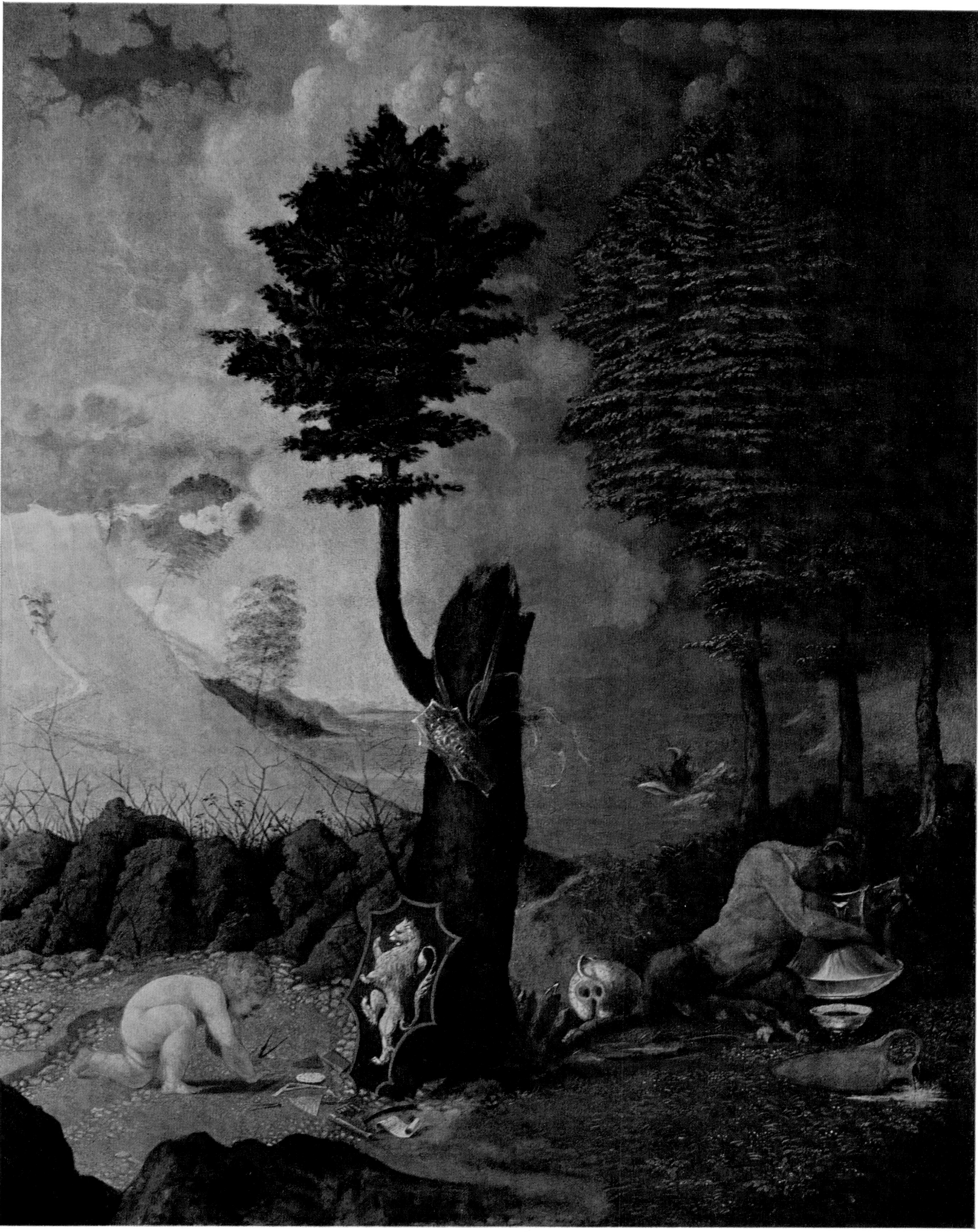

TITIAN · Venetian c. 1477-1576

Venus with a Mirror

Tomorrow let loveless, let lover tomorrow make love:
O spring, singing spring, spring of the world renew!
In spring lovers consent and the birds marry
When the grove receives in her hair the nuptial dew.
    Tomorrow may loveless, may lover tomorrow make love.

Tomorrow's the day when the prime Zeus made love:
Out of lightning foam shot deep in the heaving sea
(Witnessed by green crowds of finny horses)
Dione rising and falling, he made to be!
    Tomorrow may loveless, may lover tomorrow make love.

Bidden unarmed to go and to go naked
Lest he destroy with bow, with dart, with brand—
Yet, girls, Cupid is pretty, and you must know
That Love unarmed can pierce with naked hand!
    Tomorrow may loveless, may lover tomorrow make love.

Over sky and land and down under the sea
On the path of the seed the goddess brought to earth
And dropped into our veins created fire,
That men might know the mysteries of birth.
    Tomorrow may loveless, may lover tomorrow make love.

Anonymous
Pervigilium Veneris (3rd or 4th Century A.D.)

More than any other Renaissance artist Titian evokes the spirit of the ancient world. From his earliest masterpieces like the Bacchanals painted for the Duke of Ferrara to such late paintings as the picture reproduced, he repeatedly celebrated the power of Venus. These canvases are permeated with the same refined sensuality as that embodied in the poem *Pervigilium Veneris,* quoted above. Early records, together with many extant variations of the theme by Titian's studio and his later imitators and admirers, indicate that he painted at least three versions of the goddess of love gazing into a mirror. Only the present canvas is unanimously accepted as one of these three originals. It was bought in 1579 from Titian's son Pomponio by the Barbarigo family, Venice (in whose possession Ridolfi lists it in the seventeenth century), and passed from a branch of this family, about the middle of the last century, to the Hermitage Gallery, Leningrad. Collections: As above. *Andrew Mellon Collection,* 1937. Canvas. Height 49 in.; width 41½ in. (1.245 x 1.055). Painted c. 1555.

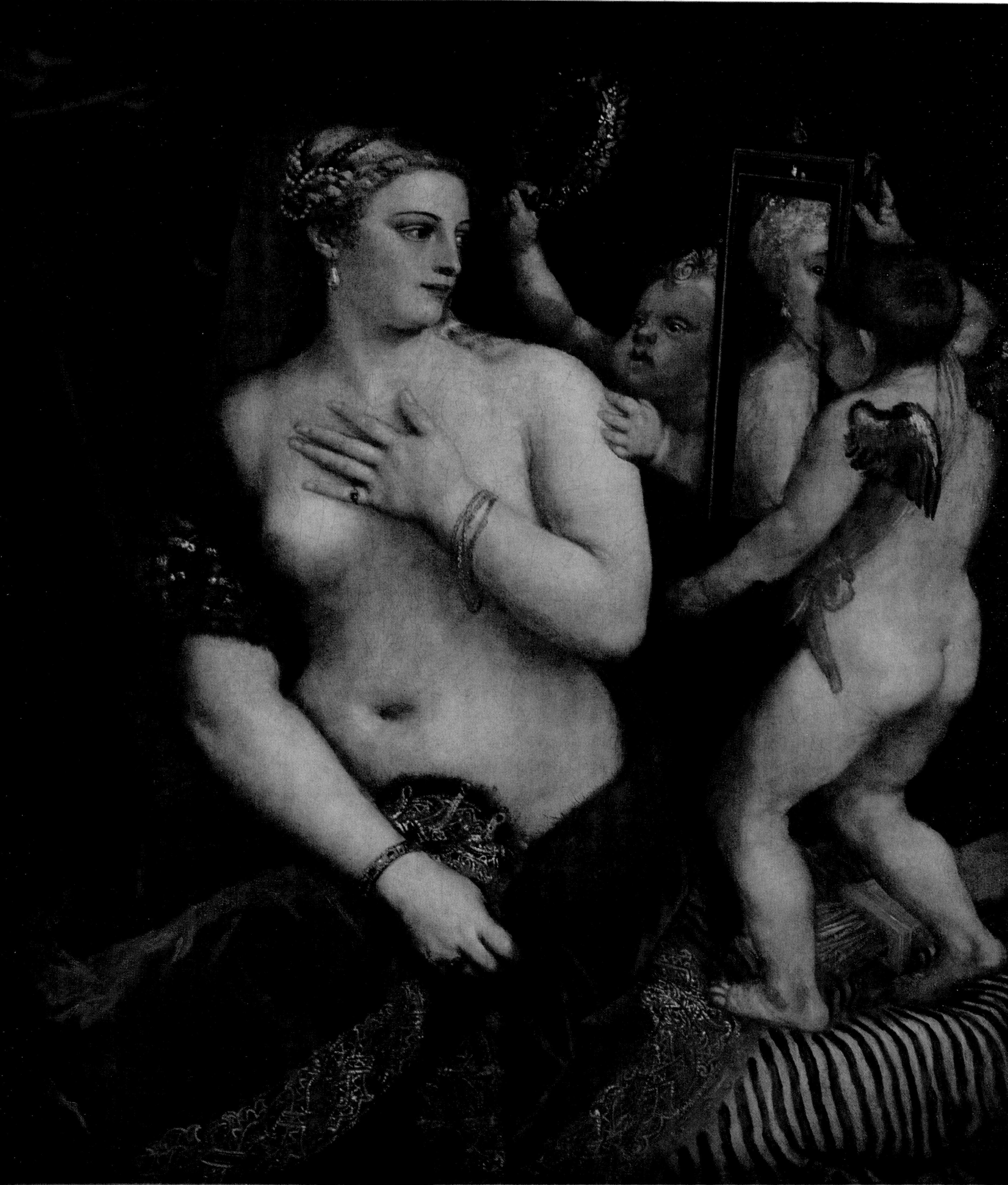

TITIAN · Venetian c. 1477-1576

Doge Andrea Gritti

The way in which Titian painted a picture was told me by Palma Giovine, who had the good fortune to have studied under the master directly. Titian prepared his pictures with a great mass of paint which served as a bed or basis for the eventual forms he was to create. I have myself seen these resolute strokes of a brush, laden with pigment, the middle tones struck in with pure red earth, the lights with white lead, and modeled into relief by touches of the same brush dipped in yellow, red, and black.

After laying this foundation he would turn the picture to the wall, and leave it there sometimes several months without looking at it. Then when he wanted to begin work on it again he would subject it to as rigorous and critical a scrutiny as he might the face of his worst enemy. If he then discovered anything that did not coincide with his intentions, he would set to work like a surgeon doctoring a patient, reducing some swelling here, redressing an arm there, adjusting or setting a limb or a foot, oblivious to the pain involved. By thus reshaping the figures he would bring them to the highest perfection; and then, while one picture was drying, he would turn his hand to another, going back to a painting again and again until his earliest layer, that first quintessence had been covered with living flesh—until only breath itself was lacking.

Never would he paint a finished figure *alla prima,* all at one time; he used to say that a poet who improvises can make neither learned nor well-formed verse. Instead, he would give great attention to the final retouches, the sauce as it were, for his creations. Rubbing his finger on the canvas he would blend here the edge of a highlight into the middle tones, or there soften the transition of one color into another. Or again, with a finger, he would lay a dab of dark paint into a corner to reinforce it, or aad a streak of red, like a drop of blood, to strengthen some weak or superficial spot. In fact, Palma assured me, in finishing a picture, Titian painted more with his fingers than with his brush.

Marco Boschini
Le ricche minere della pittvra veneziana (1674)

The painter's art in depicting each several subject seems never to get to an end, and in its embellishing it seems as if it would never stop laying on colours or taking them off—or whatever the professional painters term the process—and reach a point where the picture admits of no further improvement in respect of beauty and lucidity.

Plato
Laws (c. 360 B.C.)

Palma Giovine spent his formative years in Venice, where art was dominated by Titian, with whom he may have studied. Andrea Gritti (1454-1538), after having served the Venetian Republic as diplomat and military commander, was elected doge in 1523 and continued in that high office until his death. He was no less important to the cultural life of Venice than to its political development. At his order, a considerable number of Titian's large religious, historical, and allegorical pictures, now mostly lost, were painted. The splendid hand framed in a swirl of drapery is Titian's version of the hand of Michelangelo's Moses, of which Jacopo Sansovino is said to have brought a cast to Venice. It is undoubtedly this painting which is listed in Vertue's catalogue of the collection of Charles I of England. This identification is recorded on the back of the canvas, where, along with "CR" and a crown, an attached label reads: "Bought for his Majesty in Italy 1626." Collections: King Charles I of England; Wenzel Anton, Prince von Kaunitz-Rietburg, Chancellor of Empress Maria Theresa; Count Johann Rudolf Czernin von Chudenitz, Vienna; Czernin Gallery, Vienna. *Samuel H. Kress Collection,* 1961. Canvas. Height 52½ in.; width 40⅝ in. (1.336 x 1.032). Signed. Painted probably between 1535 and 1540.

TITIAN · Venetian c. 1477-1576

Saint John the Evangelist on Patmos

Lift up your heads, gates of my heart, unfold
    Your portals to salute the King of kings!
    Behold him come, borne on cherubic wings
    Engrained with crimson eyes and grail of gold!
Before His path the thunder clouds withhold
    Their stormy pinions, and the desert sings:
    He from His lips divine and forehead flings
    Sunlight of peace unfathomed, bliss untold.
O soul, faint soul, disquieted how long!
    Lift up thine eyes, for lo, thy Lord is near,
    Lord of all loveliness and strength and song,
The Lord who brings heart-sadness better cheer,
    Scattering those midnight dreams that dote on wrong,
    Purging with heaven's pure rays love's atmosphere!

John Addington Symonds
Animi Figura (1882)

Titian's daring treatment of space anticipates the illusionistic effects of baroque ceiling painting by more than a century. In order to appreciate fully his handling of the composition, one must remember that the artist designed the picture to be seen from below, as the central decoration of the ceiling of the assembly room in the Scuola di San Giovanni Evangelista, the headquarters of a Venetian religious confraternity. It depicts the society's patron saint, John the Divine, receiving God's inspiration to write the Book of Revelation. In the early nineteenth century when the Napoleonic government suppressed the Scuola, the whole ceiling decoration was transferred to a depository and ultimately became the property of the Accademia in Venice. In 1818, through an exchange with a collector in Turin, the central section left the Accademia. It is the only ceiling painting by Titian to be found outside Venice. Collections: Accademia, Venice; Conte Bartalazone d' Arache, Turin. *Samuel H. Kress Collection,* 1957. Canvas. Height 93½ in.; width 103½ in. (2.376 x 2.630). Painted c. 1540.

TITIAN · Venetian c. 1477-1576

Ranuccio Farnese

Titian's supreme gift was his great breadth of vision; but this is not all, there remains the lucid power which he brought to its expression. Other artists have seen as much, or possessed an even greater power of imagination, but not a greater gift in ordering their experience into a compact pictorial formula. With him a divine facility concealed a great power of concentration. There are many qualities in his work which in other channels of human endeavour would have made for success, in fact they helped him in the ordering of a singularly successful life. The vitality of the man, which enabled him to paint throughout a life of legendary length, endowed his vision with a constant energy and relish for life. Most great masters tower in the possession of some rare combination of gifts; with Titian the range is so vast, that we must turn to the qualities of a nation to find their equivalent. Viewing the major portion of his work, one is struck by the constant affirmation of splendid faculties, of a sort of optimism which colours his outlook. If the unique quality in the art of Raphael might be described as an unfailing sense of rhythm, the rhythmic sense, though great in Titian, is crossed by a greater hold upon realities which he marshals into a rhythmic whole, without Raphael's tendency to transmute them into the terms of his own convention.

Charles Ricketts
Titian (1910)

It is pleasant to look on the Picture of any Face, where the Resemblance is hit, but the Pleasure encreases, if it be the Picture of a Face that is beautiful, and is still greater, if the Beauty be softened with an Air of Melancholly or Sorrow.

Joseph Addison
The Spectator (June 30, 1712)

Ranuccio Farnese (1530-1565) was the gifted son of Pier Luigi Farnese and grandson of Pope Paul III. He was a classics student at Padua when Titian painted this portrait, in which a remarkable likeness was achieved, according to a contemporary report, in spite of the fact that the boy was able to devote very little time to sittings. Other versions of this portrait are in the Berlin Museum and in the "Brauer Collection," Florence. Collections: Cook, Doughty House, Richmond, Surrey. *Samuel H. Kress Collection,* 1952. Canvas. Height 35¼ in.; width 29 in. (0.897 x 0.736). Signed. Painted 1542, when Ranuccio was a young boy but had already been appointed Prior of San Giovanni dei Forlani at Venice, a rich property belonging to the Knights of Malta.

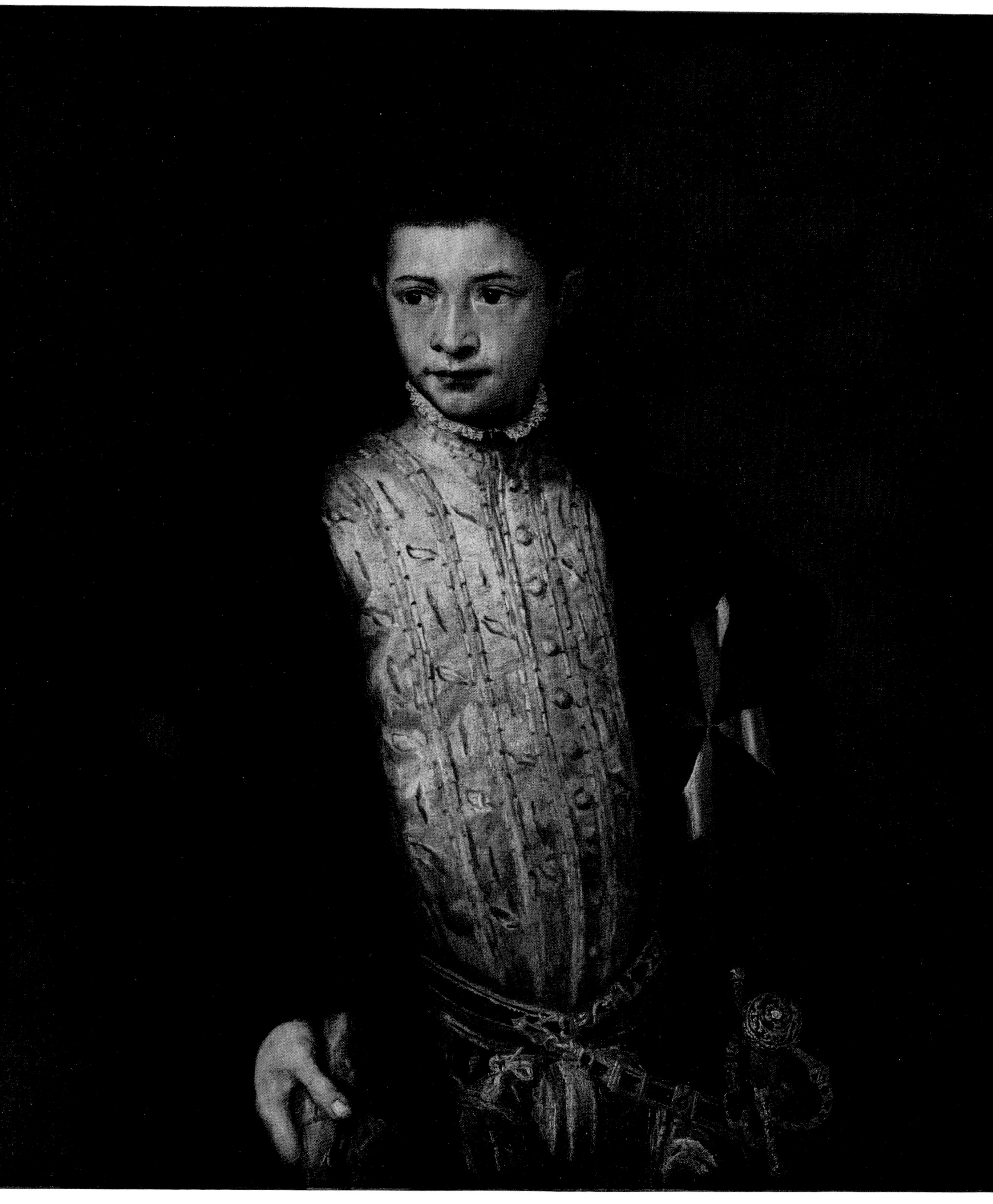

TITIAN · Venetian c. 1477-1576

Venus and Adonis

Those people are mistaken, in my judgment, who praise the admirable Titian by saying that he uses color well. If he merited no other praise but this, many a woman would surpass him. They certainly paint their faces so beautifully in white and vermilion that, as to the appearance of the colors, men are deceived by them. But if they have a long nose, a large mouth, or if their eyes, those seats of grace and beauty, are squinting or badly formed, the tints of those colors do not hide the ugliness or deformity. So the praiseworthiness in painting lies principally in the disposition of the forms so as to discover the beauty and the perfection of nature. In this, as in all other respects, the most excellent Titian is not merely divine after the manner of the world's opinion, but supremely divine and without equal as one who couples perfection of draftsmanship with liveliness of coloring to such an extent that his forms seem not painted, but real. The painter must have another quality not less necessary than all the rest: that is, the paintings he makes should so move the emotions and passions of the soul, that those who behold them are either delighted or perturbed, according to the subject, as with the works of good poets and orators. The statue of the Laocoön, which is in the Belvedere at Rome, may serve us as an example of this quality in the ancient artists. It is likewise fitting that the flesh tints be relatively delicate and soft, according to the character of the figure. For greater softness characterizes the flesh of a woman than of a man, of a youth than of an old man, of a gentleman than of a peasant, of a man accustomed to live in peace and delicately than of a soldier used to feats of arms, and so on. And the tints ought likewise to be varied as nature varies them. Just as an extreme white never pleases, so a certain tempering between white and brown contains every gradation of charm, as one sees in the Saint Catherine of our great Titian, which is in San Niccolò dei Frati Minori. Yet, on the contrary, that great diversity of colors affected by most painters today lacks verisimilitude, although it is recognized as valuable in giving relief to the figures, and delights the eyes of the ignorant. . . .

Yet, whoever establishes his art on such theories cannot go wrong; while on the contrary an infinity of painters err who do not realize these things. By rudely daubing a canvas or a panel with a portrait, or several figures done rather according to longstanding practice than to reason or art, they expect not only to be considered most excellent masters, but to surpass Raphael, Michelangelo, and Titian. And when they are not appreciated, they lament not their ignorance, but fortune, as happens also to many of us writers.

Lodovico Dolce
Letter to Gaspero Ballini (c. 1559)

Of the ten or twelve variations of this theme by Titian, the present painting is considered the last of the versions executed by him, and in many ways his most successful treatment of the subject. Collections: Lord Bristol (XVII century) and his descendants. The diarist, Evelyn, records having seen it in 1679 in the home of the Countess of Bristol and again in 1685, when it had passed by inheritance to Lady Sunderland. The latter's grandson, the first Earl Spencer, and his descendants owned the picture until it was brought to America. *Widener Collection,* 1942. Canvas. Height 42 in.; width 53½ in. (1.068 x 1.360). Painted after 1560.

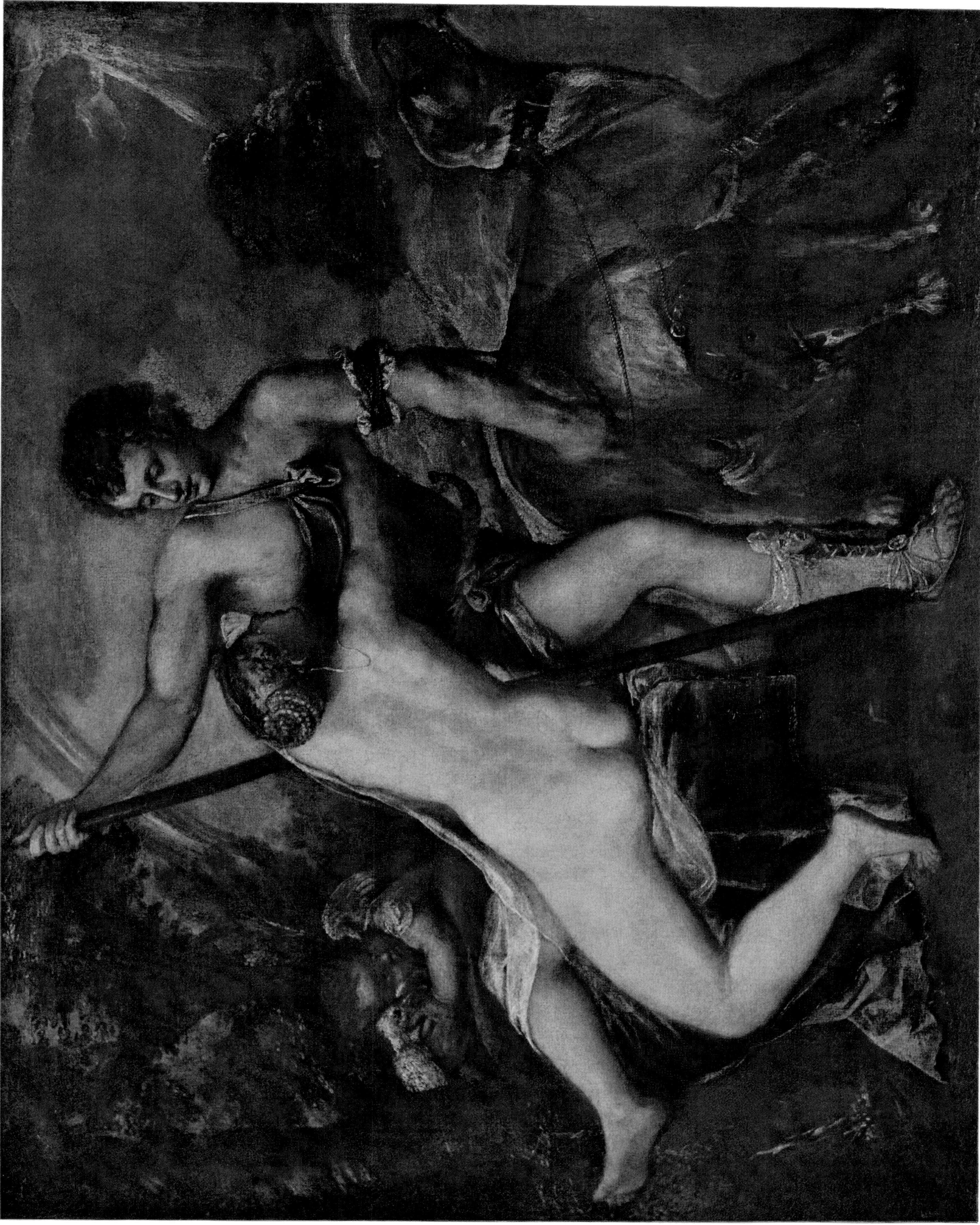

PAOLO VERONESE · Venetian 1528-1588

The Finding of Moses

The historical and outwardly significant subjects of painting have often the disadvantage that just what is significant in them cannot be portrayed visually, but must be arrived at by thought. In this respect the *nominal* significance of the picture must be distinguished from its *real* significance. The former is the outward significance, which, however, occurs only as an additional conception; the latter is that side of the Idea of humanity which is made visible to the onlooker through the medium of the picture. For example, Moses found by the Egyptian princess is the nominal significance of a painting; it represents a moment of the greatest importance in history; the real significance, on the other hand, that which is really presented to the onlooker, is a foundling child rescued from its floating cradle by a noblewoman, an incident which may have happened often. It is the costume alone which enables the scholar to recognize the particular historical case; but the costume is of importance to the nominal significance only, while it is a matter of indifference to the real significance; to the latter only the human being as such, not the arbitrary forms, are of relevance. Subjects taken from history have no advantage over those which are taken from mere possibility, and which are therefore to be called, not individual, but merely general. For what is peculiarly significant in the former is not the individual, not the particular event as such, but the universal element in it, the side of the Idea of humanity which expresses itself through it.

Arthur Schopenhauer
Die Welt als Wille und Vorstellung (1819)

Schopenhauer's aesthetics is not far removed from the theories of the Church Fathers. Though they would have given more importance to the nominalistic significance of the historical scene, they would have agreed with Schopenhauer that its real significance is its universal idea. Veronese was more modern in his point of view. Subject to him was merely an excuse for the display of formal values, the decorative effect of rich brocades, the interlocked thrust and counter-thrust of moving, gesticulating bodies, the composition of figures in space with all the complexities of linear and aerial perspective. These were his real interests and he became so indifferent to what was appropriate to the content of his scenes that he fell into difficulty with the Inquisition and barely escaped jail. Collections: Crozat (?), Paris; Louis-Michel Van Loo, Paris; Hermitage Gallery, Leningrad. *Andrew Mellon Collection,* 1937. Canvas. Height 22¾ in.; width 17½ in. (0.58 x 0.445). Painted probably in the early 1570's.

PAOLO VERONESE · VENETIAN 1528-1588

Rebecca at the Well

Veronese . . . chooses to represent the great relations of visible things to each other, to the heaven above, and to the earth beneath them. He holds it more important to show how a figure stands relieved from delicate air, or marble wall; how as a red, or purple, or white figure, it separates itself, in clear discernibility, from things not red, nor purple, nor white; how infinite daylight shines round it; how innumerable veils of faint shadow invest it; how its blackness and darkness are, in the excess of their nature, just as limited and local as its intensity of light; all this, I say, he feels to be more important than showing merely the exact *measure* of the spark of sunshine that gleams on a dagger-hilt, or glows on a jewel. All this, moreover, he feels to be harmonious,—capable of being joined in one great system of spacious truth. And with inevitable watchfulness, inestimable subtlety, he unites all this in tenderest balance, noting in each hair's-breadth of colour, not merely what its rightness or wrongness is in itself, but what its relation is to every other on his canvas; restraining, for truth's sake, his exhaustless energy, reining back, for truth's sake, his fiery strength; veiling, before truth, the vanity of brightness; penetrating, for truth, the discouragement of gloom; ruling his restless invention with a rod of iron; pardoning no error, no thoughtlessness, no forgetfulness; and subduing all his powers, impulses, and imaginations, to the arbitrament of a merciless justice, and the obedience of an incorruptible verity. . . .

Classed by one kind of merit, as, for instance, purity of expression, Angelico will stand highest; classed by another, sincerity of manner, Veronese will stand highest; classed by another, love of beauty, Leonardo will stand highest; and so on.

JOHN RUSKIN
Modern Painters (1856)

Ruskin stresses Paolo Veronese's "incorruptible verity." Veronese closely follows Genesis xxiv, which describes the recognition by Abraham's old servant of the young woman destined to be Abraham's daughter-in-law. According to the Bible, the servant of Abraham "made his camels to kneel down without the city by a well of water at the time of the evening." Then Rebecca appears and gives water to the servant and to his camels. When they have drunk she is offered gifts sent by Abraham, "a golden earring . . . and two bracelets for her hands." In sixteenth-century art nocturnes are rare, but still rarer is a nocturne which suggests an actual place, in this case the outskirts of a village of the Veneto with its buildings glimpsed in the twilight. Collections: George Villiers, second Duke of Buckingham; Archduke Leopold Wilhelm, Prague; Gemäldegalerie, Vienna. *Samuel H. Kress Collection,* 1952. Canvas. Height 57¼ in.; width 111¼ in. (1.455 x 2.827). Painted c. 1580.

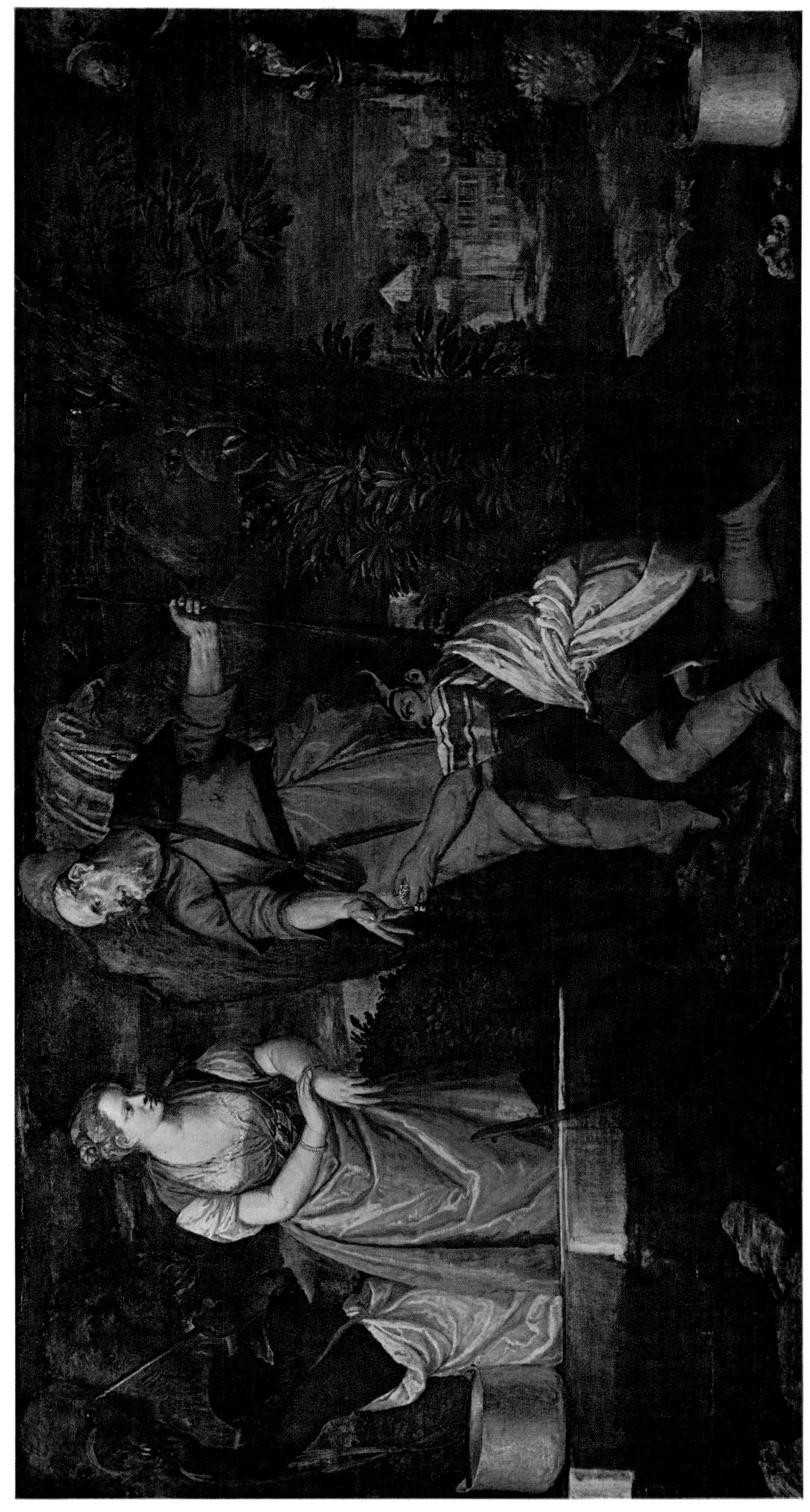

MORETTO DA BRESCIA · Brescian c. 1498-1554

Pietà

Fine art . . . only achieves its highest task when it has taken its place in the same sphere with religion and philosophy, and has become simply a mode of revealing to consciousness and bringing to utterance the Divine Nature, the deepest interests of humanity, and the most comprehensive truths of the mind. It is in works of art that nations have deposited the profoundest intuitions and ideas of their hearts; and fine art is frequently the key—with many nations there is no other—to the understanding of their wisdom and of their religion.

This is an attribute which art shares with religion and philosophy, only in this peculiar mode, that it represents even the highest ideas *in sensuous forms,* thereby bringing them nearer to the character of natural phenomena, to the senses, and to feeling. The world, into whose depths *thought* penetrates, is a supra-sensuous world, which is thus, to begin with, erected as a *beyond* over against immediate consciousness and present sensation; the power which thus rescues itself from the *here,* that consists in the actuality and finiteness of sense, is the freedom of thought in cognition. But the mind is able to heal this schism which its advance creates; it generates out of itself the works of fine art as the first middle term of reconciliation between pure thought and what is external, sensuous, and transitory, between nature with its finite actuality and the infinite freedom of the reason that comprehends. . . .

Art liberates the real import of appearances from the semblance and deception of this bad and fleeting word, and imparts to phenomenal semblances a higher reality, born of mind.

G. W. F. Hegel
Æsthetik (1835)

Hegel has assigned to art its noblest role. We have selected one of the finest paintings of the Renaissance to illustrate his text. This great pictorial achievement is a bridge "between nature with its finite actuality and the infinite freedom of the reason that comprehends." Collections: Earl of Egremont; Cook, Doughty House, Richmond, Surrey. *Samuel H. Kress Collection,* 1952. Wood. Height 69⅛ in.; width 38¾ in. (1.758 x 0.985). Painted in the 1520's.

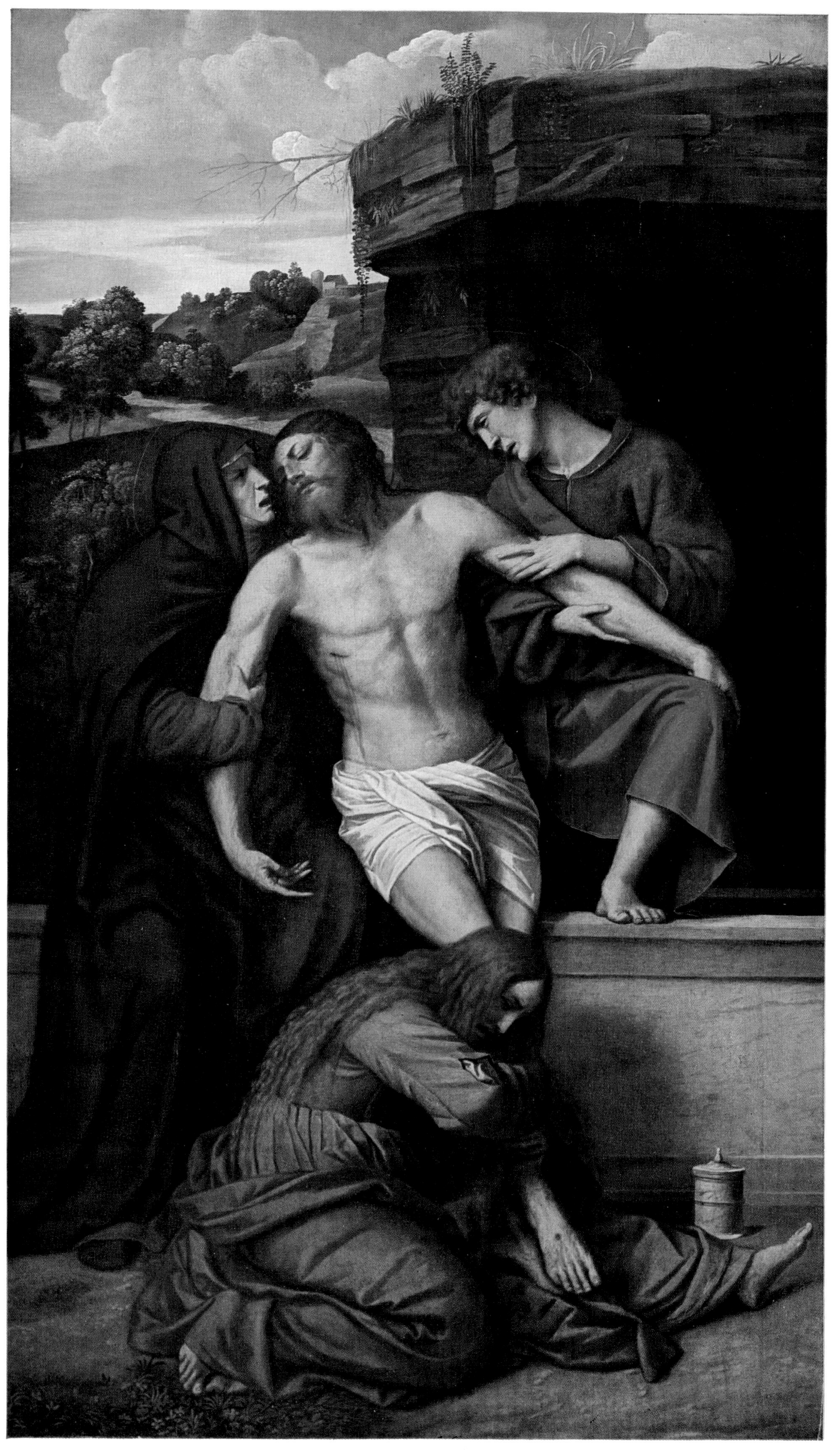

SEBASTIANO DEL PIOMBO · Venetian c. 1485-1547

Portrait of a Humanist

Magus laughs at our National Collection, devastated as it is by the sun, which corrodes the finest canvases as it penetrates window panes which act as magnifying glasses. Picture galleries can only be lighted by skylights; Magus closed and opened the shutters of his museum himself, taking as many pains and precautions with his pictures as with his daughter, his other idol. How well the old picture-fancier knew the laws of painting! According to him, masterpieces had a life of their own; they varied from day to day, and their beauty depended upon the light which came to tint them; he spoke of them as the Dutch used to speak of their tulips, and came to see a certain picture at the moment in which the masterpiece was resplendent in all its glory, when the atmosphere was clear and pure. . . .

As soon as Magus was in the sanctuary, he went straight to four masterpieces which he recognized as the most beautiful in the collection, and by masters not represented in his own. To him they were like the *desiderata* of naturalists, which cause them to undertake voyages to the ends of the earth, to the tropics, through deserts, pampas, savannahs, and virgin forests. The first picture was by Sebastian del Piombo. . . .

In the history of art, Sebastian del Piombo is like a shining point at which three schools have agreed to meet in order to contribute their finest qualities. A Venetian painter, he came to Rome to learn the style of Raphael under the direction of Michelangelo, whose aim it was to send one of his own lieutenants to do battle with that high priest of art. This idle genius, therefore, combined Venetian color, Florentine composition, and the style of Raphael in the few paintings he deigned to paint, and the sketches for them were drawn, it is said, by Michelangelo himself. . . .

Élie Magus had tears in his eyes as he looked at each of the masterpieces in turn.

"I will give you 2000 francs commission for each of these pictures, if you will get them for me for 40,000 francs", he whispered to Mme. Cibot, who was stunned at this fortune which had fallen from the sky. The admiration, or to be more exact, the delirium of Magus had caused such chaos in his mind and in his normal habits of greed that he plunged headlong into this madness, as we have seen.

Honoré de Balzac
Le Cousin Pons (1847)

Waagen, a great connoisseur, who was a contemporary of Balzac, wrote of this picture in his notes on the Lansdowne Collection, "A male portrait, very nobly conceived, and of deep harmony of colouring." Such a painting would have appealed strongly to Cousin Pons, whose collection Magus was intent on acquiring. The scholarly pursuits of the sitter are indicated by books, writing equipment, globe, and compass. Collections: Ghizzi family, Naples; Marquess of Lansdowne, Bowood Hall, Wiltshire. *Samuel H. Kress Collection,* 1961. Wood. Height 53 in.; width 39¾ in. (1.347 x 1.010). Painted c. 1520, according to Dussler and Pallucchini.

GIOVANNI BATTISTA MORONI · Brescian c. 1520-1578

"Titian's Schoolmaster"

The Master said, A gentleman takes as much trouble to discover what is right as lesser men take to discover what will pay.

The Master said, When natural substance prevails over ornamentation, you get the boorishness of the rustic. When ornamentation prevails over natural substance, you get the pedantry of the scribe. Only when ornament and substance are duly blended do you get the true gentleman.

'A gentleman can be broken, but cannot be dented; may be deceived, but cannot be led astray.'

The Master said, A true gentleman is calm and at ease; the Small Man is fretful and ill at ease.

The Master said, The gentleman calls attention to the good points in others; he does not call attention to their defects. The small man does just the reverse of this.

The Master said, 'The demands that a gentleman makes are upon himself; those that a small man makes are upon others.'

Master K'ung said, There are three things that a gentleman fears: he fears the will of Heaven, he fears great men, he fears the words of the Divine Sages. The small man does not know the will of Heaven and so does not fear it. He treats great men with contempt, and scoffs at the words of the Divine Sages.

Confucius
The Analects (6th or 5th Century B.C.)

Portraiture may be great art. There is a sense, indeed, in which it is perhaps the greatest art of any. And portraiture involves expression. Quite true, but expression of what? Of a passion, an emotion, a mood? Certainly not. Paint a man or woman with the damned 'pleasing expression,' or even the 'charmingly spontaneous' so dear to the 'photographic artist,' and you see at once that the thing is a mask, as silly as the old tragic and comic mask. The only expression allowable in great portraiture is the expression of character and moral quality, not of anything temporary, fleeting, accidental. Apart from portraiture you don't want even so much, or very seldom: in fact you only want types, symbols, suggestions. The moment you give what people call expression, you destroy the typical character of heads and degrade them into portraits which stand for nothing.

Edward Burne-Jones
Quoted, Georgiana Burne-Jones, *Memorials of Edward Burne-Jones* (1904)

Moroni has given his sitter that "expression of character and moral quality" which Burne-Jones emphasizes. The portrait epitomizes the Renaissance ideal of a gentleman, which found classic expression in Castiglione's *Il Cortegiano* (1528), and which is an ideal of some universality as Confucius bears witness. Hazlitt (*Sketches of the Principal Picture-Galleries in England,* 1824) said of the picture reproduced: "Not knowing any thing of Moroni, if we had been asked who had done it, we should have replied, *'Either Titian or the Devil.'*... but the eye in *Titian's School-master* is *an eye to look at, not to look with,* or if it looks *at* you, it does not look *through* you, which may be almost made a test of Titian's heads." The portrait was sketched by van Dyck and copied by Rubens. Collections: Palazzo Borghese, Rome; Duke of Bridgewater, Bridgewater House, London; his nephew, 2nd Marquis of Stafford, Stafford House, London; his son, 2nd Duke of Sutherland, Stafford House, in which collection it remained until it came to America. *Widener Collection,* 1942. Canvas. Height 38⅛ in.; width 29¼ in. (0.97 x 0.74). Painted c. 1575.

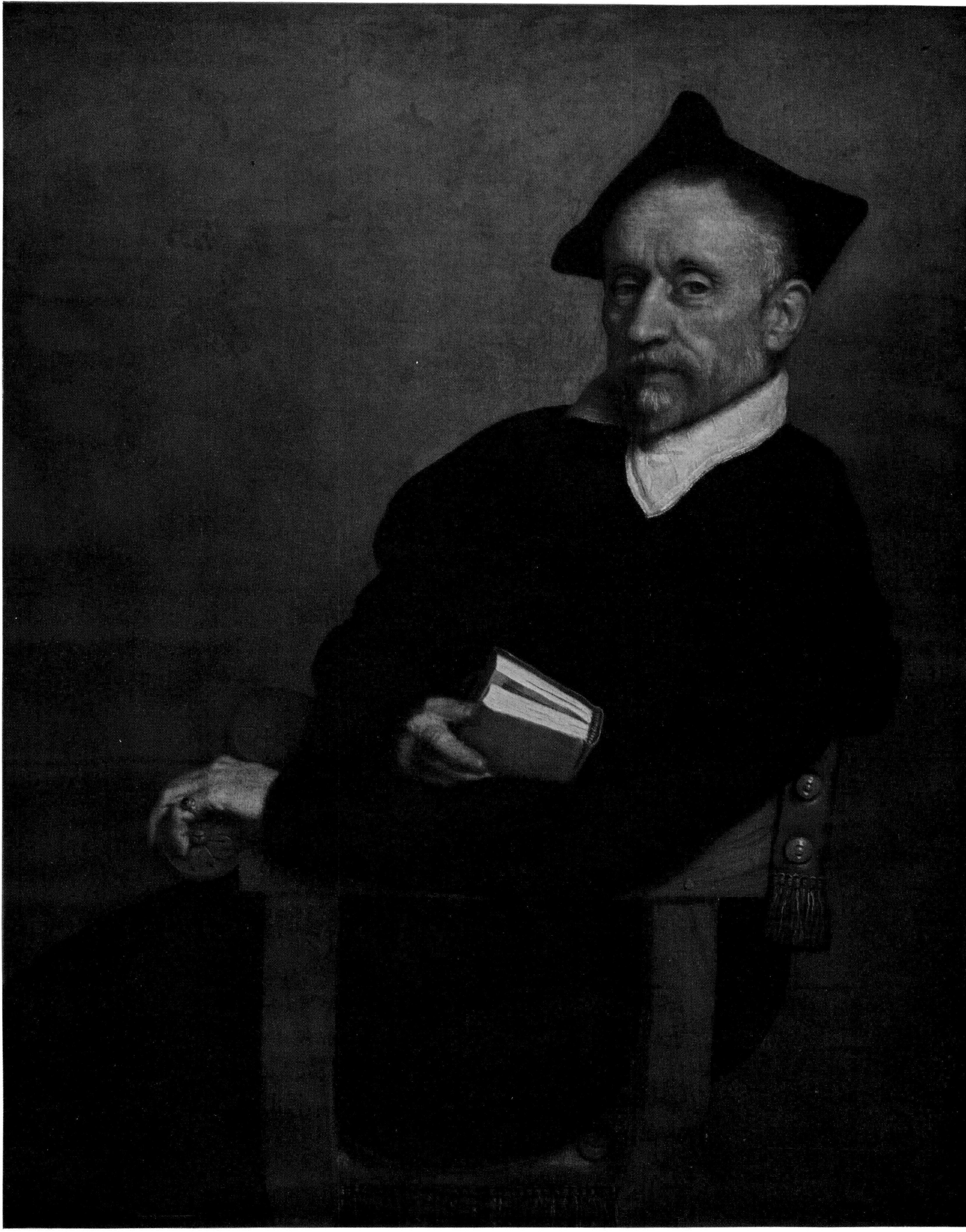

JACOPO TINTORETTO · VENETIAN 1518-1594

The Conversion of Saint Paul

Tintoretto, called by the Italians the thunderbolt of painting, because of his vehement impulsiveness and rapidity of execution, soars above his brethren by the faculty of pure imagination. It was he who brought to its perfection the poetry of *chiaroscuro,* expressing moods of passion and emotion by brusque lights, luminous half-shadows, and semi-opaque darkness, no less unmistakably than Beethoven by symphonic modulations. He too engrafted on the calm and natural Venetian manner something of the Michael Angelesque sublimity, and sought to vary by dramatic movement the romantic motives of his school. In his work, more than in that of his contemporaries, Venetian art ceased to be decorative and idyllic. . . .

The imagination of Tintoretto is too passionate and daring; it scathes and blinds like lightning.

JOHN ADDINGTON SYMONDS
Renaissance in Italy (1877)

"Extravagant, capricious, swift and resolute, with the most terrific imagination ever given to painting." It is thus that Tintoretto is described by his contemporary, Vasari. A special opportunity for exploring the far reaches of imagination was afforded by Paul's vision of the heavenly light that throws him to the ground and strikes consternation into the soldiers accompanying him. Few things are more expressive of terror than a frightened horse and the horses are everywhere in this picture, rearing, falling headlong, dashing away, with mane flying and eyes bulging, beautiful horses that show the impact of Leonardo's drawings and plastic models. Collections: Lord Kinnaird, Rossie Priory, near Inchture, Scotland. *Samuel H. Kress Collection,* 1961. Canvas. Height 60 in.; width 92⅞ in. (1.524 x 2.362). Painted shortly before 1545, according to Suida, or a little later, according to Bercken.

JACOPO TINTORETTO · VENETIAN 1518-1594

Christ at the Sea of Galilee

The prodigious and superhuman in his genius shocks ordinary or placid souls. In truth, no such man has been seen before or since; he is as unique as Michelangelo, Rubens, and Titian. You may call him extravagant, hotheaded, an improviser; you may complain of the darkness of his colors, the contortion of his figures, the disorder of his groups, the hastiness of his brush, the strain and the mannerism which sometimes debase the originality of his style; you may accuse him of the defects of his qualities—that I will permit—but never has there been such a fiery furnace, so burning, so overflowing with outbursts and sputtering of flames, with such soaring of sparks, such sudden and manifold flashes of lightning, such a continuous blazing of unexpected smoke and lights.

I really do not know how to speak of him; I cannot describe his paintings, they are too vast and there are too many of them. It is the inner impetus of his spirit that one must describe; it seems to me that one discovers in him a unique condition, a lightning stroke of inspiration. That is a strong statement, but it corresponds to precise facts, that one can cite. In certain extreme moments, confronted by a great danger, a sudden shock, a man will see distinctly in a flash, with terrible intensity, years of his life, complete landscapes and scenes, sometimes a fragment of an imagined world: the memories of those who have been suffocated, the accounts of people who have narrowly escaped drowning, the confessions of would-be suicides and of opium smokers, and the Indian Puranas all testify to this. The active power of the mind suddenly increased tenfold, a hundredfold, makes the spirit live in this epitome of a moment, more than all the rest of its life. In truth, the result of such a sublime hallucination is usually prostration and illness; but when a temperament is strong enough to bear this electric shock without breaking down, a man like Luther, Saint Ignatius, Saint Paul or any of the great visionaries, will accomplish works that are beyond human capability. Such are the outbursts of creative imagination in the great artists; with fewer counterbalances they were as strong in Tintoretto as in the greatest masters. If one has properly understood the effect of this involuntary and extraordinary state on his tragic nature, and on his color sense, the rest follows from it. . . .

In comparison with him, all painters merely imitate each other. One is always surprised by his pictures; one wonders where he found all this, in what unknown world, fantastic and yet real.

HIPPOLYTE TAINE
Voyage en Italie (1866)

There is no simpler pleasure than looking at a fine Titian, unless it be looking at a fine Tintoret.

HENRY JAMES
Italian Hours (1909)

Probably of the same period as the three paintings commissioned in 1562 for the Scuola di San Marco, now divided between the Accademia, Venice, and the Brera, Milan. In this picture, one of the most remarkable early seascapes in the history of art, Tintoretto anticipates the style of El Greco. The subject follows faithfully the scene described in John xxi. Collections: Count J. Galotti; Arthur Sachs, New York. *Samuel H. Kress Collection,* 1952. Canvas. Height 46 in.; width 66¼ in. (1.17 x 1.685). Painted c. 1560.

EL GRECO · Spanish 1541-1614

Christ Cleansing the Temple

El Greco is probably the greatest experience which could occur to any of us. It is necessarily unique and of a completely different variety from all other artistic impressions which we have gained to date. Not because El Greco is so great, but because he is new. We were brought up with Rembrandt, Rubens, Michael Angelo, with all the other great men of history. We see Goethe at the age of twelve, of twenty, of forty years. Slowly our opinion deepens. We add almost nothing. Unconsciously the sources of our inner beings flow from the contact with the great, grown habitual, and we hardly notice how the river swells because we stand upon the banks. It is never our lot to experience the direct impression of these heroes. Nobody knows when he heard Beethoven for the first time and we remember the first impression we received from Raphael as little as the first words which we spelt as children. . . .

El Greco, however, comes like a flash of lightning. He comes at a moment in which the great experiences, I will not say have come to an end, but when they have at any rate occurred. We had imagined that all that is essential was crammed into the loft and that it could only be a question—so we thought—of putting its contents straight. At best, we still expected the arrival of details, supplements, stragglers, also-rans. And then he comes like a bomb. Our calculations ever since we wore long trousers were based upon three continents: Michael Angelo, Rembrandt, Rubens. Now there is a fourth. Not an island that floats at random in the ocean, not a peninsula which has grown at the extremity of the main land; a real genuine immense continent of the same significance as the three others on which for so-and-so many centuries so-and-so many millions of men have lived; men who enjoy things and have longings like you and I, and who had and have no notion of this constellation in their immediate vicinity.

Julius Meier-Graefe
Spanische Reise (1909)

Meier-Graefe's passage written fifty years ago indicates how recently El Greco has come to be appreciated. His sudden popularity resulted from the distortions made popular by the Post-Impressionists. Today in the light of nonobjective painting, or action painting, the element of shock which impressed Meier-Graefe is gone and we see these pictures as mere variations on the great tradition of Venetian painting, which, incidentally, is a "continent" Meier-Graefe does not mention. Christ Cleansing the Temple is generally considered the earliest signed work by El Greco. It is one of his closest imitations of the Venetian masters, and consequently it is more contorted than distorted. Collections: J. C. Robinson, London; Cook, Doughty House, Richmond, Surrey. *Samuel H. Kress Collection,* 1957. Wood. Height 25¾ in.; width 32¾ in. (0.654 x 0.832). Signed. Painted c. 1570.

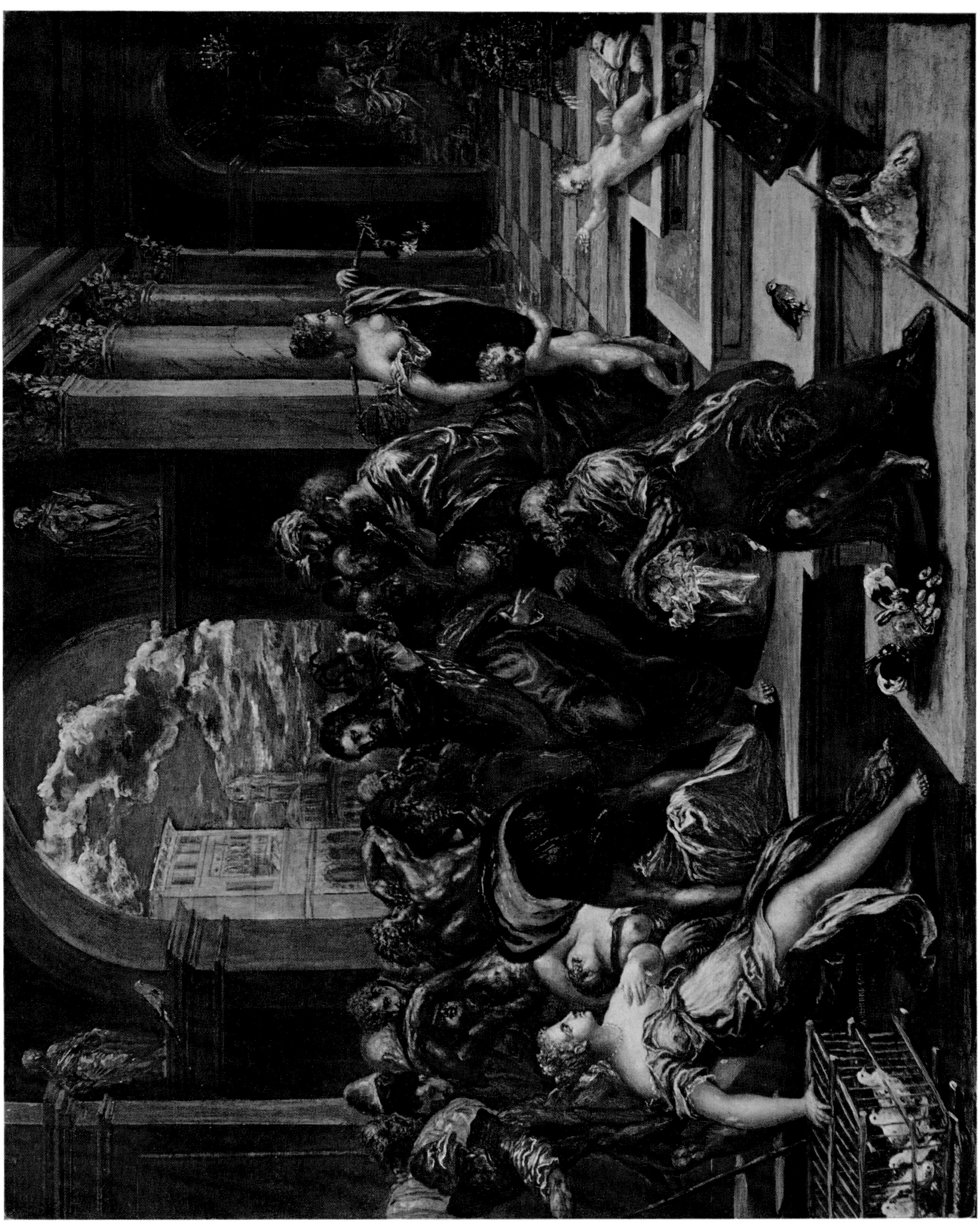

EL GRECO · Spanish 1541-1614

The Virgin with Saint Inés and Saint Tecla

There was in him to my mind a temper that exactly suited the spirit that he found prevalent to some extent in Venice, and at its height in Rome. So he became the greatest of baroque painters. Looking at the whole series of his pictures I seem to see his interest in decoration for decoration's sake grow in intensity. His contemporaries thought that he painted in an increasingly fantastic manner because he went mad. I do not believe it. More recently it has been suggested that he suffered from astigmatism and it has been said that if you put on the right glasses his vertiginous figures would assume normal proportions. I do not believe it. Their immense elongation, which, I may remind the reader, he will find also in many of Tintoretto's pictures, seems to me a natural development of treating the human form as decoration. Because El Greco was aiming at this and nothing else I think he grew more and more indifferent to fact.... If he were alive to-day I imagine he would paint pictures as abstract as the later work of Bracque, Picasso and Fernand Léger. And it may be that the interest in formal design of the present day is due to the same causes as produced baroque art in the sixteenth century. Now too we are spiritually at sixes and sevens. Afraid of the sublime, we take refuge in the multiplication table....

But of course there is more in El Greco than the fantastic patterns he devised, his grace and distinction, the elegance of his gestures and his dramatic intensity, seldom falling into theatricalism, with which as I take it he satisfied the sardonic, ironic, sumptuous, sinister side of his nature.... Then there is his colour. This, I think, was the second of the two methods by which he strove to release his spirit from its burden; and it is his colour that makes him so wonderful an artist. A painter thinks with his brushes. Such thoughts as he has that can be put into words are for the most part commonplace. Why artists are often incomprehensible to other people is that they express their profoundest feelings in a language of their own. I think El Greco put the most serious emotion of his strange, perhaps inexplicable personality into the colours that he set down on canvas. However he acquired his palette, he gave it an intensity, a significance, which were his own. Colour was his complete and unique experience. They are not so far wrong who see in him a mystic, though I cannot help thinking that to look upon him as a religious mystic is superficial. If mysticism is that state that renders you conscious of depths of truth unknown to the intellect, revealing like "glimpses of forgotten dreams" a greater significance in life and union with some larger reality, then I think you can hardly fail to find it in El Greco's painting. I seem to see as great a mystic rapture in the painting of the right side of the body of Christ in the Crucifixion in the Louvre as in any of the experiences of Santa Teresa.

W. Somerset Maugham
Don Fernando (1935)

The painting was begun in 1597, according to the records of the lawsuit brought by the donors, who considered El Greco's charges exorbitant, and was completed in 1599. It was placed in the Chapel of San José in Toledo, where it formed a companion picture to the Saint Martin and the Beggar reproduced on page 201. Collections: Chapel of San José, Toledo. *Widener Collection,* 1942. Canvas. Height 76⅛ in.; width 40½ in. (1.935 x 1.03). Inscribed with the Greek initials of El Greco's name on the forehead of the lion.

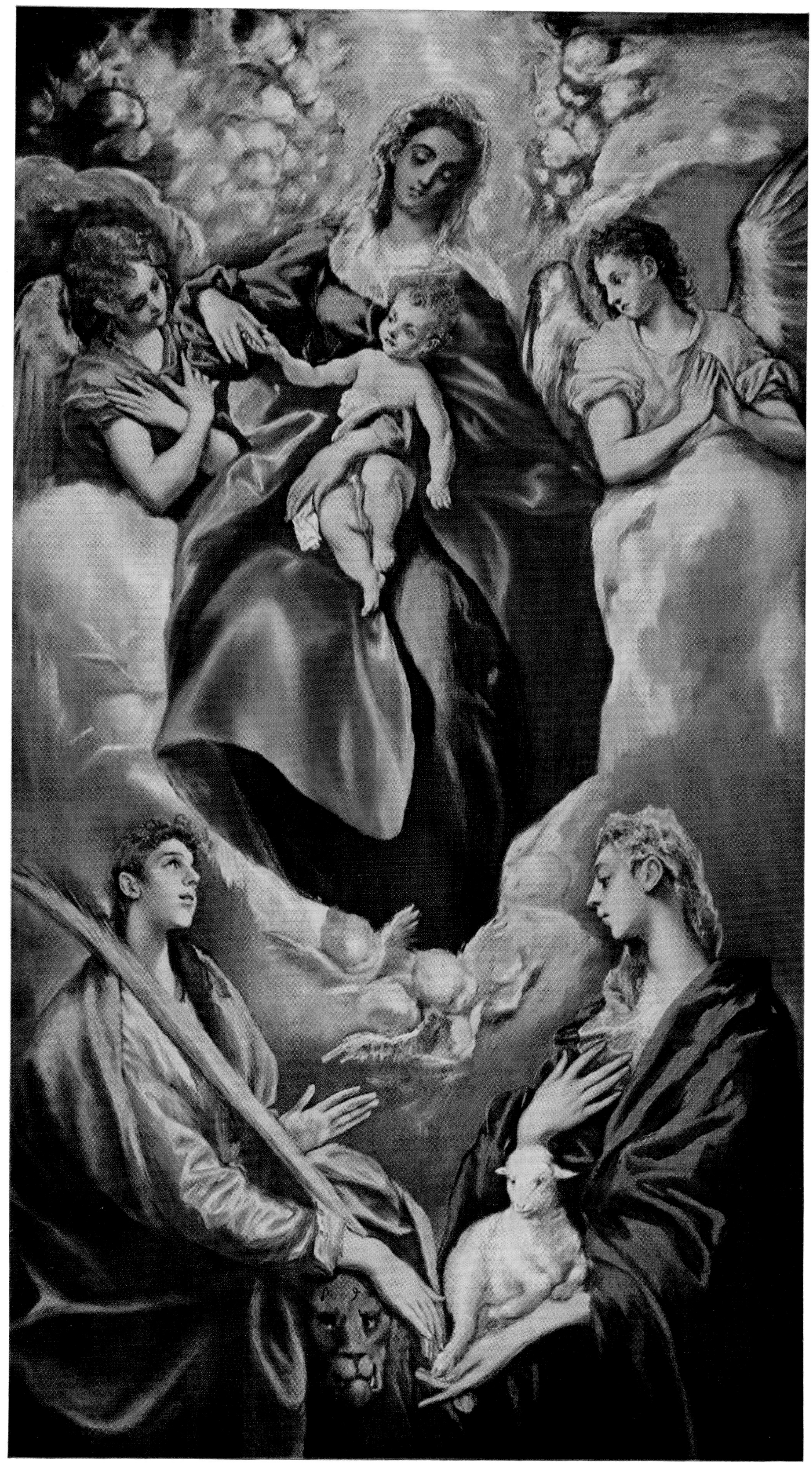

EL GRECO · Spanish 1541-1614

Saint Martin and the Beggar

Toledo is a knife. Greco has cut his name deeply into its blade. . . .

Hidden rhythm is developed from one end to the other of Greco's canvases.

Never mind about those square clouds, or that flat face, or that enormous leg. Nature must obey, and allow herself to be used to fill such spaces as this imperious master may assign to her.

Whether it is Greco or Cézanne, these skilful groupings and camouflaged problems on which the picture's harmony depends—these basement kitchens as it were—may be mistaken for either childishness or madness.

Barrès, though not so blind as to fall into that error, accounts for the deformations in Greco's pictures on sentimental grounds. He will only admit a spasm—the spiritualization of the body—instead of seeing that it is also largely a question of architecture. 'Architecture corrected by emotion.'

Greco is first and foremost a painter, and should not be confounded with the intellectual Leonardo.

Jean Cocteau
Visites à Maurice Barrès (1924)

There is no Excellent *Beauty,* that hath not some Strangenesse in the Proportion.

Francis Bacon
Essayes (1625)

Painted for the Chapel of San José, Toledo, this painting and its companionpiece (see page 199) are documented by the original contract, dated November 20, 1597, which states that El Greco is to be paid 31,328 reales. This was an unusually high price and it was necessary for El Greco to sue for payment. The fact that Saint Martin, when represented as a soldier, rides a white horse is explained by G. G. King (*Art Bulletin,* 1922), as a reference to the vision in Revelation vi: 2, in which the rider on a white horse "went forth conquering, and to conquer." Saint Martin dividing his cloak with a beggar was a favorite subject in Spain, and especially with El Greco. The present painting is probably the first of his several versions that have been preserved. Collections: Chapel of San José, Toledo. *Widener Collection,* 1942. Canvas. Height 76⅛ in.; width 40½ in. (1.935 x 1.03). Signed. Painted 1597-99.

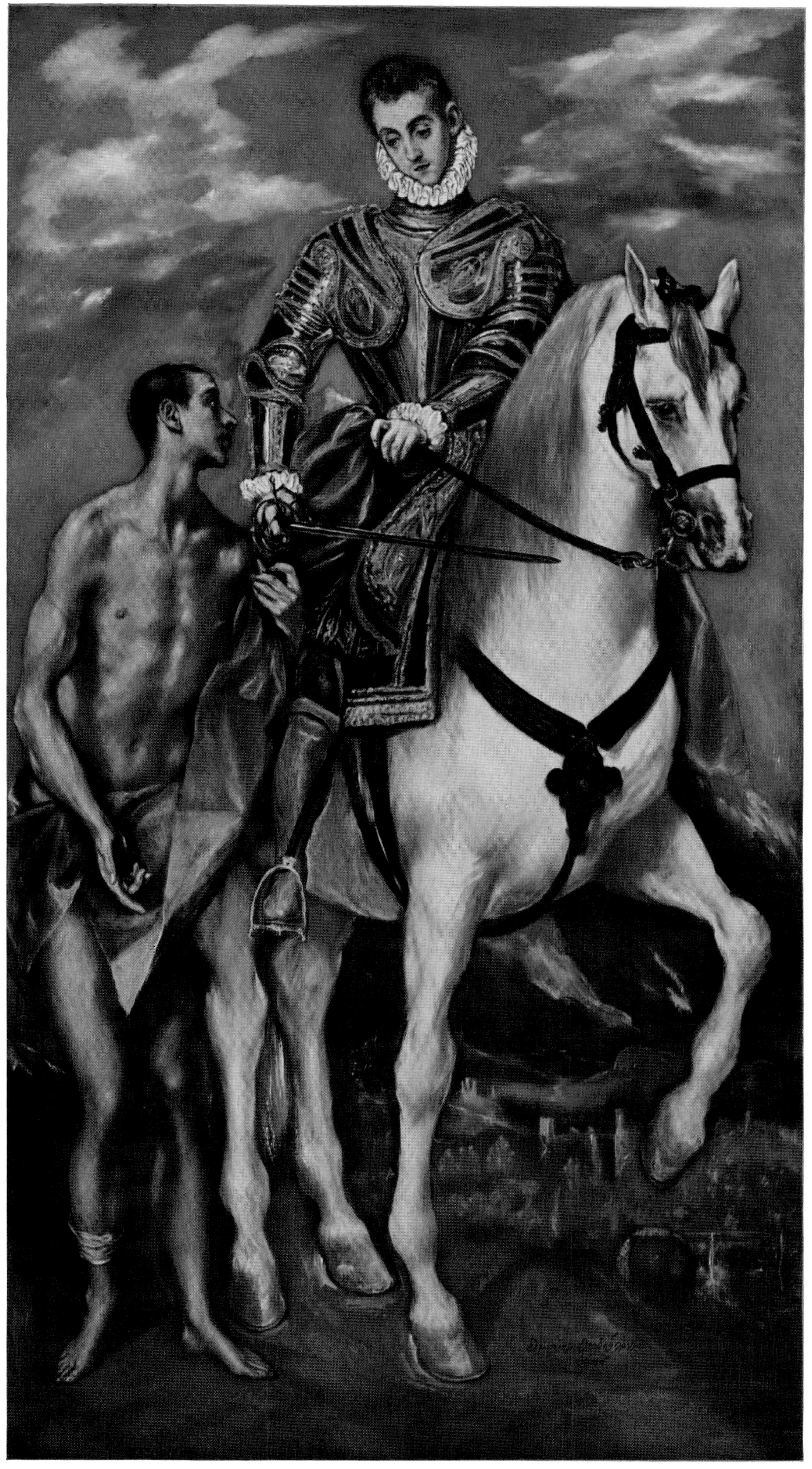

EL GRECO · Spanish 1541-1614

Laocoön

A greater omen and of worse portent
Did our unwary minds with fear torment,
Concurring to produce the dire event.
Laocoön, Neptune's priest by lot that year,
With solemn pomp then sacrificed a steer,
When, dreadful to behold, from sea we spied
Two serpents, ranked abreast, the seas divide,
And smoothly sweep along the swelling tide.
Their flaming crests above the waves they show;
Their bellies seem to burn the seas below;
Their speckled tails advance to steer their course,
And on the sounding shore the flying billows force.
And now the strand, and now the plain they held,
Their ardent eyes with bloody streaks were filled;
Their nimble tongues they brandished as they came,
And licked their hissing jaws, that spluttered flame.
We fled amazed. Their destined way they take,
And to Laocoön and his children make.
And first around the tender boys they wind,
Then with their sharpened fangs their limbs and bodies grind.
The wretched father, running to their aid
With pious haste, but vain, they next invade.
Twice round his waist their winding volumes rolled,
And twice about his gasping throat they fold.
The priest thus doubly choked, their crests divide,
And towering o'er his head, in triumph ride.
With both his hands he labours at the knots,
His holy fillets the blue venom blots;
His roaring fills the flitting air around.
Thus, when an ox receives a glancing wound,
He breaks his bands, the fatal halter flies,
And with loud bellowings breaks the yielding skies.
Their tasks performed, the serpents quit their prey,
And to the tower of Pallas made their way.
Couched at her feet, they lie protected there
By her large buckler and protended spear.

Virgil
Aeneid (c. 19 B.C.)

Although El Greco was born a Greek, he painted only one subject derived from the history or mythology of Greece, the story of Laocoön and his sons. Possibly it was the sculptured group of the Laocoön, discovered in 1506 and exhibited in the Vatican during El Greco's sojourn in Rome, that inspired him to paint his interpretation of the legend. Among the several versions of the story in Greek and Latin, Virgil's is the most famous; it is uncertain which version El Greco followed. The three figures at the right have been conjectured to be Apollo, Artemis, and Hera, deities connected with the sea, hence present at the tragedy involving Poseidon's priest. In the background is a view of El Greco's adopted home, Toledo. Collections: Probably the large painting of Laocoön listed in 1614 in the inventory of El Greco's estate in Toledo; Dukes of Montpensier, Seville; Palace of San Telmo, Seville; Infante Don Antonio de Orleans, Sanlúcar de Barrameda; E. Fischer, Charlottenburg; Prince Paul of Yugoslavia, Belgrade. *Samuel H. Kress Collection,* 1946. Canvas. Height 54⅛ in.; width 67⅞ in. (1.375 x 1.725). Painted c. 1610.

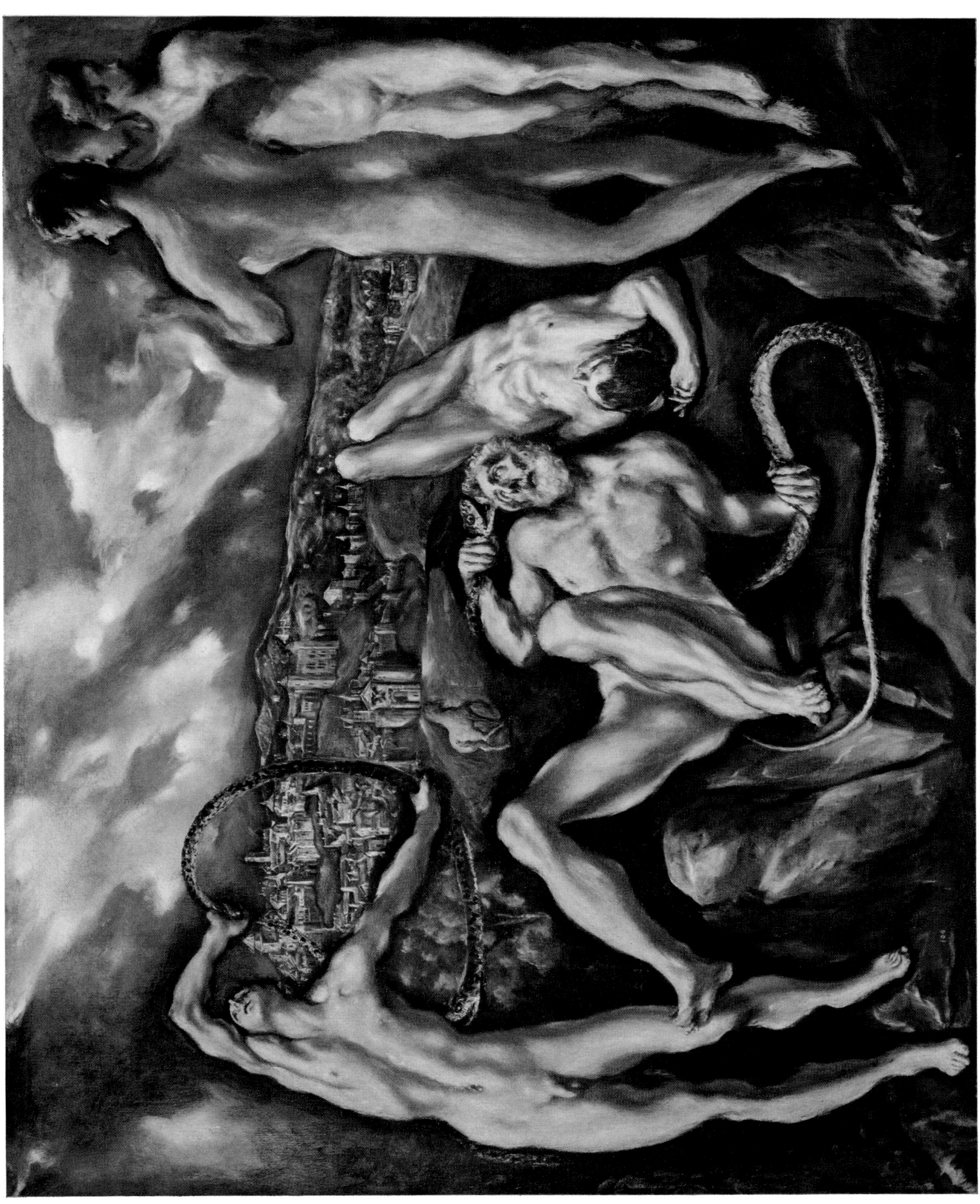

VELÁZQUEZ · SPANISH 1599-1660

The Needlewoman

Now, in the usual "pictures of the year" there is but one flesh, that shall do service under all circumstances, whether the person painted be in the soft light of the room or out in the glare of the open. The one aim of the unsuspecting painter is to make his man "stand out" from the frame—never doubting that, on the contrary, he should really, and in truth absolutely does, stand *within* the frame —and at a depth behind it equal to the distance at which the painter sees his model. The frame is, indeed, the window through which the painter looks at his model, and nothing could be more offensively inartistic than this brutal attempt to thrust the model on the hitherside of this window!

Yet this is the false condition of things to which all have become accustomed, and in the stupendous effort to bring it about, exaggeration has been exhausted—and the traditional means of the incompetent can no further go.

Lights have been heightened until the white of the tube alone remains—shadows have been deepened until black alone is left. Scarcely a feature stays in its place, so fierce is its intention of "firmly" coming forth; and in the midst of this unseemly struggle for prominence, the gentle truth has but a sorry chance, falling flat and flavourless, and without force.

The Master from Madrid, himself, beside this monster success of mediocrity, would be looked upon as mild: *beau bien sûre, mais pas "dans le mouvement"!*

Whereas, could the people be induced to turn their eyes but for a moment, with the fresh power of comparison, upon their fellow-creatures as they pass in the gallery, they might be made dimly to perceive (though I doubt it, so blind is their belief in the bad) how little they resemble the impudent images on the walls! . . . And then it might be explained to their riveted intelligence how they had mistaken meretriciousness for mastery, and by what mean methods the imposture had been practised upon them.

JAMES A. MCNEILL WHISTLER
The Gentle Art of Making Enemies (1890)

Whistler learned from "the Master from Madrid," as he called Velázquez, to paint in a restricted key. This is a practice that Alberti also stresses (see page 22). Such organization of tone was often ignored by fashionable painters like Sargent and Boldini, who frequently exaggerated high lights and illusionistic feats of modeling until their sitters often seem to step out of the frame. The painting reproduced, thought to be of Velázquez's daughter and probably identical with the "Head of a Woman Sewing" recorded in the inventory of his studio at the time of his death, is a good illustration of the principles Whistler was preaching. Collections: Amedee, Marquis de Govello de Keriaval, Château de Kerlevenant, Sarzeau, Morbihan, Brittany; Mme. Christiane de Polès, Paris. *Andrew Mellon Collection,* 1937. Canvas. Height 29⅛ in.; width 23⅜ in. (0.74 x 0.60). Painted c. 1640.

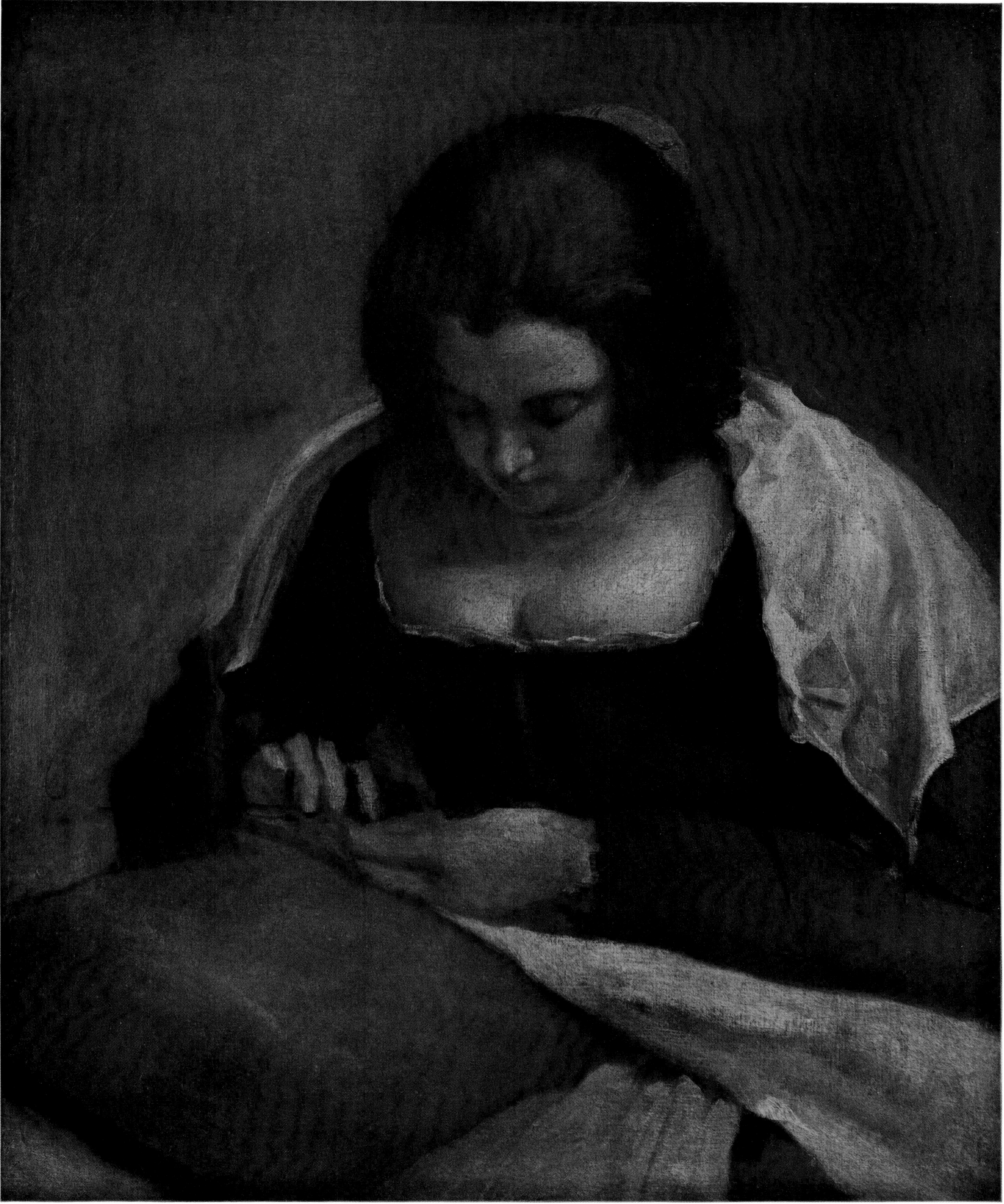

VELÁZQUEZ · Spanish 1599-1660

Pope Innocent X

Everything is done at the first stroke; no glazes, no overloaded colors, no professional tricks. The brush, freely playing in the thick pigments, where the trace of each hair is still visible, writes the forms, defines the muscles, identifies the setting, distributes light and shadow with sincerity and clarity and, at the same time, incomparable breadth. Never did a richer palette charm the eye. However, the general tone remains grave, for Velázquez does not employ colors which are in themselves brilliant. It is not by the use of blues, reds, greens and vivid yellows that he achieves that intense and luminous effect, that warm atmosphere which bathes his figures, but rather by broken tones, by skilful opposition of gradations, by an instinctive feeling for the color proper to objects. In this respect he is an unrivaled master. The Venetians and the Flemings do not have that restrained splendor, tranquil and profound, suggesting the luxury of houses which have enjoyed wealth for many generations.

However, Velázquez was realistic, like the art of his age, but how superior! He painted only from life, and having left the school of the frenzied Herrera, the Elder, to enter that of Pacheco, he would paint gourds, vegetables, game, fish and similar subjects, for practice.

The young master did not think these studies beneath his dignity. He brought to them that sovereign simplicity and that grandiose breadth which are the essence of his style, scorning all useless detail. Treated thus, these fruits might have been posed upon a golden platter on a royal sideboard; these viands, of epic import, might have figured at the Marriage at Cana.—Velázquez does not seek out beauty as did the great Italian artists, nor does he pursue ideal ugliness as do the realists of our age. He accepts nature as it is, freely, and reproduces it in its absolute truth, with a life, an illusion, and a miraculous power, so that whether beautiful, trivial, or ugly, it is always enhanced by the character and effect he bestows on it. Like the sun, which impartially sheds its light on all objects, converting a heap of straw into a mound of gold, a drop of water into a diamond, and a rag into a cloak of purple, Velázquez sheds his radiant color over all things, and without changing them gives them an inestimable value.—Touched by this brush, as by a fairy wand, ugliness becomes beauty; a deformed dwarf with a snub nose and flat wizened face delights the beholder more than a Venus or an Apollo. When Velázquez is confronted by beauty, how magnificently he expresses it, without witless flattery, preserving its bloom, its velvety quality, its grace, its charm, and augmenting it with a mysterious attraction, with a delicate and supreme strength! Have perfection pose for him, and he will paint it with a noble ease and not be overcome by it. Nothing that exists could baffle his brush.

Théophile Gautier
Tableaux à la plume (1880)

According Beruete (*The School of Madrid*) this is a preliminary study from life for the celebrated portrait in the Doria Collection, Rome. It has an immediacy and an uncompromising realism afterwards generalized in the larger work. The portrait belonged at one time to Sir Robert Walpole. His son Horace, in cataloguing the collection, noted that Innocent X was considered in his day the ugliest man in Rome. Collections: Acquired from the Walpole Collection, Houghton Hall, Norfolk, England, in 1779 for the Hermitage Gallery, Leningrad, by Catherine the Great. *Andrew Mellon Collection,* 1937. Canvas. Height 19½ in.; width 16¼ in. (0.49 x 0.42). Painted c. 1650.

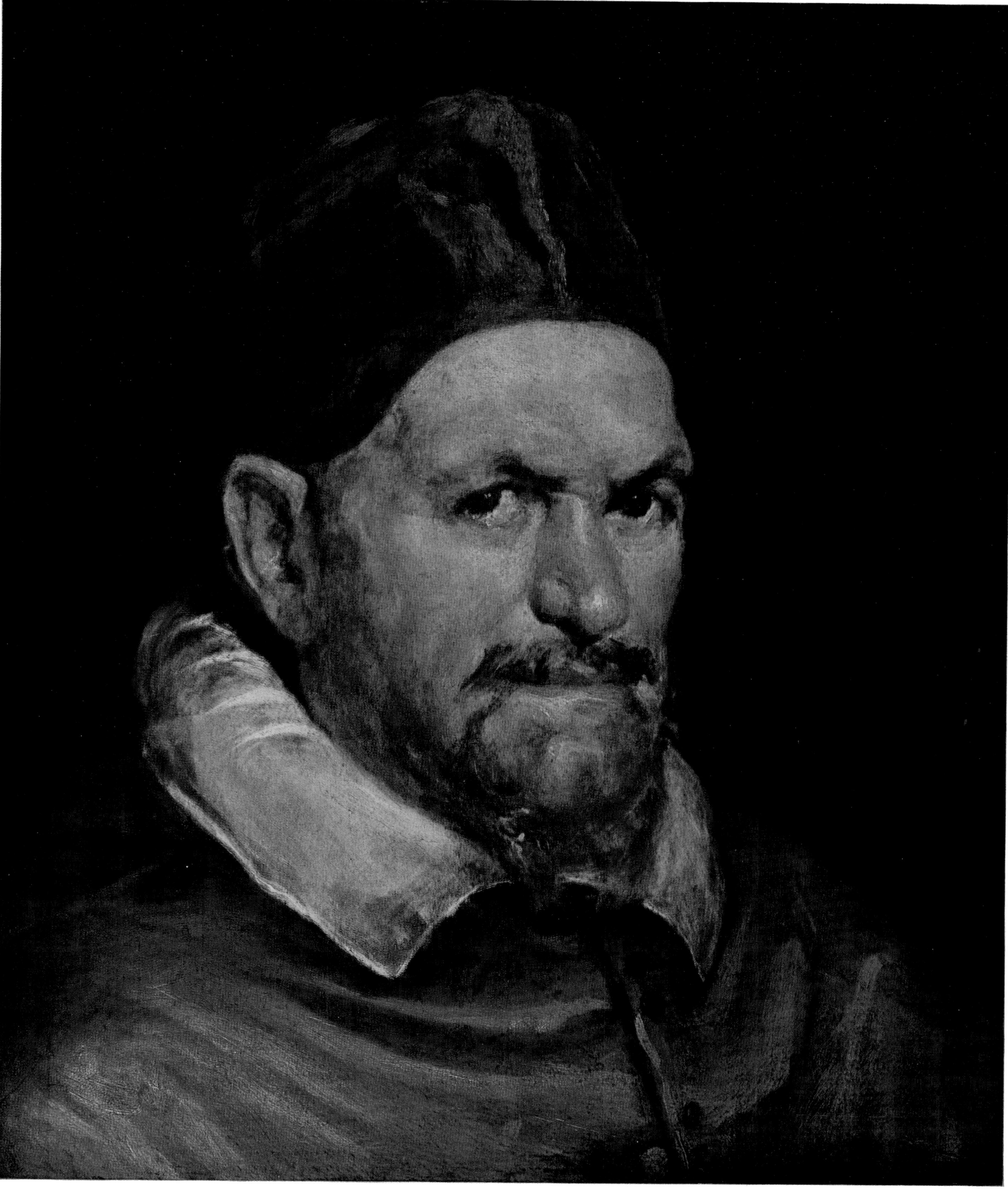

FRANCISCO DE ZURBARÁN · Spanish 1598-1664

Saint Jerome with Saint Paula and Saint Eustochium

Where he generally maintains his excellence is in the rendering of draperies or cloths. In these the touch is mostly firm and the folds are arranged with precision, emphasized especially in the shadows. The pleating is logical and very natural, yet not always convincing. Underneath the habits, human life rarely pulsates. We do not feel it hidden under the cloth, nor do we realize that a human form is concealed within. These works are a study of draperies of great value, if we consider them separately, as an admirable and picturesque reproduction, but the painter did not put into them—on account of having used the manikin excessively—anything but the wish to copy things minutely. The real essence, the life, the true spirit, was reserved by him for the expression in the eyes of saints, of ascetics and devotees in ecstasy, and of monks lost in profound meditations.

For those who lived in the cloister with an unquiet soul; for those who gave themselves up to ineffable dreams; for those who hoped for the great beyond promised to the good; for the mystic whose exaltation leads him to a sacred sacrifice; for the ascetics who annihilate in ecstasies their earthly passions; for the monks, writers, philosophers, theologians who worked for culture, Zurbarán kept the power of his expressive pencil. In their faces, as the noblest of human features, he concentrated life—contemplative, intellectual life—the emotion which overwhelms, or the creative force which culminates in a state of mingled joy and sweet pain, resulting from the mental perturbation that causes it.

D. M. Rodríguez Codolá
Arquitectura y construcción (1905)

Saint Jerome is identified by his cardinal's hat. The older of the nuns is Saint Paula, who accompanied Saint Jerome from Rome to Bethlehem, where he founded a monastery for men and Saint Paula a convent for women. Saint Jerome wrote her biography and addressed to her many of his letters of instruction. The younger nun is her daughter Saint Eustochium. Collections: Frank Hall Standish; bequeathed by Standish to King Louis Philippe, Louvre, Paris; Alphonse Oudry, Paris. *Samuel H. Kress Collection,* 1952. Canvas. Height 96½ in.; width 68⅛ in. (2.451 x 1.73). According to Soria, painted c. 1640, perhaps for the convent of Saint Paula of the Jeronymite Nuns in Seville, where extensive decorations by other artists are documented in the years shortly before and after 1640.

MURILLO · Spanish 1617-1682

A Girl and Her Duenna

He was an artist of feminine and receptive temperament, a realist indeed, but with no virile force, inapt to express the vigorous dramatic qualities which most natively find expression in Spanish art. But his hand was highly accomplished and his taste showed a finer sensibility than is common in Spain; he was sensitive to beauty, especially to the idyllic beauty of homely landscape scenes (though he was here largely a follower of Bassano), and to the plebeian charm of the Spanish peasant. His quick eye and ready hand were forced to adapt themselves to the needs of a city in which beauty was dedicated almost altogether to the service of religion. That circumstance, though it led to the production of pictures which made Murillo's fame, has yet been unfortunate for his reputation in the highest sense. Of all Spanish painters, Murillo alone, the genuine child of Andalusia, may be said to represent the spirit of what we term the "South." For that very reason, perhaps, he was not so typically and essentially Spanish as Ribera was. He was without the Spanish dramatic aptitude, without the sincerity of intense religious feeling. Murillo's famous Virgins in the clouds, after the manner of Ribera's great Salamanca "Conception," however delicious the glowing haze in which they live, are nearly always pretty peasant girls, posing in beautiful robes that do not belong to them, and simulating ecstatic emotions they have never felt. His other religious pictures are similarly gracious and charming, similarly unconvincing. When we can forget that we are looking at a religious picture, or when the painter was free to devote himself to frankly secular subjects, we can better enjoy the qualities of his art. It is true that his beggar-boys are just as deliberately and self-consciously picturesque as his saints are deliberately and self-consciously holy. Still, no other Spanish painter has so agreeably seized the peasant life of Spain, or rather of Andalusia, at the points where it fell in harmoniously with his own pretty mannerisms; in this field, indeed, he sometimes seems both sensitive and sincere, able to present life for what it is worth. Even the absence of dramatic instinct helped him here. His love of beauty and refinement, especially when manifested in a plebeian shape, his idyllic feeling for the beauty of pastoral repose in a patriarchal age. . . . his softly bright and luminous colouring, his facile skill in realistic detail—all these things must make Murillo a fascinating and peculiar figure in Spanish painting, though they cannot enable us to place him beside Velazquez and Ribera.

Havelock Ellis
The Soul of Spain (1908)

Traditionally known as Las Gallegas, the Galicians, because the painting is said to portray two notorious courtesans of Seville, sisters who had come to the city from the province of Galicia. A slightly smaller repetition of this painting was in the Munro-Ferguson Collection at Novar, Ross-shire. Collections: The Duke of Almodóvar, Madrid; Lord Heytesbury, Wiltshire. *Widener Collection,* 1942. Canvas. Height 50¼ in.; width 41¾ in. (1.277 x 1.061). Painted c. 1670.

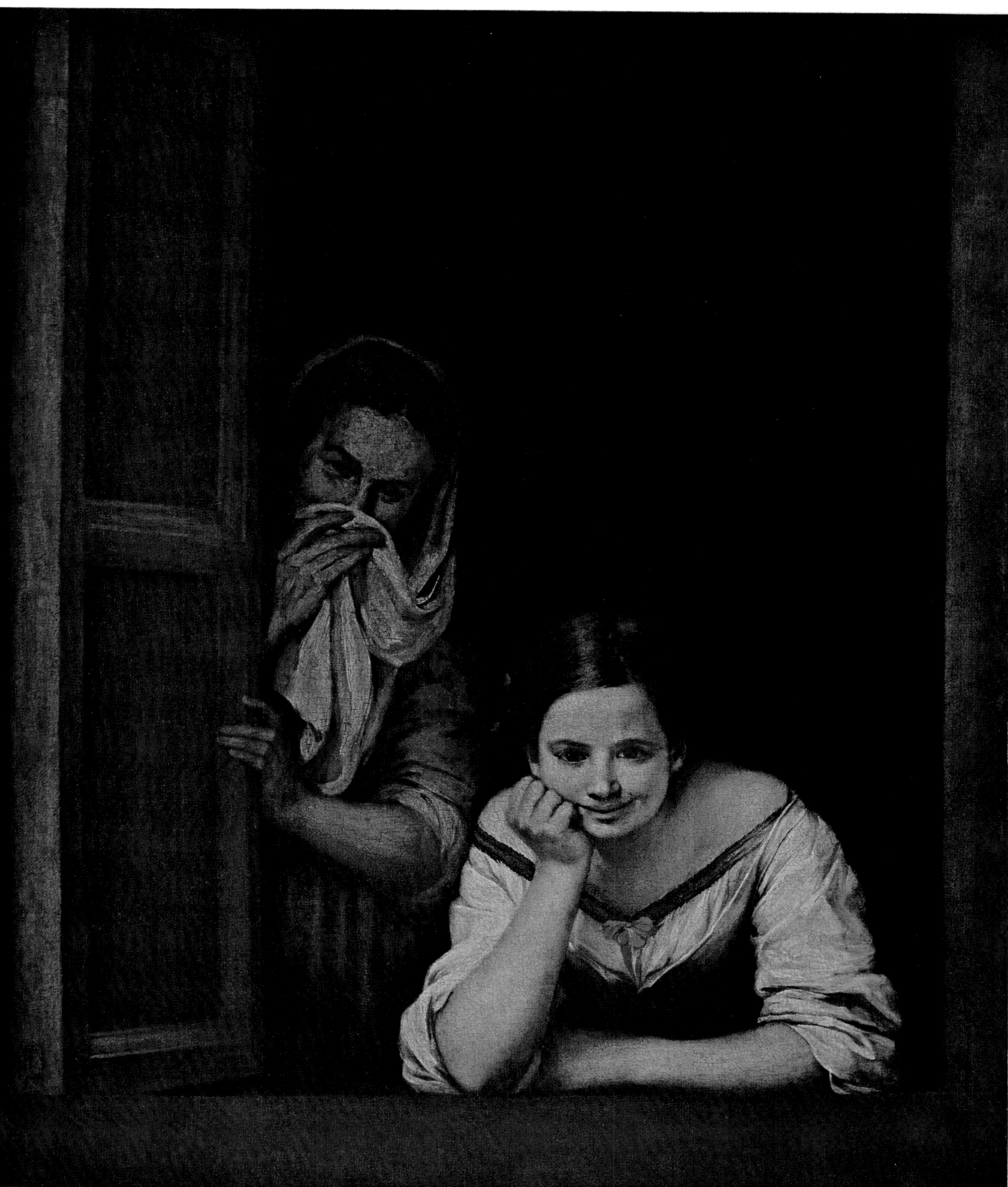

MURILLO · Spanish 1617-1682

The Return of the Prodigal Son

If there be a real law of Nature, that is to say any instinct that is universally and permanently rooted in animals and men (which is not beyond dispute), I may say that, in my opinion, next to the anxiety for self-preservation and avoiding what is harmful, which is possessed by every animal, the affection which the begetter has for his offspring takes the second place. And, because Nature seems to have recommended to us this affection, looking to the extension and advance of the successive parts of this her machine, it is not to be wondered at if the love of children towards their parents, since it goes backwards, is not so great.

To which may be added that other Aristotelian consideration, that the man who benefits another loves him better than he is loved by the other; and that he to whom a thing is owing loves better than he who owes. Every artisan loves his work better than he would be loved by the work if it had feeling; since Being is a thing to be cherished, and Being consists in motion and action. Wherefore every one in some sort lives in his work. He who benefits another does a beautiful and worthy deed; he who receives, only a useful one. Now the useful is much less to be loved than the beautiful. The beautiful is stable and permanent, affording him who has exercised it a constant gratification. The useful is easily lost and escapes, nor is the memory of it either so fresh or so pleasing. Those things are most dear to us that have cost us most; and it is more difficult to give than to take.

Michel de Montaigne
Essais (1595)

The French military commander, Marshal Soult, carried back from the conquest of Spain hundreds of paintings which are now scattered over Europe. Among those looted pictures, which were sold after the collapse of Napoleon, was the Prodigal Son. Originally it formed part of the decoration of the church built by the Brotherhood of La Caridad in Seville in connection with their Hospital of Saint George. The present canvas, together with Moses Striking the Rock (still in La Caridad), Abraham and the Angels (formerly in Stafford House and now in the National Gallery of Canada, Ottawa), and the Charity of San Juan de Dios (La Caridad), hung on the Gospel side of the nave. On the opposite side its counterpart was Christ Healing the Paralytic (National Gallery, London), and the other compositions were the Miracle of the Loaves and Fishes (La Caridad), Saint Peter in Prison (Hermitage, Leningrad), and Saint Elizabeth of Hungary Healing the Sick (now in La Caridad). Collections: La Caridad, Seville; Marshal Soult, Paris; Duke of Sutherland, Stafford House, London. *Gift of the Avalon Foundation,* 1948. Canvas. Height 93 in.; width 102¾ in. (2.363 x 2.61). Painted between 1670 and 1674.

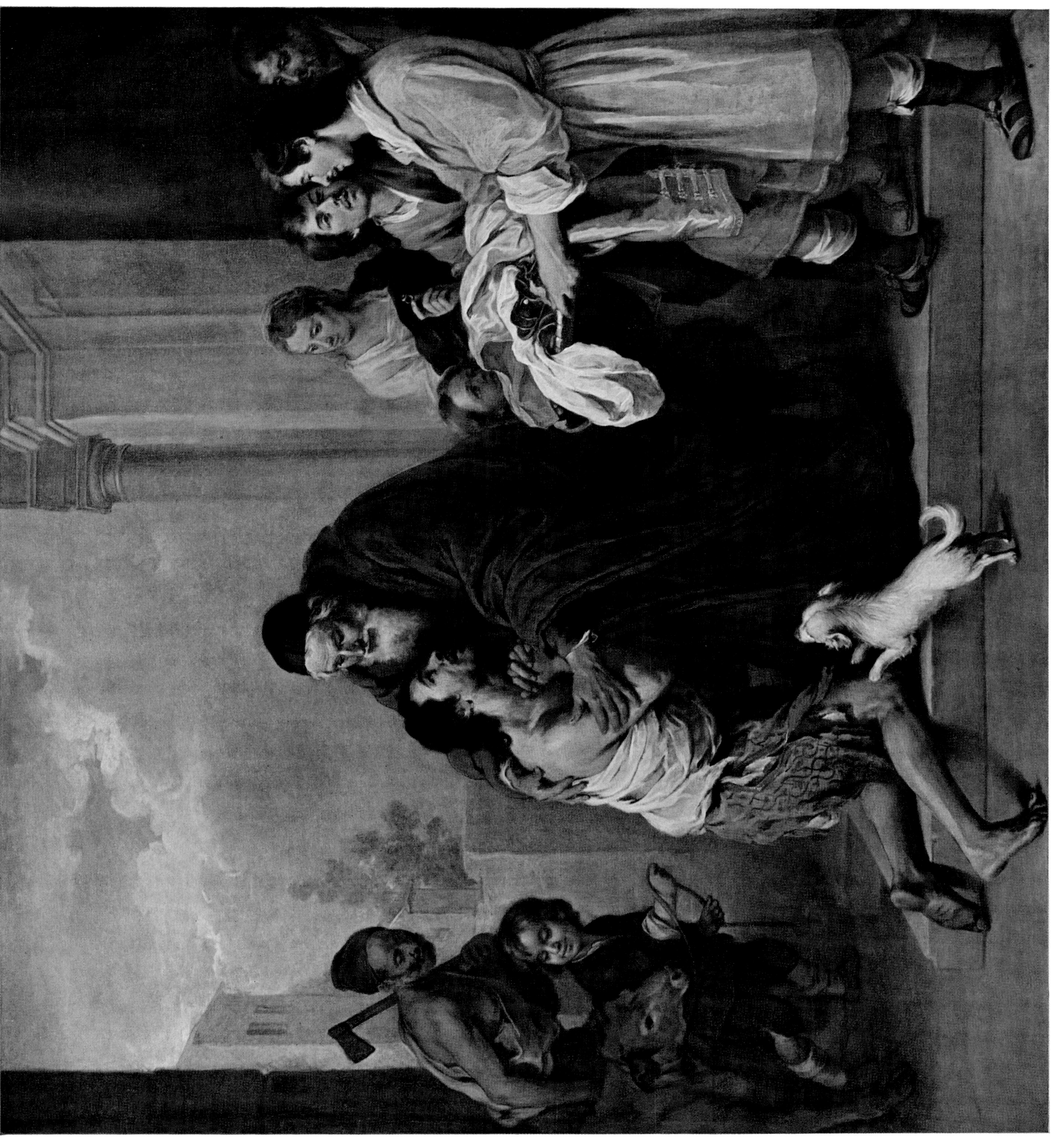

JUAN DE VALDÉS LEAL · Spanish 1622-1690

The Assumption of the Virgin

Hark! she is call'd, the parting houre is come.
Take thy Farewell, poor world! heaun must goe home.
A peice of heau'nly earth; Purer & brighter
Then the chast starres, whose choise lamps come to light her
While through the crystall orbes, clearer then they
She climbes; and makes a farre more milkey way.
She's calld. Hark, how the dear immortall doue
Sighes to his syluer mate rise vp, my loue!
Rise vp, my fair, my spottlesse one!
The winter 's past, the rain is gone.
  The spring is come, the flowrs appear
No sweets, but thou, are wanting here.
    Come away, my loue!
    Come away, my doue! cast off delay,
    The court of heau'n is come
    To wait vpon thee home; Come come away!
    The flowrs appear.
Or quickly would, wert thou once here.
The spring is come, or if it stay,
'Tis to keep time with thy delay.
The rain is gone, except so much as we
Detain in needfull teares to weep the want of thee.
    The winter 's past.
    or if he make lesse hast,
His answer is, why she does so.
If sommer come not, how can winter goe....
Goe then; goe Gloriovs.
    On the golden wings
Of the bright youth of heaun, that sings
Vnder so sweet a Burthen. Goe,
Since thy dread son will haue it so.
And while thou goest, our song & we
Will, as we may, reach after thee.
Hail, holy Queen of humble hearts!
We in thy prayse will haue our parts.

Richard Crashaw
In the Gloriovs Assvmption of Ovr Blessed Lady (1652)

Mario Praz in his essay *The Flaming Heart* points out that Crashaw has "a strain of feminine tenderness by which some of his poems seem to be related to Murillo's delicate and mellow sacred paintings. The exceeding *morbidezza* of these lyrics, the lavish use of such adjectives as 'sweet,' 'dear,' the refined grace of the similes and the diluted fluency of the verse, seem to proceed from that world where tender saints with motherly fondness stretch out their soft arms." Valdés Leal rivaled Murillo during his lifetime. Both worked in Seville, but Valdés Leal's extravagantly gesticulating figures correspond even more closely than Murillo's sweet and tranquil saints to Crashaw's conceits, to his verbal turbulence. Collections: Marquise Landolfo, Carcano, Paris; Dr. Carvalho, Paris. *Samuel H. Kress Collection,* 1961. Canvas. Height 84⅜ in.; width 61½ in. (2.151 x 1.563). Signed. Painted c. 1670.

FRANS HALS · Dutch c. 1580-1666

Balthasar Coymans

Drop the catalogue and use your own eyes. The first impression is profound; not that Hals was profound in the sense of Rembrandt's profundity, but because of the almost terrifying vitality of these portraits. Prosaic men and women, great trenchermen, devourers of huge pasties, mowers down of wine-bottles and beer-tankards, they live with such vitality on the canvases of Hals that you instinctively lower your voice. The paint-imprisoned ghosts of these jolly officers, sharpshooters, regents, and shrewd-looking old women regents are not so disquieting as Rembrandt's misty evocations. They touch hands with you across the centuries, and finally you wonder why they don't step out the frame and greet you. Withal, no trace of literalism, of obvious contours or tricky effects. Honest, solid paint, but handled by the greatest master of the brush that ever lived—save Velasquez. How thin and unsubstantial modern painting is if compared to this magician, how even his greatest followers, Manet and Sargent, seem incomplete. Manet, with his abridgments, his suppressions, his elliptical handling, never had the smiling confidence of Hals in facing a problem. The Frenchman is more subtle, also more evasive; and there is no hint in him of the trite statement of a fact that we encounter in Bartholomew Van der Helst—himself a great painter. Hals had not the poetic vision of Rembrandt, but he possessed a more dexterous hand, a keener eye. Judged according to the rubric of sheer paint, sheer brush-work, not Rubens, not Van Dyck, was such a virtuoso. Despite his almost incredible swiftness of execution, Hals got closer to the surfaces of what is called "actual" life than any of the masters with the exception of the supreme Spaniard. . . .

What a colourist! What nuances he produces on a restrained key-board! The tones modulate, their juxtaposition causes no harsh discords. The velvet black, silvery grays, whites that are mellow without pastiness, and the reds and yellows do not flare out like scarlet trumpets; an aristocratic palette. Really you begin to realise that what you formerly considered grandfather tales are the truth. The great painters have been and are not with us to-day. It is not a consoling pill to swallow for apostles of "modernity." Hals is more modern than Sargent. . . .

Hals shows us not the magic of life but the normal life of daylight in which move with dignity men and women undismayed by the mysteries that hem them about. He has a daylight soul, a sane if not poetic soul, and few painters before him so celebrated the bravery of appearances, the beauty of the real.

James Huneker
Promenades of an Impressionist (1910)

By means of the coat of arms, van Lennep (*Burlington Magazine,* 1908) has verified the traditional connection of this portrait with the Coymans or Koeymans family. The date indicates that the sitter must be Balthasar (1618-1690), Lord of Streefkerk and Nieuw Lekkerland and Alderman of Haarlem. Collections: Coymans Family, Haarlem; Mrs. Frederick Wollaston, London; Rodolphe Kann, Paris; Mrs. Collis P. Huntington, New York; Archer E. Huntington, New York. *Andrew Mellon Collection,* 1937. Canvas. Height 30¼ in.; width 25 in. (0.77 x 0.64). Dated 1645.

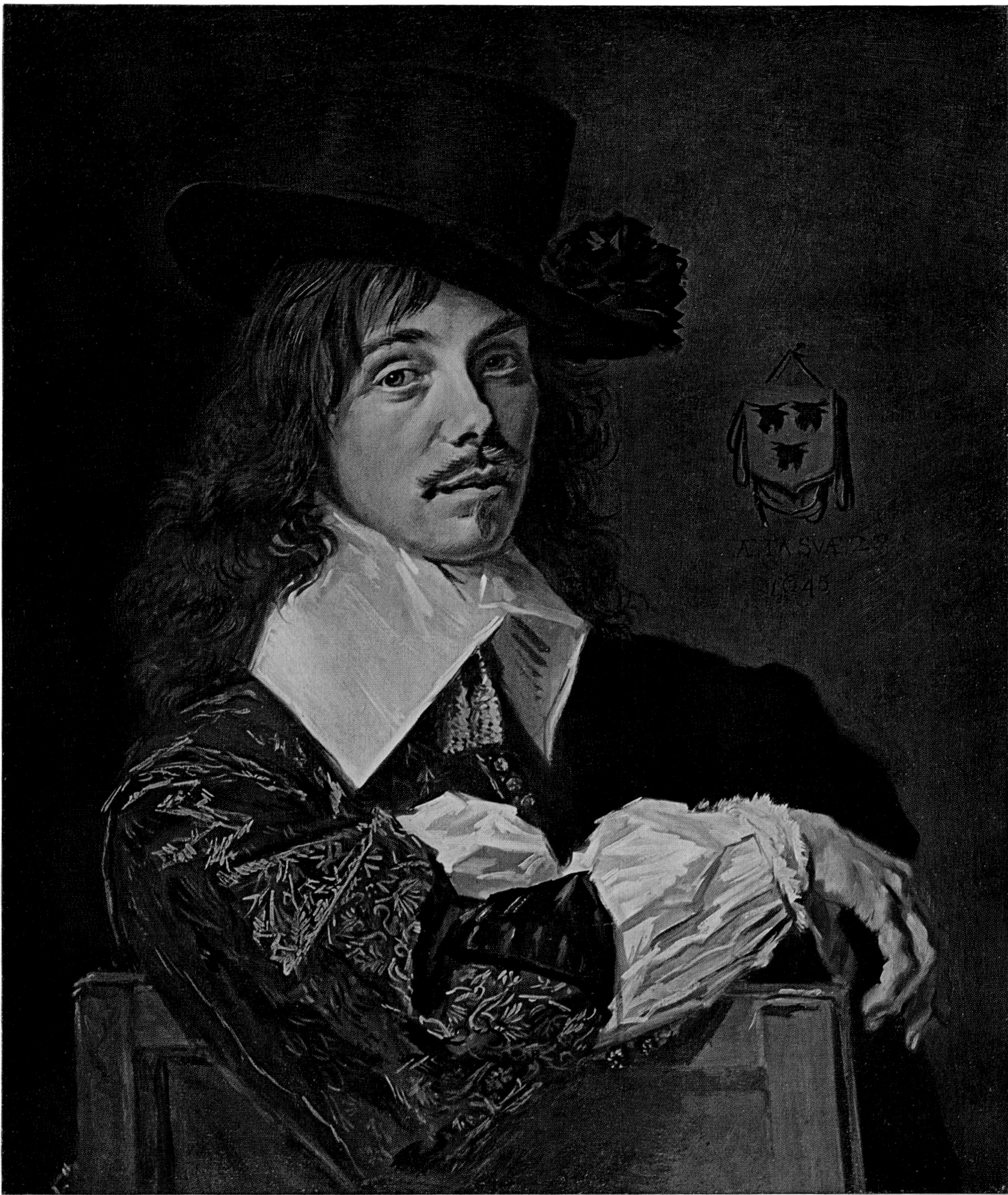
1645

FRANS HALS · Dutch c. 1580-1666

Portrait of an Officer

The appreciation of art should not be considered as merely a pleasurable pastime. To apprehend beauty is to work for it. It is a mighty and an entrancing effort, and the enjoyment of a picture is not only in the pleasure it inspires, but in the comprehension of the new order of construction used in its making. . . .

By the *spring* in the drawing of the eyelash the quick action of the eye may be suggested. The upper eyelid and lash generally cast a shadow scarcely observed yet very effective on the eyeball. The white of the eye is more often the same color as the flesh about it than the average painter is likely to think it to be. The pupil is larger in quiet light, becoming very small by contraction when looking into brilliant light. The highlight in the pupil is a matter of drawing although best done with one quick touch. Its direction, shape, edges, and its contrast in color and value to the pupil give shape, curve, brilliancy or mark the contrary. The right brush, the right paint, a perfect control of the hand are necessary for this. For some, a maul stick to steady is of great value here. (There is a time and place for all things, the difficulty is to use them only in their proper time and places.)

The highlight on the end of the nose is likewise a matter of important drawing, although generally executed in a simple quick touch. By its shape it defines the three angles of the end of the nose.

The lines and forms in the clothes should be used to draw the body in its sensitive relationship with the head. The wrinkles and forms of the clothes are building material not for tailoring in your hands but for established basic lines rising to the head. There is an orchestration throughout the whole canvas. Nothing is for itself, but each thing partaking of the other is living its greatest possibility, is surpassing itself with vitality and meaning and is part of the making of a great unity. So with the works of the great masters.

Robert Henri
The Art Spirit (1923)

Henri was never able to practice what he preached with the skill Frans Hals shows in paintings like this of an officer, which brilliantly illustrates every point he makes. It has been suggested that the view through the window shows the sea and that the sitter was a naval officer. Collections: Catherine II, Empress of Russia; Hermitage Gallery, Leningrad. *Andrew Mellon Collection,* 1937. Canvas. Height 33¾ in.; width 27 in. (0.86 x 0.69). Painted c. 1640.

REMBRANDT · Dutch 1606-1669

A Polish Nobleman

I had seen an old head by Rembrandt at Burleigh House, and if I could produce a head at all like Rembrandt in a year, in my lifetime, it would be glory and felicity and wealth and fame enough for me! The head I had seen at Burleigh was an exact and wonderful fac-simile of nature, and I resolved to make mine (as nearly as I could) an exact fac-simile of nature. I did not then, nor do I now believe, with Sir Joshua, that the perfection of art consists in giving general appearances without individual details, but in giving general appearances with individual details. Otherwise, I had done my work the first day. But I saw something more in nature than general effect, and I thought it worth my while to give it in the picture. There was a gorgeous effect of light and shade: but there was a delicacy as well as depth in the *chiaro scuro* which I was bound to follow into all its dim and scarce perceptible variety of tone and shadow. Then I had to make the transition from a strong light to as dark a shade, preserving the masses, but gradually softening off the intermediate parts. It was so in nature; the difficulty was to make it so in the copy. I tried, and failed again and again; I strove harder, and succeeded as I thought. The wrinkles in Rembrandt were not hard lines, but broken and irregular. I saw the same appearance in nature, and strained every nerve to give it. If I could hit off this edgy appearance, and insert the reflected light in the furrows of old age in half a morning, I did not think I had lost a day.... How many revisions were there! How many attempts to catch an expression which I had seen the day before! How often did we try to get the old position, and wait for the return of the same light! ... The picture was never finished, and I might have gone on with it to the present hour.

William Hazlitt
Table Talk; or Original Essays on Men and Manners (1821)

The painting at Burleigh House mentioned by Hazlitt has vanished from the literature on Rembrandt. This does not matter. What counts is the insight of a great critic into the methods of a great artist. Hazlitt had the advantage of being himself a painter. This professional knowledge expressed in prose of utter lucidity makes his artistic criticism the most rewarding in English literature with one possible exception, Ruskin, who was also a painter. Collections: Hermitage Gallery, Leningrad. *Andrew Mellon Collection,* 1937. Wood. Height 38⅛ in.; width 26 in. (0.97 x 0.66). Signed, and dated 1637.

REMBRANDT · Dutch 1606-1669

Self-Portrait

The self-portrait from the Widener Collection, now in the National Gallery in Washington, shows Rembrandt's appearance . . . in 1650. This date can be called the end of his middle period, or equally well, the beginning of his late one. The artist looks considerably older here. The characteristic locks of bushy brown hair by his cheekbone have begun to turn gray. As for the costume, it is the richest we have yet seen. Rembrandt here wears no overcoat and exhibits freely the precious gold embroidery of his fancy dress. Equally ornate is the brocade cap under the red beret. Red and gold tones are fused into a warm coloristic harmony. Rembrandt's romantic interest in precious things is shown most pointedly in the large pearl that dangles from the artist's right ear. This is a pictorial touch of the most delicate charm. But in spite of the importance given to outward display in this picture, the psychological content is dominant. Here again there is an interesting relationship between two contrasting features: the artist's obvious delight in picturesque attire and glittering materials and, on the other hand, his critical and deeply questioning expression. Whether or not we call these features contradictory, they are here united in one personality with an extraordinary effectiveness and betray Rembrandt's double disposition to romanticism and to psychological penetration.

In comparison to the self-portrait of 1640, the pictorial organization is again tremendously enriched. The area of attraction through light, color, and textural qualities is extended over a wider field, and the treatment is more varied, from subtle glazing to full impasto. The dominance of the artist's features within this rich pictorial performance relies upon larger compositional accents which lead up from both sides to his head: from the left the diagonal of the sloping shoulders directs our attention to the earring and to the questioning glance of his eyes; on the right, one instinctively relates the half-tone area of the gloved hand resting upon an ornate walking stick to the same tonality in his slightly shadowed face.

Within the development of Rembrandt's self-portraits we may say that this Widener picture shows, in addition to richly romantic implications, a significant advance from self-description to self-analysis.

Jakob Rosenberg
Rembrandt (1948)

The year 1650 was a critical period in Rembrandt's life. In that year a miserable breach-of-promise suit ended with the confinement in an insane asylum of Geertje Dircx, whom Rembrandt had employed as a nurse for his son Titus. Also his financial situation was deteriorating and the finery here so conspicuously displayed he was eventually forced to sell. Out of the deepening shadows of this portrait Rembrandt casts on the spectator a glance still defiant but at the same time self-questioning. Collections: Sebastien Erard, Paris; W. Williams Hope, London; Sir Anthony de Rothschild, London. *Widener Collection,* 1942. Canvas. Height 36¼ in.; width 29¾ in. (0.92 x 0.755). Signed, and dated 1650.

REMBRANDT · Dutch 1606-1669

The Mill

Rembrandt's "Mill" is a picture wholly made by chiaroscuro; the last ray of light just gleams on the upper sail of the mill, and all other details are lost in large and simple masses of shade. Chiaroscuro is the great feature that characterizes his art, and was carried farther by him than by any other painter, not excepting Correggio. But if its effects are somewhat exaggerated by Rembrandt, he is always so impressive, that we can no more find fault with his style than we can with the giant forms of Michael Angelo. Succeeding painters have sometimes, in their admiration of "The Mill," forgotten that Rembrandt chose the twilight to second his wishes, and have fancied that to obtain equal breadth, they must leave out the details of nature in broad daylight; this is the danger of mistaken imitation.

John Constable
Lectures on Landscape Painting (1836)

As the keen stimulus derived from good figure painting may be compared to the excitement of an active intellectual life, so the effect of landscape upon us may be compared to that of a country holiday. The periods in which contemplation takes the place of action may not, from a material point of view, have been the most important in our lives; they may have included no serious crisis of our fortunes, they may recall no decisive triumphs. Nevertheless, in after years it is to these times of repose that our minds revert most pleasurably and most definitely. The details of our troubles and our strivings are apt to become vague memories, until it seems as if the whole of our active existence had been one long uneasy dream, and our holidays the only moments in which we were awake to the reality of life.

Landscape, then, might be described as the pictorial interpretation of man's communion with nature, and its functions are, in their degree, analogous to those of that communion. The mission of landscape is thus to soothe the spirit rather than to excite it, to open out a prospect of quiet, of solitude, or of space. It can stimulate, too, but it stimulates by the indirect process of nature herself—by a gradual attraction rather than by any sudden shock or striking exhibition of force. It can exhilarate by movement, though the movement will not be the strong sweep of the passions, or the agitation of a troubled spirit, but the tonic ebb and flow of the fresh air of heaven. Landscape can also accomplish that purging of the emotions by pity and fear, which for more than two thousand years has been recognised as the function of all tragic art, though it does not do so by the heroic strife or godlike rest of those magnified images of our own humanity which have been the recognised puppets of all the great figure painters, great sculptors, and great poets. The tragic power of landscape lies in its command of the irresistible forces of nature—the storm, the cataract, or the angry sea—and those hardly less tremendous emblems of her repose, the mountains and the twilight.

C. J. Holmes
Constable and His Influence on Landscape Painting (1902)

The Mill has had a strong influence on English landscape painting. Turner admired it greatly, and the notes in his sketchbook show it was the basis of his conception of Rembrandt's handling of light. Charles Turner engraved it in his *Gems of Art*. Collections: Duc d'Orléans, Paris; William Smith, London; Marquess of Lansdowne, Bowood Hall, Wiltshire, England. *Widener Collection,* 1942. Canvas. Height 34½ in.; width 41½ in. (0.875 x 1.055). Painted c. 1650.

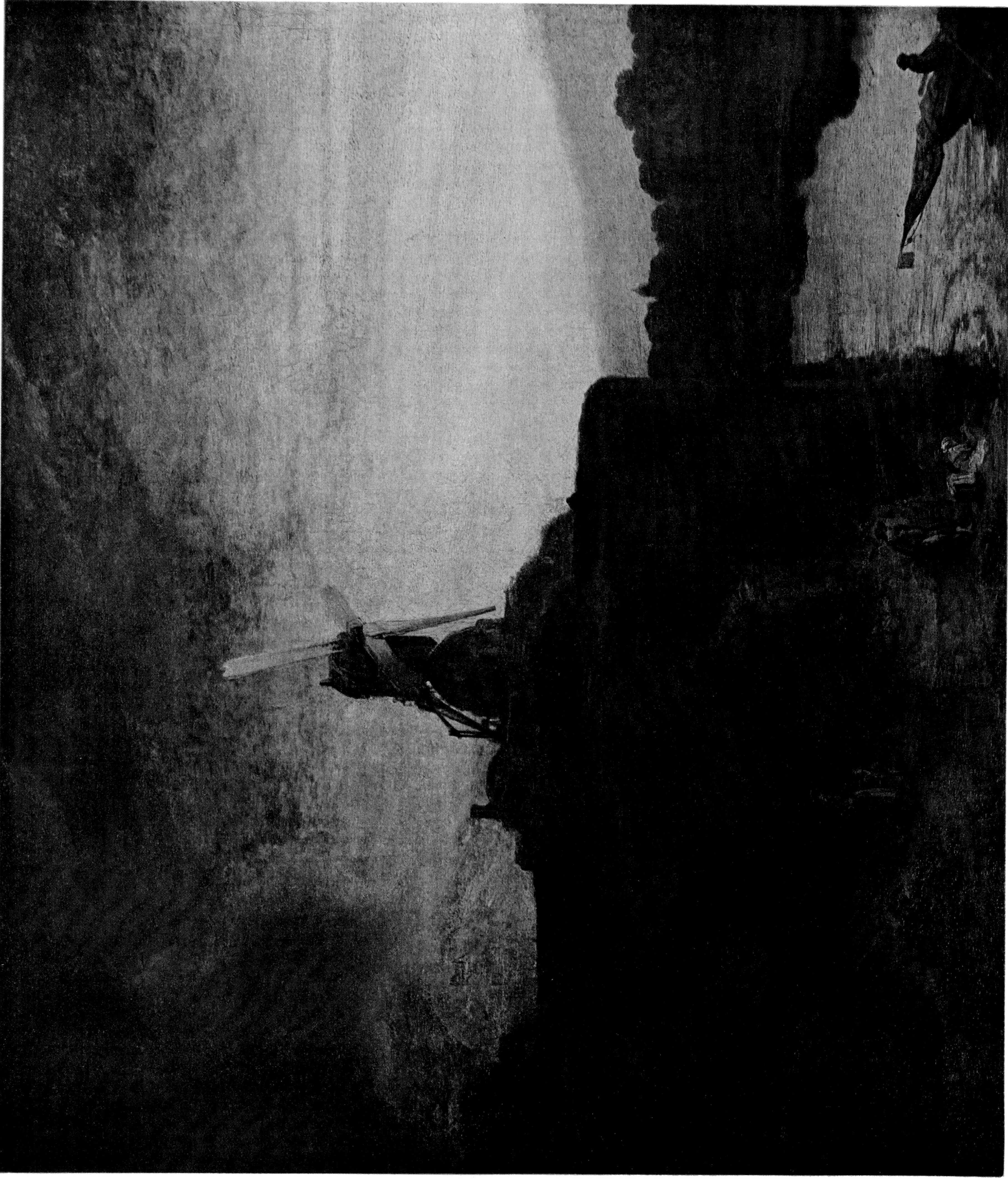

REMBRANDT · Dutch 1606-1669

A Girl with a Broom

Conditions being as they were [in *Holland*], it was out of the question for the painter to wait for the customer who would order a picture for his drawing-room. Paintings were done in the artist's studio in ignorance of who would buy them and where they would go. Art dealing flourished, the link between producer and consumer was broken. There were two alternatives open to the painter in this situation. He could make up his mind to work for the market, or he could in the absence of personal patrons forget about the consumer entirely and regard his art as an unconditioned intercourse with his genius and his conscience....

The danger underlying this was increased by the taste of the art dealer's clientele. It has been said before that these Dutch merchants only rarely had a trained taste, although very often a real collecting passion. Otherwise art dealers and other traders dabbling in art could not have piled up such surprising numbers of pictures. It is recorded that a certain painter and art dealer at Rotterdam left 200 pictures, and that the owner of a slop-shop when he died possessed 1500 pictures. To satisfy the taste of such amateurs a painter had to adapt himself to their powers of comprehension. The more exacting an artist was, the less likely would it be that his works would meet with response in so amorphous a market. In Roman Catholic countries the artist who wanted to express deeper feeling would enshrine the best of his genius in altar-pictures. That was barred in Holland, and if Rembrandt felt driven to express his philosophy in paintings from the Gospels, there was no steady demand for works of this kind, and he had to wait for the appreciative patron who would see such a picture and buy it. In France, where at all times the national genius prevails over the individual, this situation might have appeared tolerable, in the Germanic country it was bound to end in tragedy. Rembrandt, the greatest genius that Holland ever produced, was its victim. As long as his art was comprehensible to the wealthy bourgeois of Amsterdam, he was admired. When he grew in spiritual intensity, when his speech became more and more the intimate meditation of a recluse, success deserted him.

Nikolaus Pevsner
Academies of Art, Past and Present (1940)

Even Rembrandt, in an effort to maintain his prosperity, tried occasionally to paint popular pictures. And yet when he selects a subject as trite as a child with broom and bucket leaning on a fence, some mysterious transformation takes place. The little girl looks at us from the gloom of the darkened canvas with an expression of haunting interrogation, with a demand in her deep set eyes for some explanation we cannot give. Thus in a trivial scene from everyday life, we feel overtones of sadness; and the artist, perhaps in spite of himself, once again creates that somber mood which seems to have perplexed and troubled the diminishing number of his patrons. Collections: Louis-Antoine Crozat, Baron de Thiers, Paris; Catherine II, Empress of Russia; Hermitage Gallery, Leningrad. *Andrew Mellon Collection,* 1937. Canvas. Height 42¼ in.; width 36 in. (1.07 x 0.91). Signed, and dated 1651.

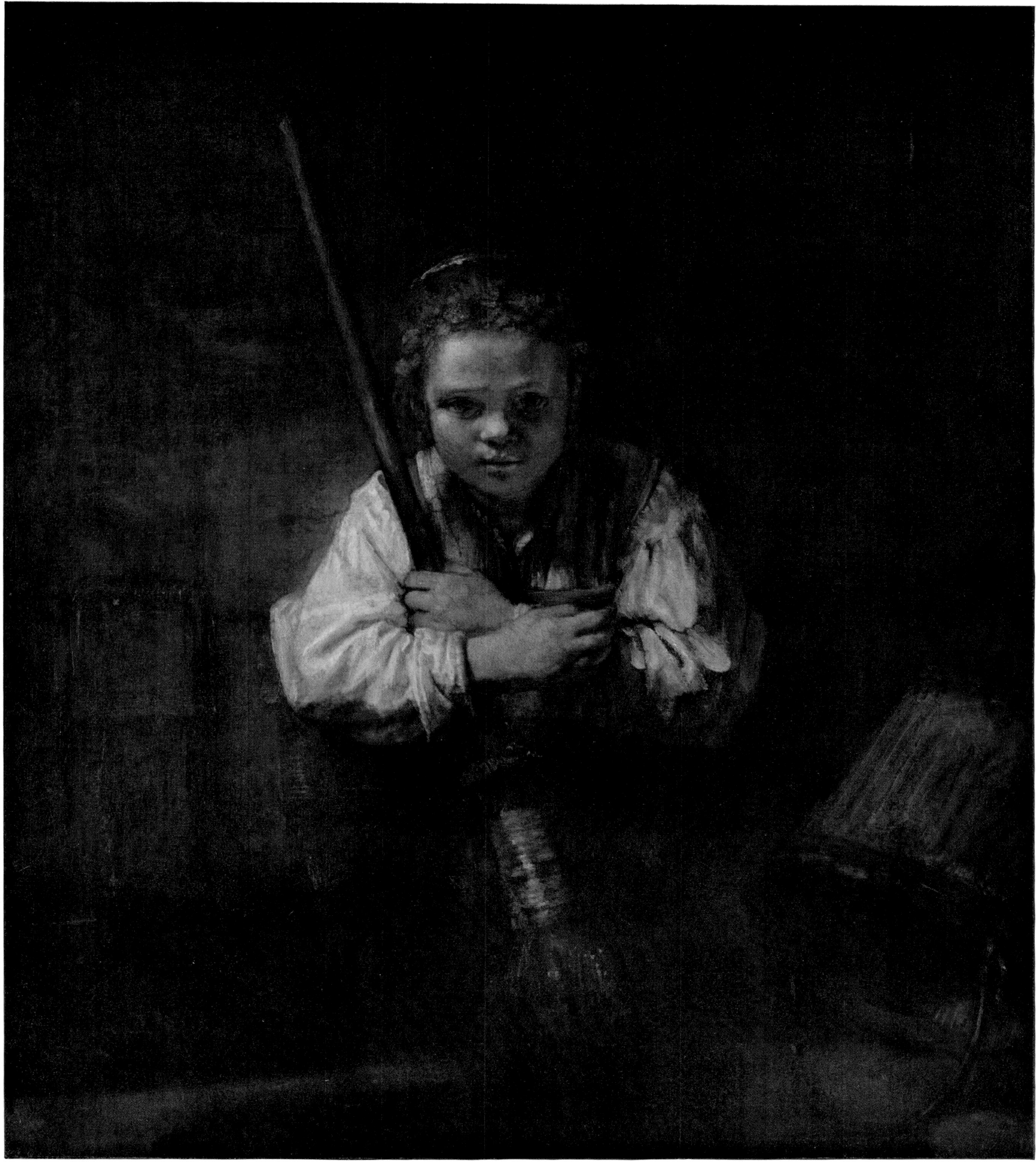

REMBRANDT · Dutch 1606-1669

The Descent from the Cross

Desire for nothing known in my maturer years,
When joy grew mad with awe, at counting future tears.
When, if my spirit's sky was full of flashes warm,
I knew not whence they came, from sun or thunder-storm.

But, first, a hush of peace—a soundless calm descends;
The struggle of distress, and fierce impatience ends;
Mute music soothes my breast—unuttered harmony,
That I could never dream, till Earth was lost to me.

Then dawns the Invisible; the Unseen its truth reveals;
My outward sense is gone, my inward essence feels:
Its wings are almost free—its home, its harbour found,
Measuring the gulf, it stoops—and dares the final bound.

Oh! dreadful is the check—intense the agony—
When the ear begins to hear, and the eye begins to see;
When the pulse begins to throb, the brain to think again;
The soul to feel the flesh, and the flesh to feel the chain.

Yet I would lose no sting, would wish no torture less;
The more that anguish racks, the earlier it will bless;
And robed in fires of hell, or bright with heavenly shine,
If it but herald death, the vision is divine!

Emily Jane Brontë
Poems (1846)

"The mystic attitude is not of calm control or angry revolt and self-assertion," D. S. MacColl (*Nineteenth Century Art,* 1902) remarks in what might be a gloss upon both Emily Brontë's poem and Rembrandt's painting. "It is a loss, a surrender of self in ecstatic contemplation, looking through the thing to something beyond it. Since things are signs of more than themselves to the mystic, he is often content with a symbol, the sign of a sign." Collections: Viscountess Hampden; J. A. Beaver, Lancashire; E. W. Parker, Skirwith Abbey, Cumberland; F. von Gans, Frankfort-on-Main. *Widener Collection,* 1942. Canvas. Height 56¼ in.; width 43¾ in. (1.43 x 1.11). Signed, and dated 165(1?).

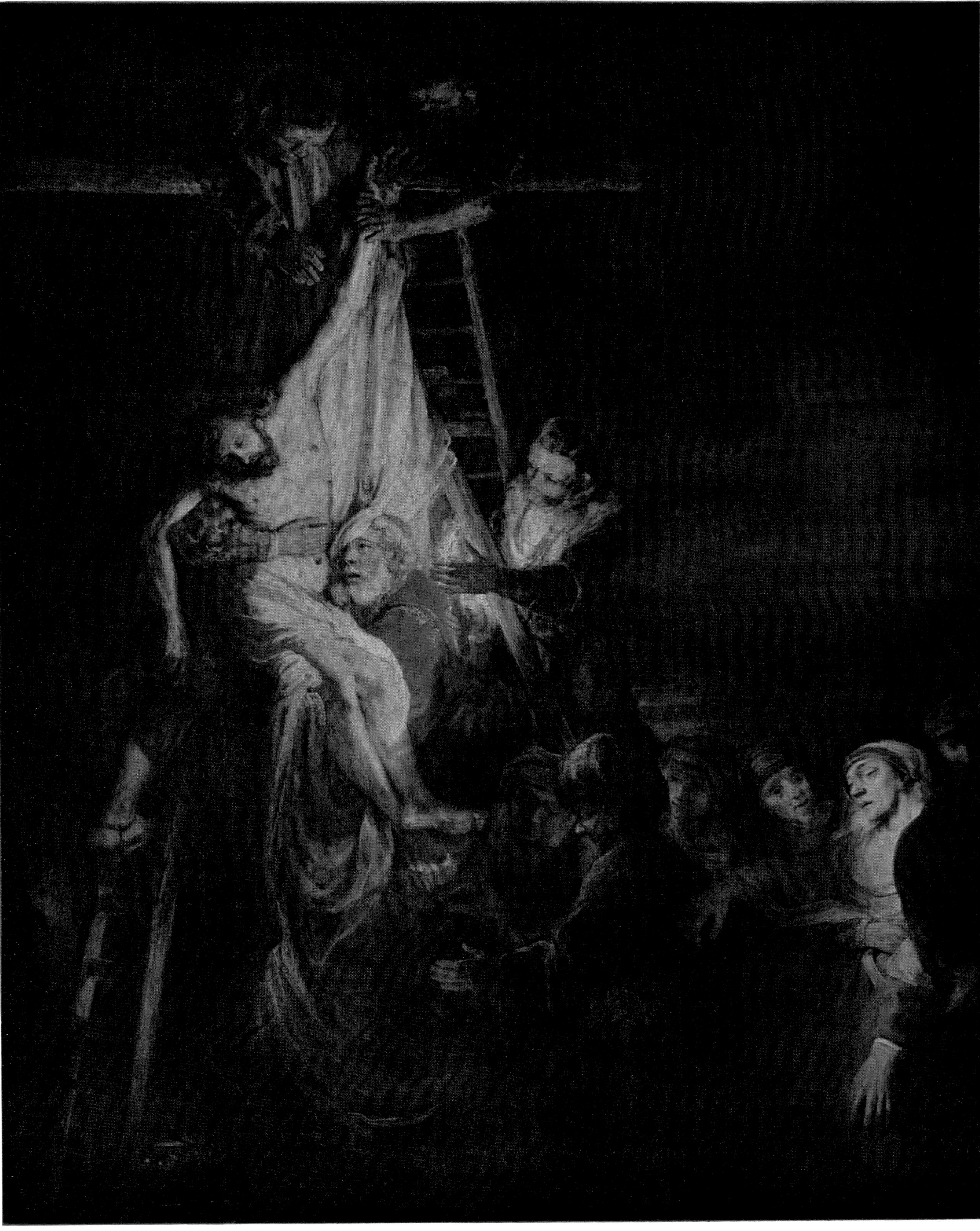

REMBRANDT · Dutch 1606-1669

Joseph Accused by Potiphar's Wife

Phraxanor — My lord—my lord—the man that you did love
Hath much abus'd me.
Potiphar — Ha!—if it be so—
Phraxanor — If!—
When Phraxanor has said there is no if....
Potiphar — Wherefore did you not give him to the guard?
Phraxanor — Aye, there it is: his art and guile are such
(Being more dangerous because unknown)
That I dar'd trust my honour in no hand
But my dear lord's; and therefore I bore all
(Tho' somewhat ruffled) patient as I could....
Joseph — The truth is this:
The character my lady hath bestow'd
Is borrow'd of herself and fix'd on me
To feed her disappointment and revenge.
She would have tempted me, but I refus'd
To heap up shame on my so honour'd lord....
Potiphar — I have a mind to cut thee all to pieces—
Or tear thee limb from limb, and strew thy bones
About the walk where executions are
Done in the city. Hark! sweet mercy's gate
Now jarreth in my breast to shut thee out,
A stranger thence for ever....
Go to thy dungeon, go.

Charles Jeremiah Wells
Joseph and His Brethren (1824)

This is a scene Baroque artists delighted to represent. Usually Joseph is shown fleeing from his would-be seductress, who leaps from her bed and grabs at his coat, here shown on the bedpost. But Rembrandt has treated the story at the level of highest tragedy. The aging beauty, the beautiful youth, the puzzled husband, all seem bemused by passions beyond their comprehension. One senses Rembrandt's deep compassion for each of the actors in this archetypal domestic drama. Collections: Catherine II, Empress of Russia; Hermitage Gallery, Leningrad. *Andrew Mellon Collection,* 1937. Canvas. Height 41⅞ in.; width 38½ in. (1.06 x 0.98). Signed, and dated 165(5?).

REMBRANDT · Dutch 1606-1669

Self-Portrait

As we know, the sensual and the aesthetic do not necessarily coincide, though they may overlap. Rembrandt made no attempt to squeeze his subjects into the mould of Beauty as prescribed by an alien tradition: he took people as he found them and he found them good. Only in his younger days, amused by exotic display, he dressed himself and his models up in pseudo-oriental finery; but maturing, discarded this nonsense in favour of the fashions of his time, with always, it is true, a predilection for the de-moded and well-worn habiliments of the very poor.

Later a plain chemise, a blanket or a few rags were all he needed, his ward-robe being empty (if he had one). But the forms they dissembled were no less alive, and for him life was all that mattered. The brooding femininity of Hendrickje calls for no bedizenment; her eyes provide adequate jewelry as they gaze out of the shadows and convey a secret which her mouth re-iterates, silent but smiling within the golden penumbra of her master's vision.

Blackmailed, ruined, ostracized and deserted by his rich patrons, the artist removes to the Jewish quarter and there with his partner and his Bible continues to paint with ever increasing power. Does Jan Six venture to visit his old friend? No. What of his numerous pupils, above all Nicolas Maes? We are not told. And thus in gloom and mystery, illuminated solely by the transposed sunlight of his genius, the greatest Dutchman dies, content, we must think, that like Poussin he had "neglected nothing."

Augustus John
A Note on Rembrandt
The Burlington Magazine (1942)

Few autobiographies are as searching as Rembrandt's self-portraits. Starting with the self-portrait of 1652, Rembrandt shows an increased interest in psychological interpretation. His self-portraits from this date until his death constitute an almost unbroken record of his life. The picture reproduced is, in prose and costume, most closely related to the self-portrait dated 1659 in the collection of the Duke of Sutherland (formerly the Earl of Ellesmere), London. Two other self-portraits (Museum, Aix-en-Provence, and National Gallery, London) also show Rembrandt at about the age of fifty-three. Collections: Duke of Buccleuch, London. *Andrew Mellon Collection,* 1937. Canvas. Height 33¼ in.; width 26 in. (0.84 x 0.66). Signed, and dated 1659.

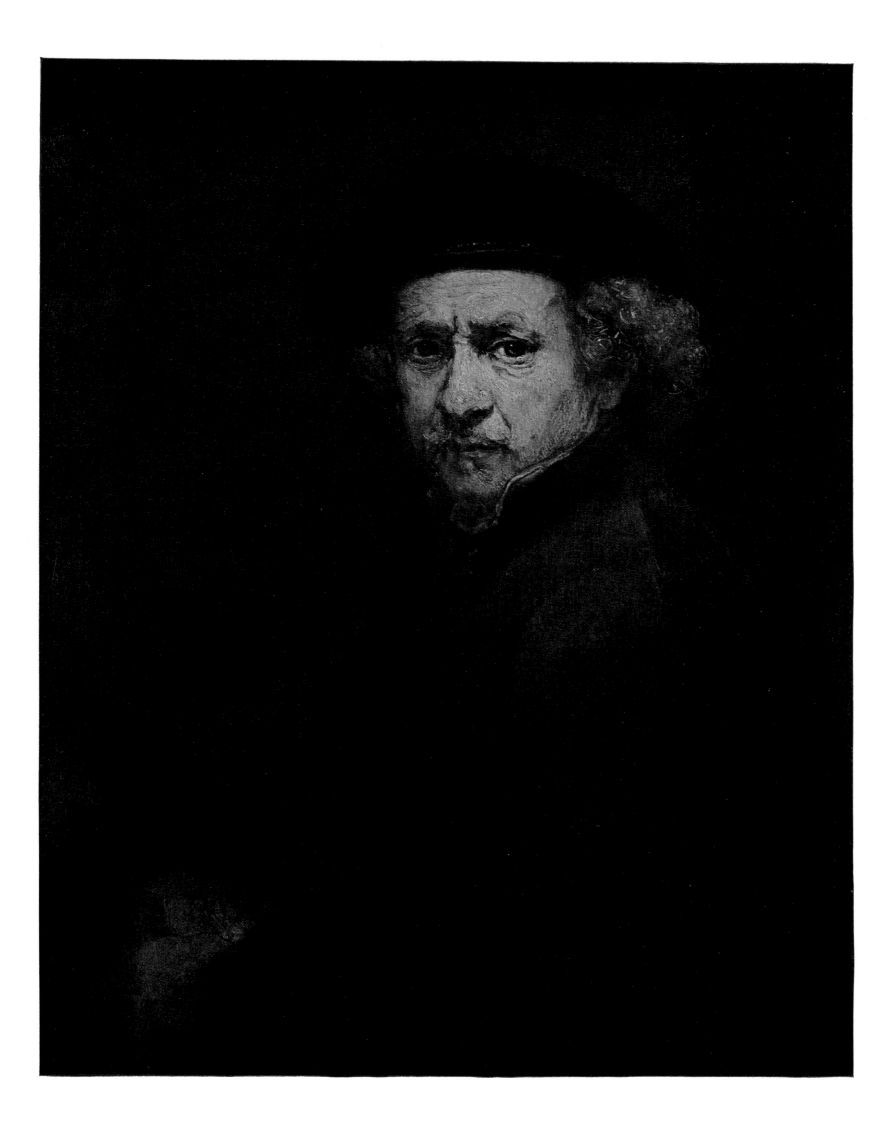

REMBRANDT · Dutch 1606-1669

Lucretia

Hir frendės axen what hir aylen myghte,
And who was dede, and she sytte aye wepynge.
A worde for shame ne may she forthe out brynge,
Ne upon hem she durstė nat beholde,
But attė laste of Tarquyny she hem tolde
This rewful case, and al thys thing horrýble.
  The wo to telle hyt were an ímpossible
That she and al hir frendės made attones.
Al haddė folkės hertys ben of stones,
Hyt myght have makėd hem upon hir rewe,
Hire hertė was so wyfely and so trewe.
She sayde that for hir gylt, ne for hir blame,
Hir housbonde shulde nat have the foulė name,
That noldė she nat suffren by no wey.
And they answerdė alle upon hir fey,
That they foryaf hyt hyr, for hyt was ryght;
Hyt was no gilt; hit lay not in hir myght,
And seyden hire ensamples many oon.
But al for noght, for thus she seyde anoon:
'Be as be may,' quod she, 'of foryifynge;
I wol not have no foryift for nothinge.'
But pryvely she kaughtė forth a knyfe,
And therwithal she rafte hir-selfe hir lyfe;
And as she felle adoun she kaste hire loke,
And of hir clothės yet she hedė toke;
For in hir fallynge yet she haddė care,
Lest that hir fete or suchė thynge lay bare,
So wel she lovėde clennesse, and eke trouthe!

Geoffrey Chaucer
The Legende of Good Women (c. 1385)

Glossary: *ne,* nor; *rewe,* row; *noldė,* would not; *foryaf,* forgave.

Rembrandt, like Chaucer, was a great narrative artist, able to draw his audience into the mood of the scene, to make the spectator feel Lucretia's stunned bewilderment as she moves forward to her death. In the Minneapolis Institute of Arts there is another version of the subject painted in 1666 which shows Lucretia in much the same pose, but with blood running from her wound. Collections: Lapeyrière, Paris; H. Phillips, London; Michael Zachary, London; H. A. J. Munro of Novar, London; Prince Paul de Demidov, San Donato, near Florence; Léon Gauche, Paris; M. C. D. Borden, New York; Herman Heilbuth, Copenhagen. *Andrew Mellon Collection,* 1937. Canvas. Height 47¼ in.; width 39¾ in. (1.20 x 1.01). Signed, and dated 1664.

REMBRANDT · Dutch 1606-1669

Portrait of a Lady with an Ostrich-Feather Fan

What then did those immortals see, the writers who aimed at all which is greatest, and scorned the accuracy which lies in every detail? They saw many other things, and they also saw this, that Nature determined man to be no low or ignoble animal; but introducing us into life and this entire universe as into some vast assemblage, to be spectators, in a sort, of her entirety, and most ardent competitors, did then implant in our souls an invincible and eternal love of that which is great and, by our own standard, more divine. Therefore it is, that for the speculation and thought which are within the scope of human endeavour not all the universe together is sufficient, our conceptions often pass beyond the bounds which limit it; and if a man were to look upon life all round, and see how in all things the extraordinary, the great, the beautiful stand supreme, he will at once know for what ends we have been born. So it is that, as by some physical law, we admire, not surely the little streams, transparent though they be, and useful too, but Nile, or Tiber, or Rhine, and far more than all, Ocean; nor are we awed by this little flame of our kindling, because it keeps its light clear, more than by those heavenly bodies, often obscured though they be, nor think it more marvellous than the craters of Etna, whose eruptions bear up stones and entire masses, and sometimes pour forth rivers of that Titanic and unalloyed fire. Regarding all such things we may say this, that what is serviceable or perhaps necessary to man, man can procure; what passes his thought wins his wonder.

Hence, when we speak of men of great genius in literature, where the greatness does not necessarily fall outside the needs and service of man, we must at once arrive at the conclusion, that men of this stature, though far removed from flawless perfection, yet all rise above the mortal: other qualities prove those who possess them to be men, sublimity raises them almost to the intellectual greatness of God. No failure, no blame; but greatness has our very wonder. What need still to add, that each of these great men is often seen to redeem all his failures by a single sublimity, a single success; and further, which is most convincing, that if we were to pick out all the failures of Homer, Demosthenes, Plato, and the other greatest writers, and to mass them together, the result would be a small, an insignificant fraction of the successes which men of that heroic build exhibit everywhere. Therefore every age and all time, which envy itself can never prove to be in its dotage, has bestowed upon them the assured prizes of victory.

Longinus
On the Sublime (1st or 2nd Century A.D.)

In the Portrait of a Lady with an Ostrich-Feather Fan Rembrandt has touched the sublime. Here is an example of the Grand Style—that "perfection of expression in every direction and kind"—at its peak. There is a possibility that this picture and its pendant, the Portrait of a Gentleman with a Tall Hat and Gloves, also in the National Gallery of Art, represent the painter Ter Borch and his wife some ten years later than they are shown in Ter Borch's own paintings in the Rijksmuseum, Amsterdam. Collections: Prince Youssoupoff, Leningrad. *Widener Collection,* 1942. Canvas. Height 39¼ in.; width 32⅝ in. (0.995 x 0.83). Signed, and dated 166(7?).

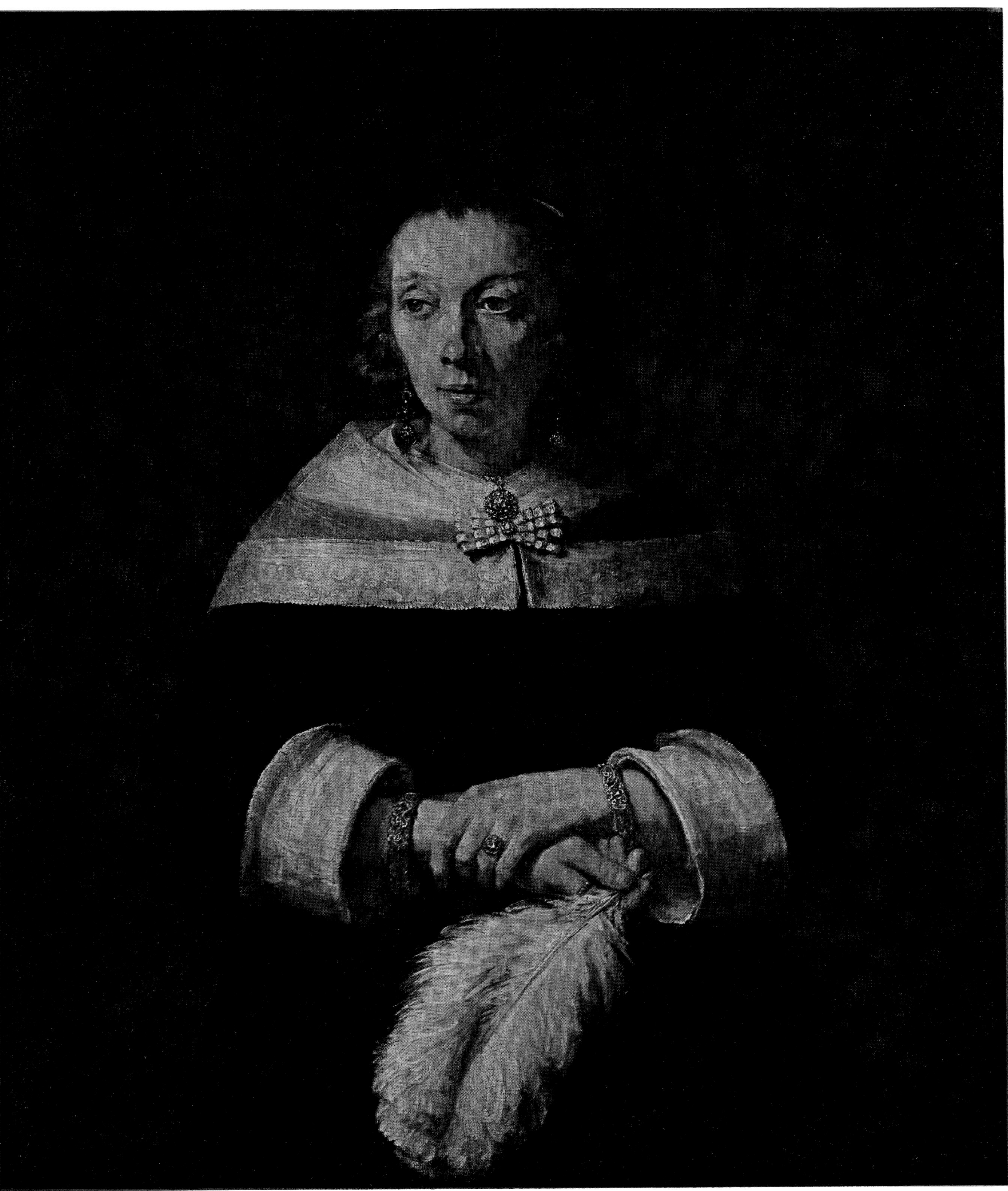

PIETER JANSZ. SAENREDAM · Dutch 1597-1665

Cathedral of Saint John at 's-Hertogenbosch

All Dutch painting is concave; I mean that it consists of curves described round a point determined by the interest of the picture—of circular shade, around a dominating light. It is drawn, coloured, and illumined like an orb, with a strong powerful base, a vanishing ceiling and rounded corners converging to the centre; from which it follows that it is deep, and that there is distance between the eye and the objects that are reproduced in it. No painting leads with greater certainty from the foreground to the background, from the border to the horizons. We live in the picture, we walk about in it, we look into its depths, we are tempted to raise our heads to look at its sky. Everything unites to produce this illusion—the accuracy of the aerial perspective, the perfect relationship of the colouring and the values with the plane the object occupies. All painting foreign to this school of the ceiling, the aerial envelope, of the far-off effect, is a picture which seems flat and laid without relief on the canvas.

Eugène Fromentin
Les Maîtres d'autrefois (1876)

Several Dutch painters specialized in rendering church interiors. Among these artists Saenredam was the greatest master of light and air; yet it is probable that his pictures were painted in his studio and based on drawings sometimes done years before. The present painting is dated 1646 in the choir enclosure on the left. But the drawing for the picture, which is in the British Museum, was sketched fourteen years earlier. Collections: Paris of Ixtassou, near Bayonne; Jonkheer J. A. G. Sandberg, Wassenaar, near Leiden. *Samuel H. Kress Collection,* 1961. Wood. Height 50⅝ in.; width 34¼ in. (1.288 x 0.87). Signed, and dated 1646.

PIETER DE HOOCH · Dutch 1629-c. 1683

A Dutch Courtyard

I venture to propose the probably rash idea that, if the Dutch painters avoid narrative subjects, of literary and dramatic significance, if they make use of anonymous actors supplemented by generalized landscapes, it is because they wish to represent not actions, not events, but moods. As the landscapes that I have just been describing give us a sense of space, so the intimate scenes of which I am now going to speak make us conscious of time. They are the reservoir of evanescent feelings. We do not merely glance at a painting by . . . . Vermeer, or Pieter de Hooch with condescending approval; we are immediately within it, we live there. We are entrapped. We are enclosed in it. We feel the form of it on us like a garment. We are saturated with its atmosphere, which we absorb through all our pores, through all our sensibilities, and, as it were, through the inlets of our very being. And, indeed, the dwelling where we are has a soul. It receives, separates and distributes the exterior ray, as does our own. It is completely filled with the stillness of the present moment. In it we witness the process that goes on within ourselves, by which outer reality is translated into light and shadow, the step-by-step motion of the daylight which rises and descends upon the wall that we present to it within our consciousness. The series of rooms and courts, the glimpse yonder of the garden through an open door, or of the sky through a transom, far from distracting us, gives us a more peaceful enjoyment of our seclusion and security. This is our reserved domain. As a sudden touch sets aglow in us a memory or an idea, as steadily increasing illumination models a figure and gives it volume, so the Dutch artist is expert in withholding and in using this mystic dowry that the passing hours pour out to him. . . . The waterlike transparency of windowpanes, the variations in the density of the air, the complex interaction of walls, and the reflections of reflections that are thrown back from one wall to the other, the checkered trellis-work that slants across a wall and that the fixed eye of a mirror records in reverse, the contrast in the midst of a room between the lighted and unlighted parts, between what has just been lighted up and that which is getting dark, the furnishings, heavy, dull-faced chests and glowing coppers, which give character to the whole—all this composes a kind of talisman, a kind of intimate formula or secret charm, and makes one understand how the people who live here cannot escape from this domestic paradise.

Paul Claudel
Introduction à la peinture hollandaise (1935)

Beyond the wall of de Hooch's courtyard is the Nieuwe Kerk in Delft. A masterpiece of true visual effect, this canvas conjures up a domestic paradise of eternal, sun-drenched felicity. The best genre painters in Holland were in varying degrees scientific investigators of such images, which the eye conveys to the mind. It is significant in this connection that the Dutch also are credited with the practical discovery of both the compound microscope and the telescope, one about 1590 and the other about 1608. Another version of this picture, lacking the cavalier holding the beer jug, is in the Mauritshuis, The Hague (formerly Ten Cate Collection, Almelo, Holland). Collections: Possibly S. A. Koopman, Utrecht; Lionel and Alfred de Rothschild, London; Countess of Carnarvon, Newbury, England. *Andrew Mellon Collection,* 1937. Canvas. Height 26¾ in.; width 23 in. (0.68 x 0.59). Painted c. 1660.

JAN STEEN · Dutch c. 1626-1679

The Dancing Couple

We arrived late at Roterdam, where was at that time their annual Mart or Faire, so furnish'd with pictures (especially Landscips, and Drolleries, as they call those clownish representations) as I was amaz'd: some of these I bought and sent into England. The reason of this store of pictures, and their cheapenesse proceede from their want of Land, to employ their Stock; so as 'tis an ordinary thing to find, a common Farmor lay out two, or 3000 pounds in this Commodity, their houses are full of them, and they vend them at their Kermas'es to very greate gaines.

John Evelyn
Diary (Aug. 13, 1641)

Hippoclides, a young Athenian chosen by Clisthenes of Sicyon as husband for his daughter. At the final banquet Hippoclides not only insisted on dancing, but even stood on his head on the table and waved his legs in the air. Clisthenes was disgusted and cried, "O son of Pisander, you have danced away your marriage." The young man smiled and said, "Hippoclides don't care," which became a proverb.

John Lemprière
Classical Dictionary (1949)

Evelyn's "common Farmor" may not have had much appreciation of art, but he felt sure the art he owned would eventually appreciate in monetary value. However, two or three thousand pounds in the seventeenth century was a great sum of money. To spend it on pictures indicates that in Holland there must have been an extraordinary excess of capital—a fact hinted at by Evelyn in his remark about the "want of Land, [for farmers] to employ their Stock." Collections: J. Bisschop, Rotterdam; Hope family, Amsterdam and then London. *Widener Collection,* 1942. Canvas. Height 40⅜ in.; width 56⅛ in. (1.025 x 1.425). Signed, and dated 1663.

AELBERT CUYP · Dutch 1620-1691

The Maas at Dordrecht

One of the first circumstances that struck me wherever I went was what you had prepared me for, the resemblance that every thing wore to the Dutch and Flemish pictures. On leaving Ostend, not only the people, the houses, and trees, but whole tracts of country, reminded one of the landscapes of Teniers; and, on getting further into the country, this was only relieved by the pictures of Rubens, Wouvermans, and some other masters, taking his place. I thought I could trace the particular districts in Holland where Ostade, Jan Stein, Cuyp, and Rembrandt had studied, and could fancy the very spot where pictures of other masters had been painted. Indeed, nothing seemed new to me in the whole country; for I had been familiar with it all upon canvas: and, what one could not help wondering at was, that these old masters should have been able to draw the materials of so beautiful a variety of art from so contracted and monotonous a country.

Sir David Wilkie
Letter to Sir George Beaumont (Dec. 12, 1816)

If I might point out to you another defect, very prevalent of late, in our pictures, and one of the same contracted character with those you so happily illustrate, it would be that of the *want of breadth,* and in others a perpetual division and subdivision of parts, to give what their perpetrators call space; add to this a constant disturbing and torturing of every thing, whether in light or in shadow, by a niggling touch, to produce fulness of subject. This is the very reverse of what we see in Cuyp or Wilson, and even, with all his high finishing, in Claude.

I have been warning our friend Collins against this, and was also urging young Landseer to beware of it; and in what I have been doing lately myself have been studying much from Rembrandt and from Cuyp, so as to acquire what the great masters succeeded so well in, namely, that power by which the chief objects, and even the minute finishing of parts, tell over every thing that is meant to be subordinate in their pictures. Sir Joshua had this remarkably, and could even make *the features of the face* tell over every thing, however strongly painted. I find that repose and breadth in the shadows and half-tints do a great deal towards it. Zoffany's figures derive great consequence from this; and I find that those who have studied light and shadow the most never appear to fail in it.

Sir David Wilkie
Letter to Sir George Beaumont (Feb. 14, 1823)

In the *Commemorative Catalogue of the Exhibition of Dutch Art, Burlington House,* 1929, it is suggested that "the event represented is probably Charles II in the Dordrecht roads, May 24th, 1660, during his journey from Breda .... to The Hague and thence to England." Collections: Alexis de la Hante; Sir Abraham Hume, and his descendants, until sold by Adelbert Wellington, third Earl Brownlow, Ashridge Park, England. *Andrew Mellon Collection,* 1940. Canvas. Height 46¼ in.; width 67 in. (1.15 x 1.70). Signed. Painted c. 1660.

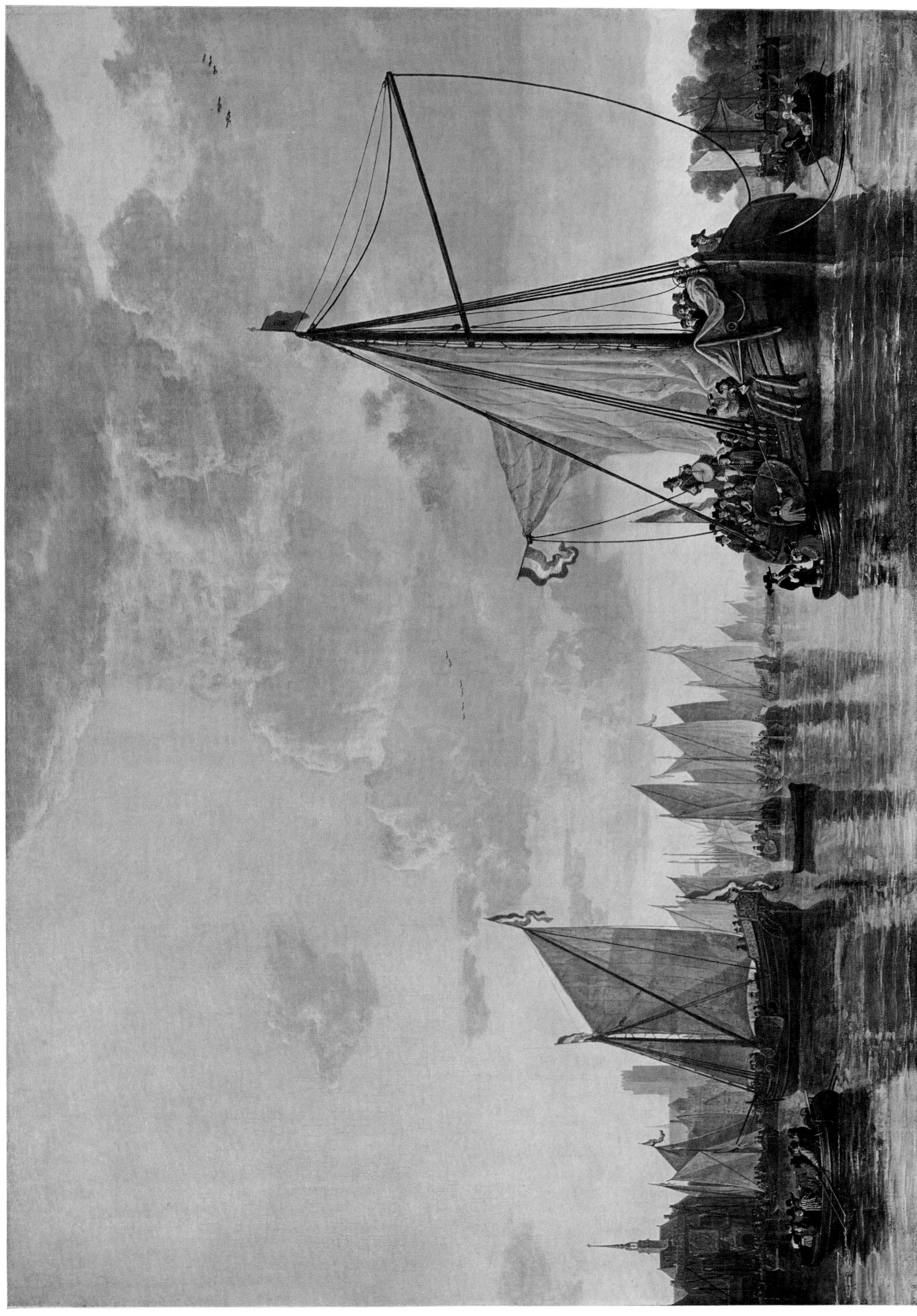

AELBERT CUYP · Dutch 1620-1691

Horsemen and Herdsmen with Cattle

Cuyp, soleil déclinant dissous dans l'air limpide
Qu'un vol de ramiers gris trouble comme de l'eau,
Moiteur d'or, nimbe au front d'un bœuf ou d'un bouleau,
Encens bleu des beaux jours fumant sur le coteau,
Ou marais de clarté stagnant dans le ciel vide.
Des cavaliers sont prêts, plume rose au chapeau,
Paume au côté; l'air vif qui fait rose leur peau,
Enfle légèrement leurs fines boucles blondes,
Et, tentés par les champs ardents, les fraîches ondes,
Sans troubler par leur trot les bœufs dont le troupeau
Rêve dans un brouillard d'or pâle et de repos,
Ils partent respirer ces minutes profondes.

[Cuyp! Setting sun melting in the limpid air, like the surface of a pond stirred by a flight of gray doves; liquid gold nimbus on the head of a birch tree or an ox; blue incense of lovely days drifting like smoke over the hillside; tranquil pools of light in the empty sky. Horsemen with their rose-feathered hats are ready, hand on hip. The brisk air which gently colors their skin stirs their silken blond locks. And enticed by glowing fields and cool waters, leaving undisturbed by their hoof-beats the dreamy herd of cattle in the quiet golden haze, they are off to savor these unfathomable moments.]

Marcel Proust
Les Plaisirs et les jours (1896)

The landscape suggests the scenery in the northern part of the Rhine Valley. Collections: The present painting, with a pendant of a similar subject, is first recorded in the J. van der Linden van Slingeland Collection, Dordrecht, in 1752. In 1785 it was purchased by M. Dubois of Paris. It passed into the collection of William Smith, who sold it to Edward Gray in 1830. In 1834 it was in the collection of Alexander Baring, who became Lord Ashburton. It remained in the Ashburton Collection until 1907. *Widener Collection,* 1942. Canvas. Height 47⅜ in.; width 67½ in. (1.20 x 1.715). Signed. Painted c. 1660/70.

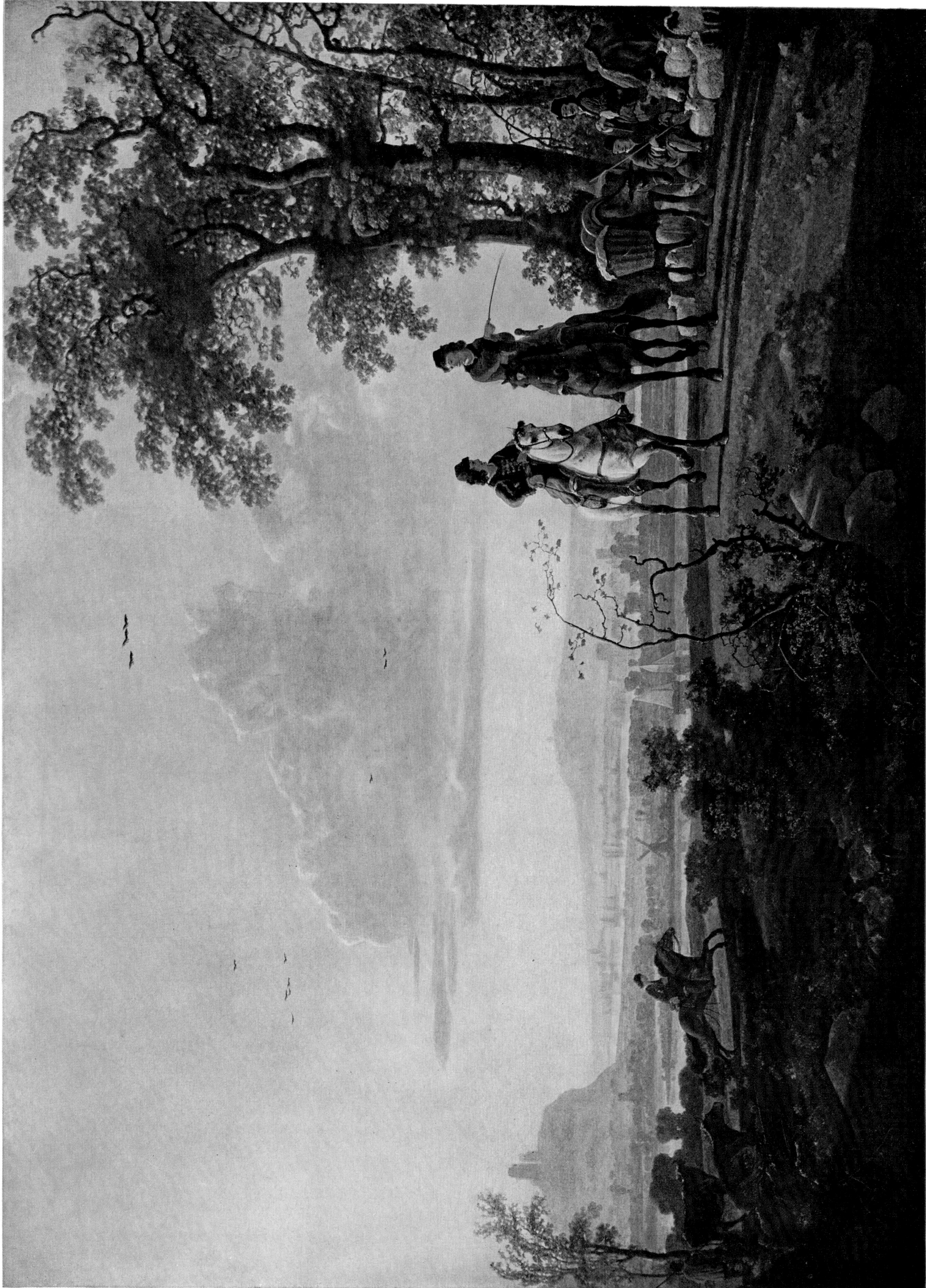

MEINDERT HOBBEMA · Dutch 1638-1709

A Wooded Landscape

We now come to the landscape of fact which directly influenced, or even created nineteenth-century vision, the landscape of seventeenth-century Holland. It bears no resemblance to Breughel, and its kinship with the backgrounds of Bellini and Pollaiuolo depends solely on similarity of aim, for these early Italian landscape painters were entirely unknown in Holland. How can we account for it? There is no single answer, and even a series of convincing looking reasons omits the vital principle upon which all movements in art depend. We may, however, give answers in three different modes which help to an understanding of the situation.

First, sociological. The landscape of fact, like all portraiture, is a bourgeois form of art. Seventeenth-century Holland was the great, we may say, the heroic epoch of bourgeoisie, and its art reflected the desire to see portrayed *recognisable* experiences. . . .

Secondly, philosophical. This was an age in which men once more felt free to ask questions about the workings of nature. The curiosity of the Renaissance had been repressed by the Counter-Reformation, though never quite destroyed. Now that the wars of religion were over—in Holland at least—a revival of science was possible. This was the great age of botany, when the details of nature were examined and classified by Christian Huyghens. It was the age in which the range of man's sight was enormously extended. In Italy Milton had met the Tuscan artist with his optic glass discovering new worlds; in England Newton evolved his theory of light. And as so often happens, art anticipated intuitively what science was beginning to formulate. . . .

Thirdly, the reasons within the art itself. By 1600 the tradition of mannerist landscape was exhausted. It was still conventionally accepted by grand collectors, as we may see by examining those pictures of their galleries, which were so frequently painted in the seventeenth century, and which show that fashionable taste in the seventeenth century took as much pleasure in mediocre art as it does today. Meanwhile, the old Netherlandish love of representing the thing seen had never been completely smothered and was there to reassert itself when the pressure of fashion was relaxed.

Kenneth Clark
Landscape into Art (1949)

Hobbema specialized almost exclusively in landscape painting until, at the age of thirty, he married and gave up his art to become a collector of excise taxes on liquor. In describing this picture Waagen said, "Seldom has the power of art in expressing the effect of the low afternoon sun in the light clouds in the sky, on tree, bush, and meadow, been exhibited with such astonishing power, transparency, and freshness as in this picture." There is general agreement that the figures are by Hobbema himself. A painting of similar dimensions, also signed and dated 1663, in Sir Alfred Beit's Collection, Wicklow, Ireland, has frequently been suggested as a pendant. A smaller version of the present design with slight variations is in the Wallace Collection, London. Collections: Charles Cobbe, Dublin; Holford, Dorchester House, London; J. Pierpont Morgan, New York. *Andrew Mellon Collection,* 1937. Canvas. Height 37½ in.; width 51⅜ in. (0.95 x 1.30). Signed, and dated 1663.

GERARD TER BORCH · Dutch 1617-1681

The Suitor's Visit

I spent some time watching them, and soon saw the redshanks courting. It was one of the most entrancing of spectacles. Redshanks, cock as well as hen, are sober-coloured enough as you see their trim brown bodies slipping through the herbage. But during the courtship all is changed. The cock-bird advances towards the hen with his graceful pointed wings raised above his back, showing their pure-white under-surface. He lifts his scarlet legs alternately in a deliberate way—a sort of graceful goose-step—and utters all the while a clear far-carrying trill, full of wildness, charged with desire, piercing and exciting. Sometimes as he nears the hen he begins to fan his wings a little, just lifting himself off the ground, so that he is walking on air.

Julian Huxley
Bird-Watching and Bird Behaviour (1930)

Nearly all Ter Borch's pictures are interiors. He takes us into a Dutch room, where he shows only a bare wall, perhaps adorned with a map or interrupted by a fireplace. In the foreground. . . . are a carpet-covered table and one or two chairs. The figures, which are quiet and unemotional, are endowed with the same apparent plainness and simplicity. This extreme reserve, decidedly premeditated, is united with an unaffected grace and a certain grandeur, for which the choice garments and their fashionable styling are necessary conditions. It gives Ter Borch's pictures their air of distinction. Thanks to his unobtrusive, aristocratic manner and his cultured breeding the artist knows how to depict his countrymen in an aspect that none of his colleagues has shown us. He portrays them with a plausible cool dignity and elegance, but their society does not chill us; on the contrary, it arouses in us an intimate response, so that in this world of quiet and easy manners we feel at home. We are interested in what is going on and, with Goethe, are tempted to reconstruct the story.

Wilhelm von Bode
Die Meister der Holländischen und Vlämischen Malerschulen (1919)

Collections: Charles-Auguste-Louis-Joseph, Duc de Morny, Paris; Marqués de Salamanca, Madrid; Adolphe de Rothschild, Paris; Maurice de Rothschild, Paris. *Andrew Mellon Collection,* 1937. Canvas. Height 31½ in.; width 29⅝ in. (0.80 x 0.75). Painted c. 1658.

JACOB VAN RUISDAEL · Dutch 1628/29-1682

Forest Scene

Towards evening, Goethe invited me to take a drive. Our road lay over the hills through Upper Weimar, by which we had a view of the park towards the west. The trees were in blossom, the birches already in full leaf; and the meadows were one green carpet, over which the setting sun cast a glow. We sought out picturesque groups, and could not look enough. We remarked that trees full of white blossoms should not be painted, because they make no picture, just as birches with their foliage are unfit for the foreground of a picture, because the delicate leaf does not sufficiently balance the white trunk; there are no large masses for strong effects of light and shade. "Ruysdael," said Goethe, "never introduced the birch with its foliage into his foregrounds, but only birch trunks broken off, without any leaves. Such a trunk is perfectly suited to a foreground, as its bright form comes out with most powerful effect."

Johann Peter Eckermann
Gespräche mit Goethe (May 2, 1824)

As Babbitt (*Rousseau and Romanticism,* 1919) has pointed out, "Romanticism gave a great impulse to landscape painting," and the creed of the Romantic landscapist is expressed in Wordsworth's familiar lines:

One impulse from a vernal wood
May teach you more of man,
Of moral evil and of good,
Than all the sages can.

Images which would evoke these impulses "from a vernal wood "Romanticism gave a great impulse to landscape painting," and tury and became the basis of the landscape painting of the nineteenth century, as developed by Constable and Turner, by the Barbizon School, by the Impressionists, and by many others. Collections: Sir Hugh Hume Campbell, London. *Widener Collection,* 1942. Canvas. Height 41½ in.; width 51½ in. (1.055 x 1.31). Signed. Painted c. 1660-65.

Q
759 STACKS 155740
U 58
v.1

U.S. NATIONAL GALLERY OF ART

Q
759 STACKS 155740
U 58
v.1

U.S. National Gallery of Art
A pageant of painting from the
National Gallery of Art

Ryan Library, Iona College
New Rochelle, N. Y.

DISCARDED